Milwaukee Sketchbook

Indigo Custom Publishing

Publisher	Henry S. Beers
Associate Publisher	Richard J. Hutto
Executive Vice President	Robert G. Aldrich
Operations Manager	Gary G. Pulliam
Editor-in-Chief	Joni Woolf
Art Director/Designer	Julianne Gleaton
Director of Marketing and Public Relations	Mary D. Robinson

Printed in India

Library of Congress Control Number: 2004116300

ISBN 10: 0976287544
ISBN 13: 9780976287544

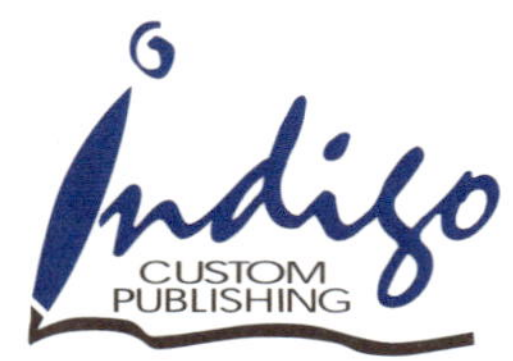

Indigo custom books are available at quantity discounts
with bulk purchase for educational, business, or sales promotional use.
For information, please write to:
Indigo Custom Publishing, 3920 Ridge Avenue, Macon, GA 31210, or call 866-311-9578.
www.indigopublishing.us

Milwaukee Sketchbook

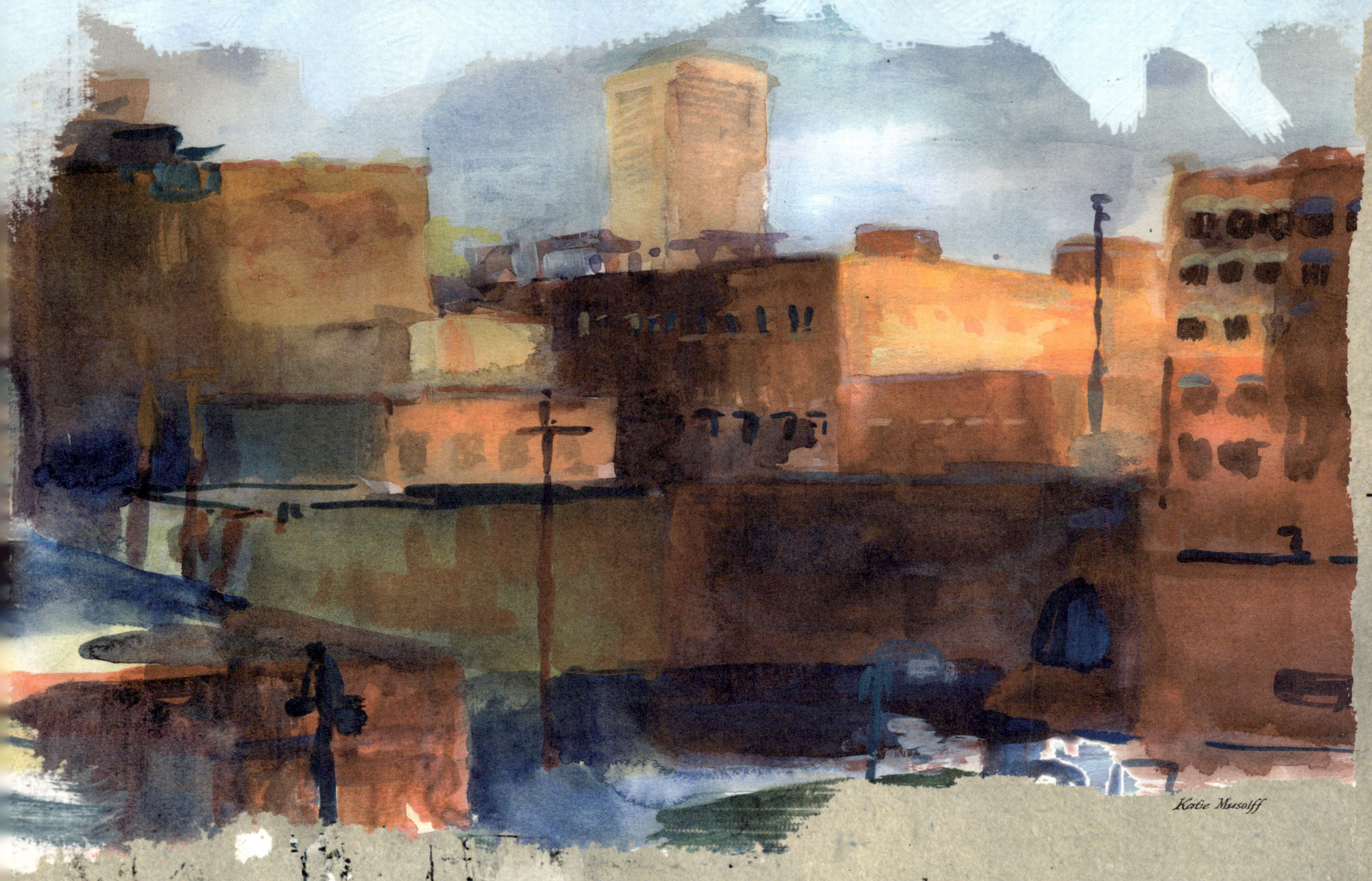

Text and captions by Fran Bauer
Paintings by students at The Milwaukee Institute of Art & Design

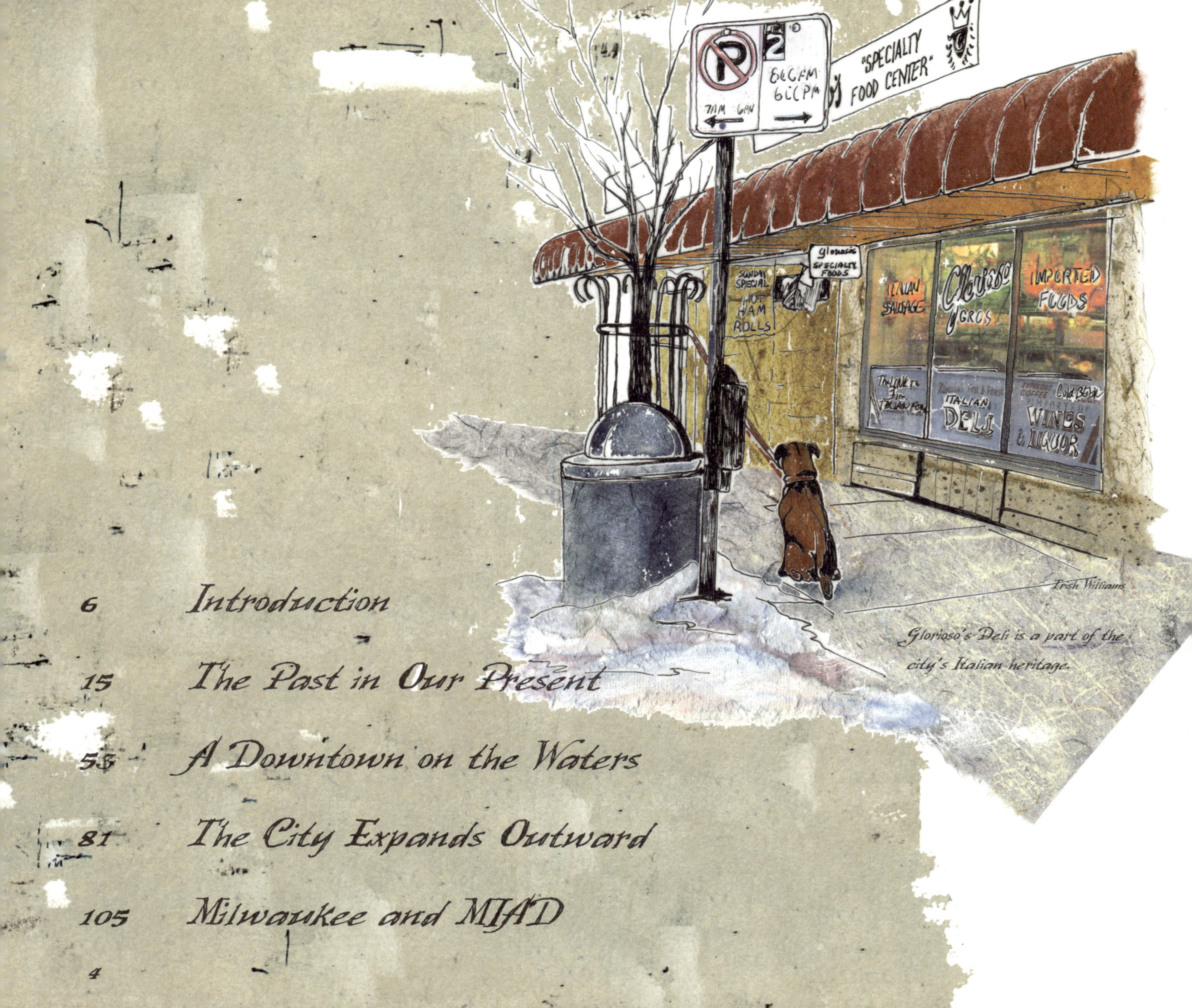

Glorioso's Deli is a part of the city's Italian heritage.

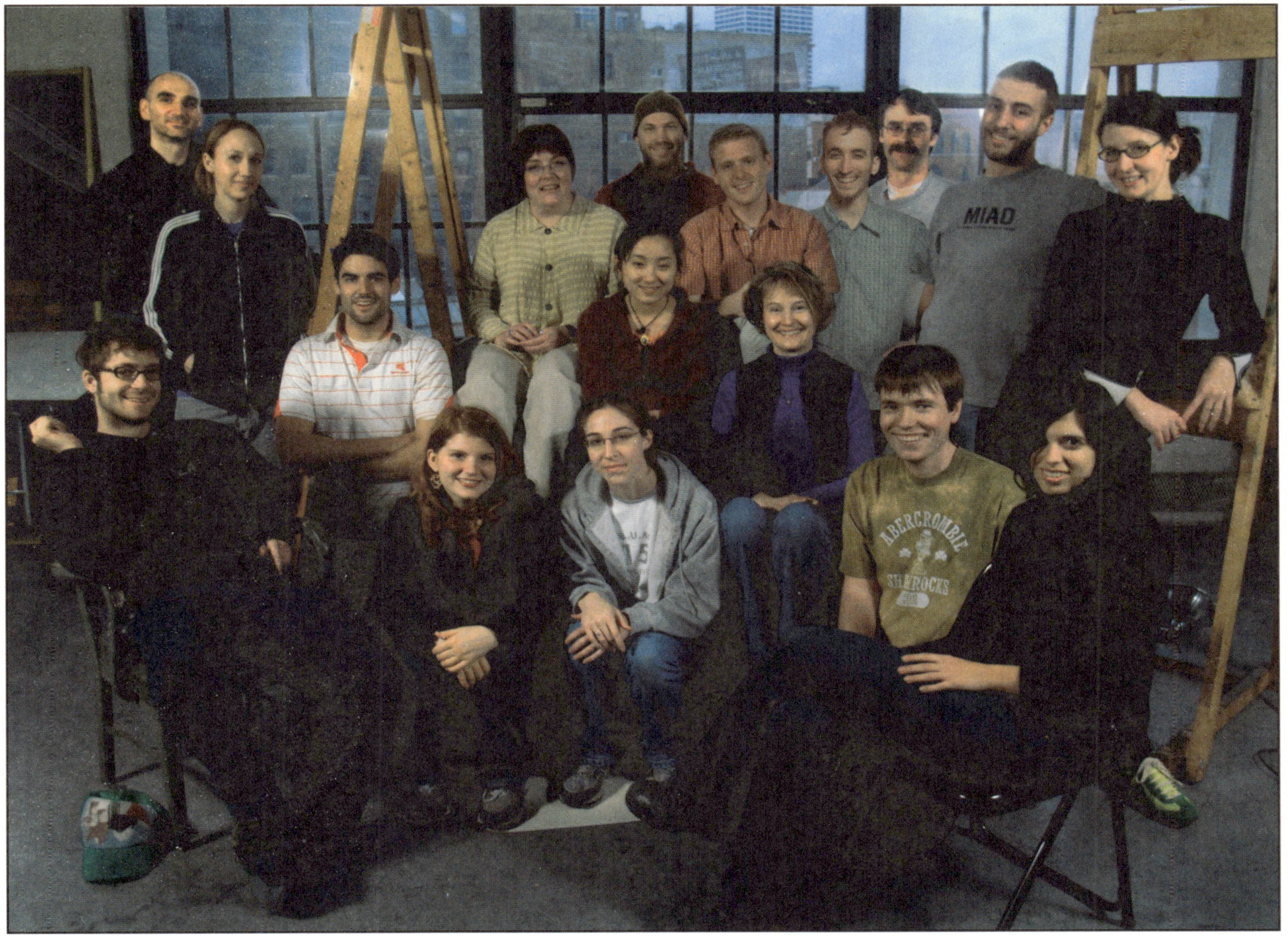

Front row, seated: Kevin Soens, Briana MacWilliam, Jessica Case, Brook Slane, Katie Musolff. Second row, seated: Andrew Perez, Doua Cheng, Trish Williams. Standing, back row: Prof. Michael Howard, Rebecca Staszak, Denise Wallner, Corbett Toomsen, David Lamps, Jason McDowell, Mark Dziewior, Andrew Serge Bernier, Prof. Christiane Grauert.

If you are interested in obtaining individual prints of any of the artworks featured in this book, visit www.miad.edu/sketch or call 414.276.7889. All prints are reproduced with pigmented, archival inks on high-quality acid-free paper. Each print is custom- produced to the artist's specifications.

The Past in our Present

It's fun to walk a community like Milwaukee, looking for places you think are distinctive enough to be considered local landmarks.

For a year, a group of fifteen art students at the Milwaukee Institute of Art & Design did just that, sketchbooks in hand. The students had some help from a group of longtime Milwaukeeans who offered their own lists of places they considered memorable.

The real surprise for the students was in seeing with their own eyes how history comes alive on Milwaukee's streets when you really begin to look for it, according to their teachers Christiane Grauert and Michael Howard. The views selected by these young artists don't tell the full story of Milwaukee. This is more a slice of life in the ongoing story of a city that's now 158 years old and counting.

Not all these landmarks are old. For example, the new wing added in 2001 to the Milwaukee Art Museum is now the city's signature piece. Today, the building and its bold designer, Spanish architect Santiago Calatrava, are attracting world-wide attention for this new pavilion with its movable sunscreen that poises like a bird over its lakefront location.

Baseball fans might pick Miller Park, the new home of the Milwaukee Brewers, which blends a nostalgic façade with the ultimate in high tech amenities, a retractable roof.

For others the most memorable landmark still is City Hall, a towering statement of civic pride built in 1895, at a time when more than half the city's population traced its ancestry to Germany. Local historian John Gurda calls the building "the single most enduring expression of the Germanism that lies at the foundation of modern Milwaukee."

So, take the time to look closely at the community that's all around you. It's amazing who you might meet, what you'll see and how varied your own list of favorites is sure to become.

The heart of Milwaukee's downtown was largely a vast swamp when fur trader Solomon Juneau settled here in 1818, and in the following years built a log cabin on the east banks of the Milwaukee River. The site where he once traded with local Indians is now near one of the city's busiest intersections at Wisconsin and Water.

It's hard to picture Milwaukee as three pitched camps. But that's what it became by the mid-1830s as the feisty Byron Kilbourn settled west of the river and

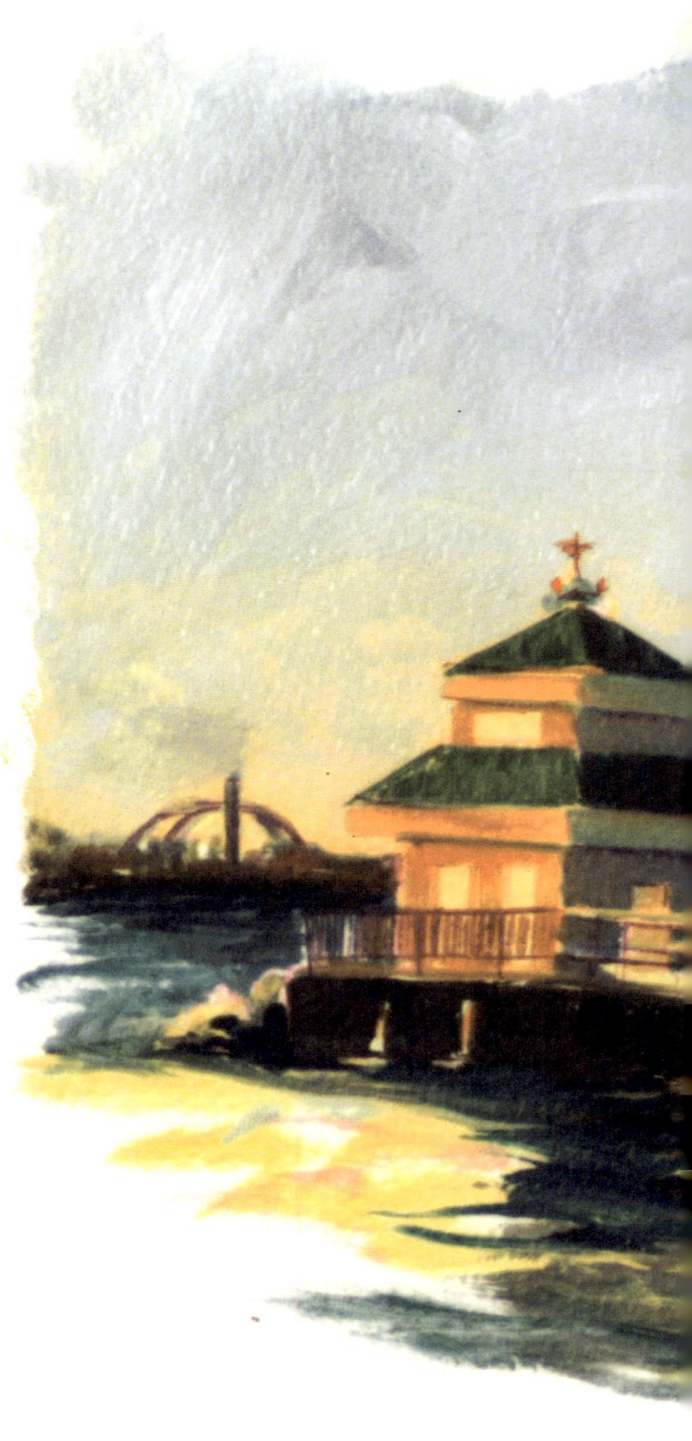

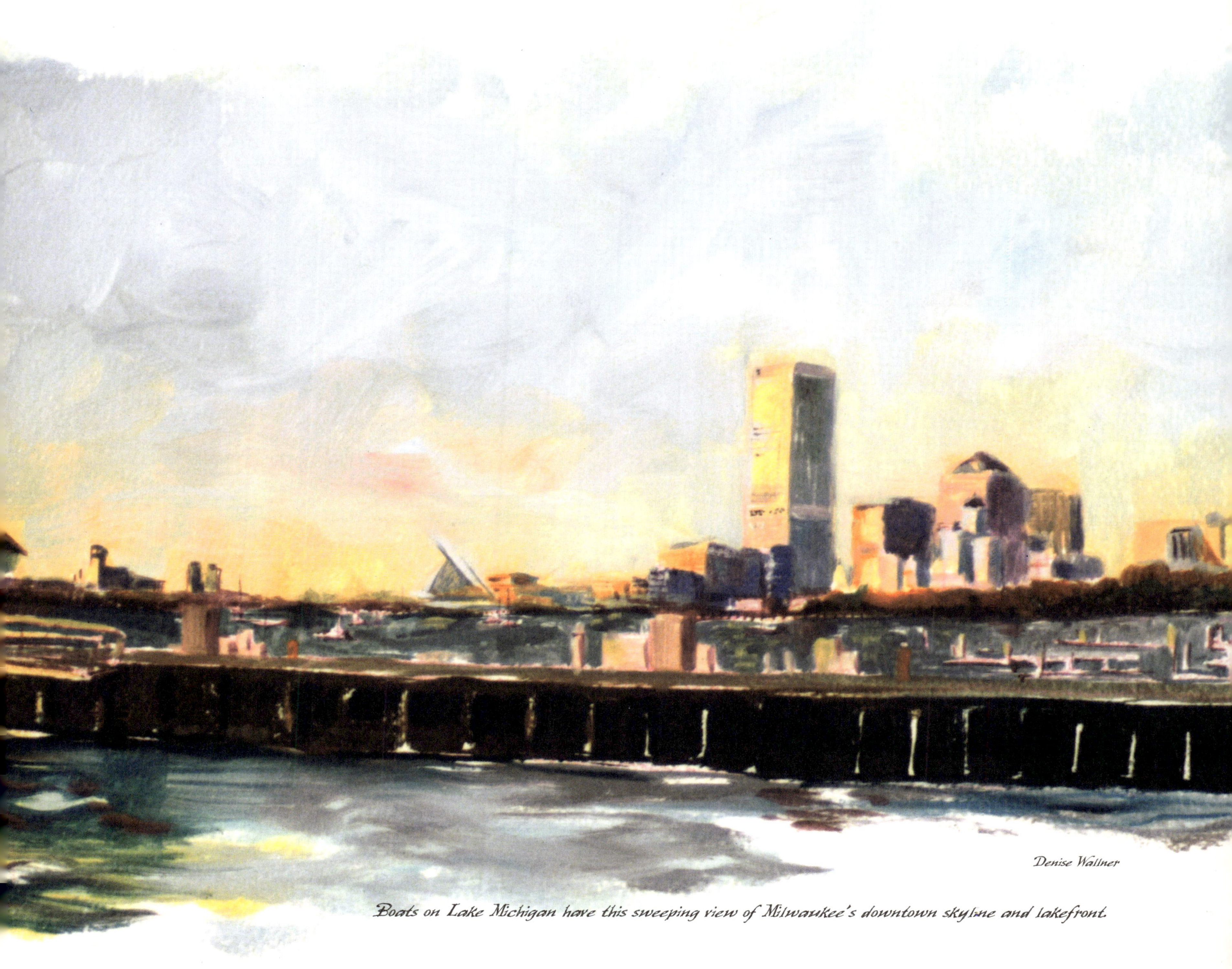

Denise Wallner

Boats on Lake Michigan have this sweeping view of Milwaukee's downtown skyline and lakefront.

tried to isolate and outdo the settlement Juneau was establishing on the opposite bank. The portly George Walker staked his claim south of the river in an area that still bears his name, Walker's Point.

Competition grew fierce as each of these early settlers vied to become the heart of this new city. Even today, most downtown bridges still cross the river at an angle because those early founders couldn't image a day when their streets would ever meet.

Though tempers flared and shots were fired, the competing settlers finally joined forces to become a city in 1846, two years before Wisconsin became a state.

By then, a young Scotsman named Alexander Mitchell already was making a name for himself, managing what became the Marine Bank as settlers poured into the new city intent on starting businesses and building homes. Mitchell soon realized how important a role railroads would play in forging the city's future, and by 1865 he'd bought up competing lines to create what ultimately became the Milwaukee Road system. He also envisioned Milwaukee becoming a world center of the wheat trade and a leading miller of flour (a title that eventually moved to Minneapolis).

To show off his business empire, Mitchell in the 1870s built both an elaborate headquarters for himself and a new home next door for the Chamber of Commerce, turning E. Michigan into the city's first financial hub. The building he built and leased to the Chamber featured an elaborate three story grain exchange room where fortunes were often made and lost on the turn of a trade. Today, those volatile deals have long been silenced, and the grain exchange room in the Mackie Building has been lovingly restored as a popular site for receptions and parties.

In 1883, tragedy struck the financial district when the city's leading hotel burned to the ground. But a new landmark soon rose from its ashes, the home offices of the Northwestern Mutual Life Insurance Company, which had been founded two years earlier in 1857 in Janesville. By 1914, Northwestern Mutual had built its own monumental home office on Wisconsin Ave. near the lakefront where it has grown steadily. Northwestern Mutual now insures more than 3 million policyholders and clients, making it the nation's leader in the field.

At the other end of town lay the Menomonee Valley. In the 1860s it was still a marshy swamp until a group of businessmen banded together to dredge canals and fill in the marsh, producing hundreds of acres of prime industrial land with dock frontage and the best in railroad service.

Before the muck was even dry, men whose names still dominate the city's business scene had begun turning the valley into an industrial hub. Still familiar today are names like John Plankinton, the butcher who with his partner Frederick Layton opened one of the first meat packing houses. Later as their packing house in the valley grew, it was plant manager Patrick Cudahy who turned the meat packing firm into one of the largest in the nation, producing pork products that still sell under his name.

Tanners like Guido Pfister and Frederick Vogel were quick to take advantage of all the hides available from the meatpackers, and Albert Trostel and August Gallun soon followed. With these German trained craftsmen leading the way, Milwaukee soon became a leader in producing shoes and boots and prospered in the 1860s by outfitting Union soldiers in the Civil War.

Milwaukee's most celebrated industry was of course the beer that was soon to make the city famous. Jacob Best began the first brewery back in 1840, but his beer was slow to prosper until Frederick Pabst took charge, renamed the brewery for himself and turned up the production, making Pabst the nation's largest brewery by 1874. His closest competitor was Joseph Schlitz, followed by Milwaukee's third largest brewer, Valentin Blatz. Joining them in 1855 was Frederick Miller, who founded what is now the nation's second largest brewery that still bears his name.

The Miller Brewing Company is now the city's only remaining major brewery. Though it is no longer locally owned, it still produces and bottles much of its beer from the west side site where it first began. In comparison, competitors like Schlitz, Pabst and Blatz are long closed. Most of their ornate brew houses have now been converted to more modern uses as office parks, restaurants, and condominiums.

The 1880s also saw the rise of another industry, the production of heavy machinery, which was soon to outpace beer as Milwaukee's leading industry. Leading the way was entrepreneur Edward Allis who, in the1860s, bought a bankrupt machine shop and began building his empire. As demand grew for his electric motors, gasoline engines and steam turbines, he expanded west into open countryside. By 1902 his factory was surrounded by the suburb now known as West Allis.

His firm, Allis Chalmers, was for years the state's largest corporation and the region's leading private employer until suffering a breathtaking crash in the 1980s. The sprawling 130-acre plant site has now been converted to offices and retail shops still surrounded by hundreds of sturdy homes built by the workers once employed there.

The world's largest four-sided clock that serves as both a beacon and landmark on Milwaukee's south side also marks the spot where Lynde Bradley in 1902 rented shop space and with the help of his brother Harry designed the electrical motor controls that grew into what is now Rockwell Automation.

Meanwhile on the west side, two men who had been working together in a bicycle factory, William Harley and Arthur Davidson, began experimenting with a motorized bike. Working in a shed that Davidson's father had built on the west side, they developed a company that in 1907 became the Harley-Davidson Motor Company. Thus began a tradition that still draws Harley riders by the thousands to rallies that fill Milwaukee's streets.

The daring of Milwaukee's early entrepreneurs helped to shape the city into a place where jobs were plentiful, giving it the image of the blue collar stronghold that it remains today. Local historian John Gurda, in his book "The Making of Milwaukee," describes Milwaukee as a "workingman's city, a place that offered

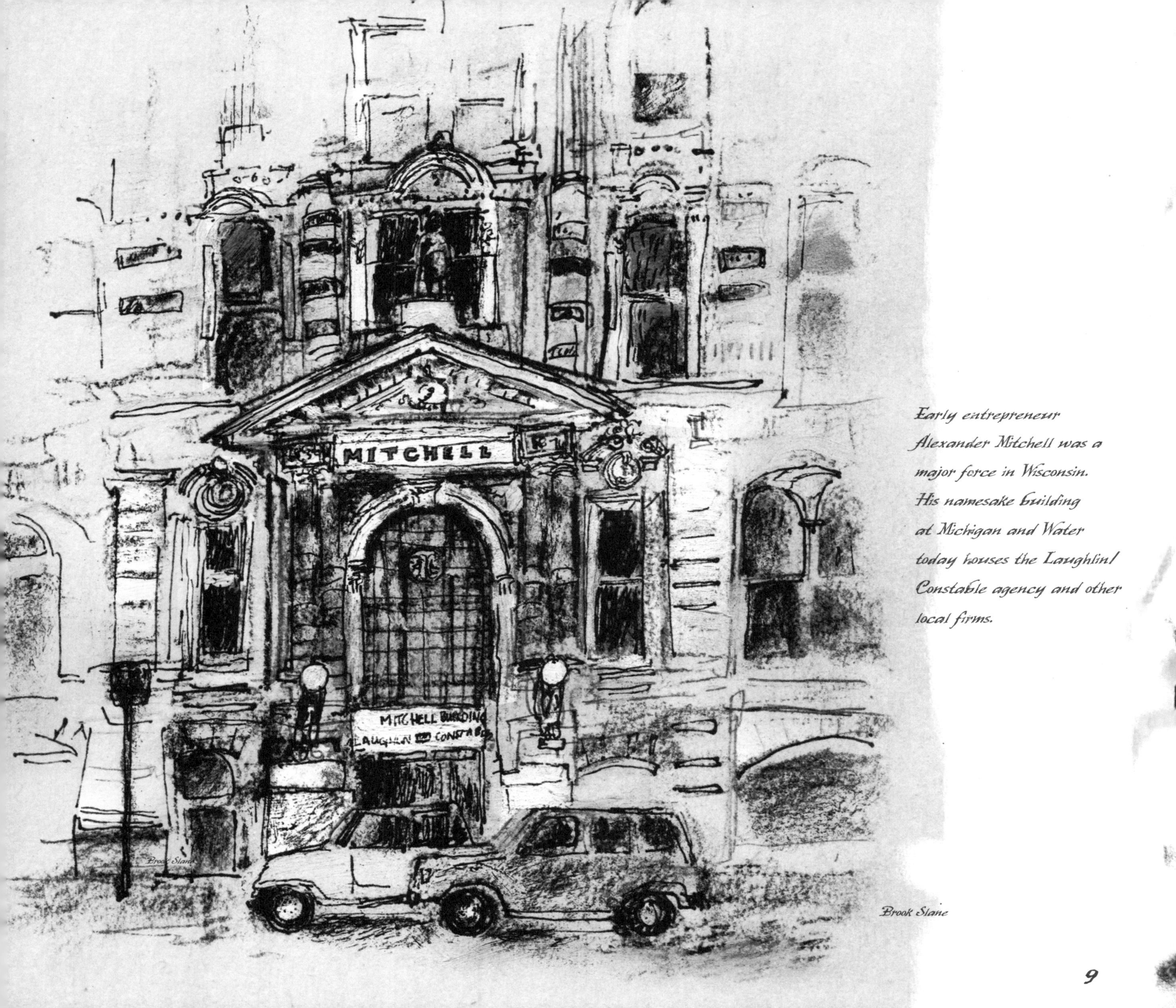

Early entrepreneur Alexander Mitchell was a major force in Wisconsin. His namesake building at Michigan and Water today houses the Laughlin/ Constable agency and other local firms.

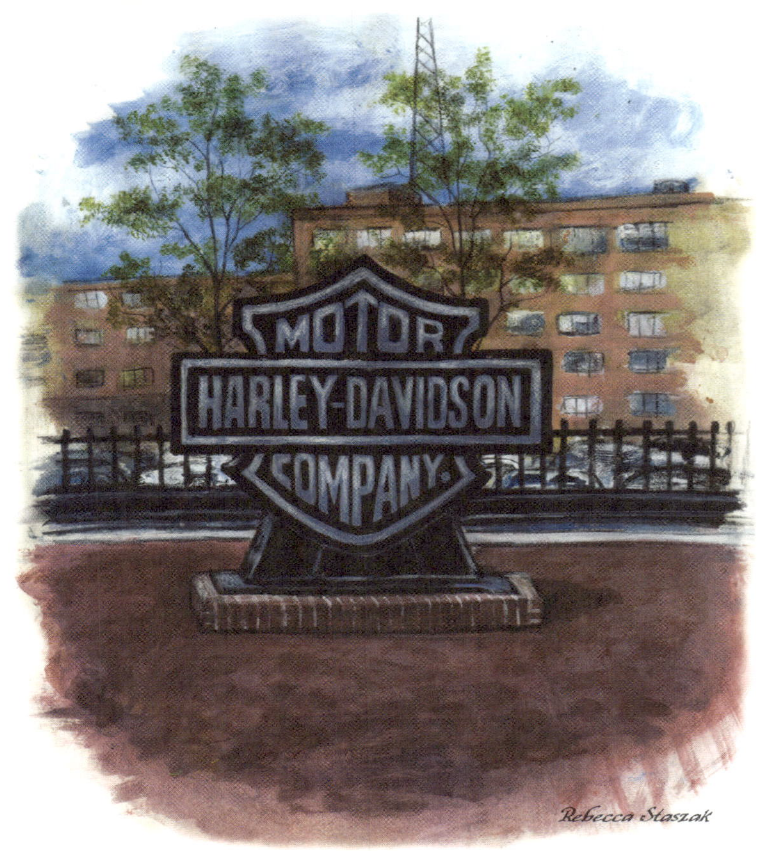

William Harley and Arthur Davidson were working together in a bicycle factory when they got the idea for a motorized bike. By 1907, they had moved to the west side where their home office is still located today.

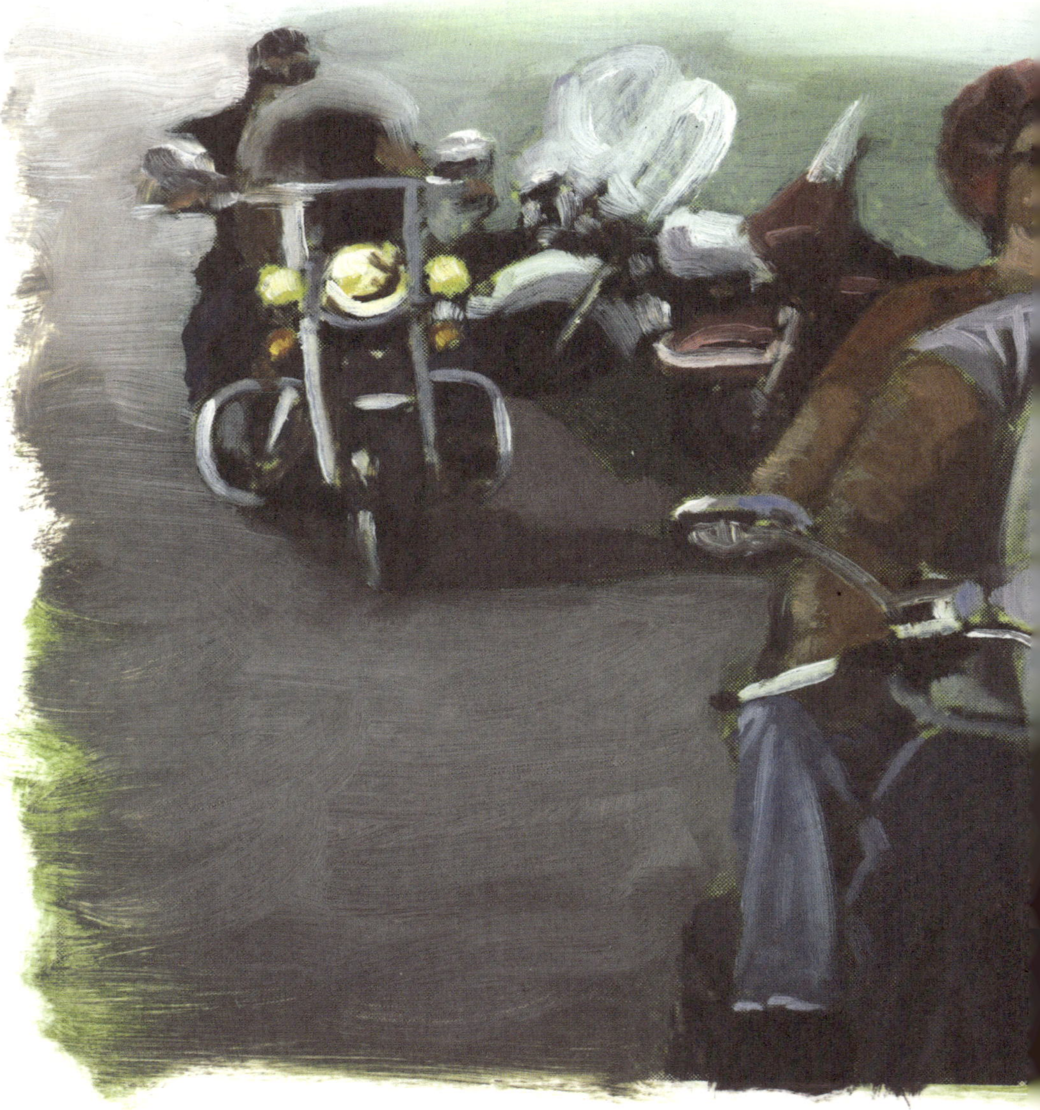

To celebrate its anniversaries, Harley invites its Harley Owners Groups (HOGs) from across the US to ride home to Milwaukee together. No other city welcomes Harley riders like Milwaukee does.

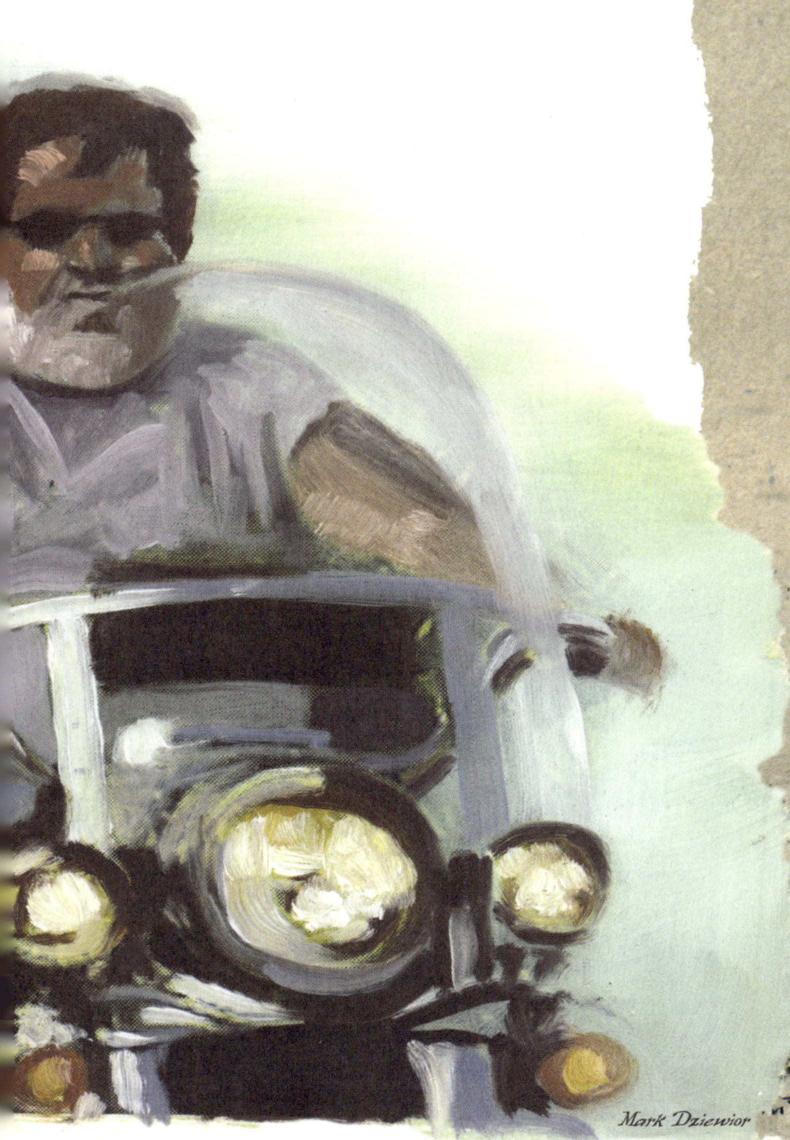

even the poorest newcomer good air, good water, cheap living and a place to found a home of his own."

Yet the Germans, who dominated the city on every social and economic level, also made sure it was a city that knew how to have a good time. For example, on many a local corner, the city's German brewers opened competing taverns that served only their own brand of beer. There were lush beer gardens, music halls and restaurants to cater to the fun loving Germans.

The Germans were eager to make friends with the other ethnic groups settling in the city. So in 1852, they invited all their fellow Milwaukeeans to the city's first ethnic festival. It drew 10,000 people to a day filled with music, dancing, outdoor games and of course drinking some of Milwaukee's favorite beers and wines.

The idea of a civic festival was to return in 1933, when this beer capital celebrated the end of Prohibition with a fest in the auditorium Downtown. The event was so successful that it continued on the lakefront until the outbreak of war in 1941.

In 1967, Henry Maier, who was then mayor, promoted turning Milwaukee into a city of festivals. But it wasn't until 1970 when the city took over an abandoned Nike missile site on Milwaukee's lakefront that Summerfest began to blossom into the annual 11-day music festival which now draws some of the nation's top jazz, rock, country, and blues performers.

By the late 1960s, new expressways had taken a large bite out of Milwaukee's old Third Ward near the lakefront, displacing a tightly knit Italian community. Still stung by the loss of its home, in 1978 their community decided to hold a reunion on Summerfest grounds. Festa Italiana is now the largest of a series of ethnic festivals that fill the grounds all summer and help keep each group's traditions alive.

Building The City Beautiful

It took time for Milwaukee to realize that it was truly "a great city on a great lake" as an earlier slogan had proclaimed. Not until the 1920s did extensive landfill create the beaches, marinas, and elegant Lincoln Memorial Drive that now curves along much of the city's lakefront.

Instead, it was really the Milwaukee River - not Lake Michigan - that Milwaukeeans headed to when they wanted to have fun. The river had been central to city life ever since the Potawatomi Indians came by canoe to trade their pelts to Solomon Juneau in the city's earliest days. But what attracted people to canoe there in the late 1800s was the long narrow pond created by the old North Avenue dam, which was soon lined with beer gardens, swimming schools, amusement parks, and the summer homes of wealthy German entrepreneurs, according to local historian Tom Tolan.

Although the last swimming school didn't close until 1940, the river had already become a polluted open sewer, ending its glory days. In1997, the dam was finally

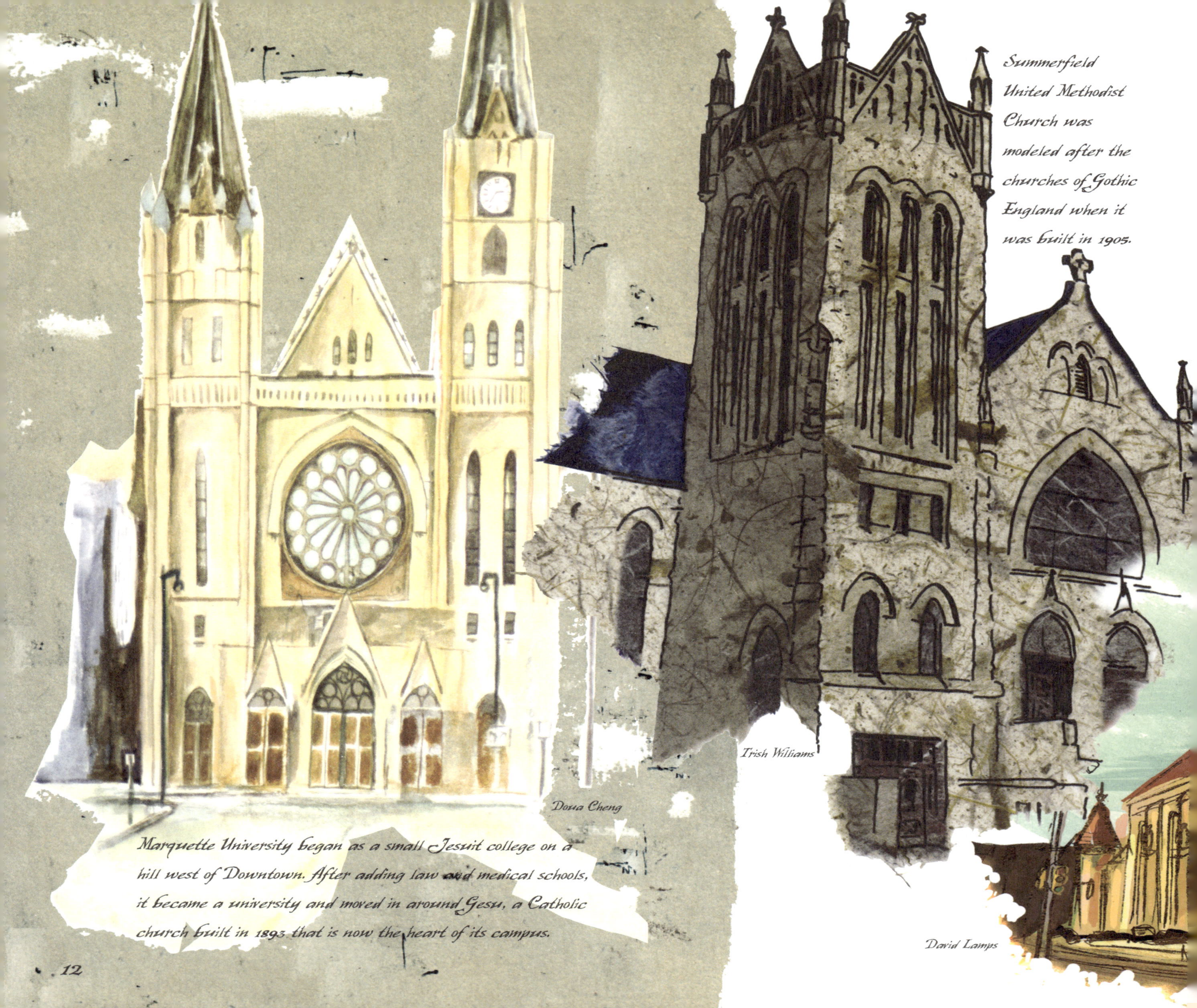

Summerfield United Methodist Church was modeled after the churches of Gothic England when it was built in 1905.

Marquette University began as a small Jesuit college on a hill west of Downtown. After adding law and medical schools, it became a university and moved in around Gesu, a Catholic church built in 1893 that is now the heart of its campus.

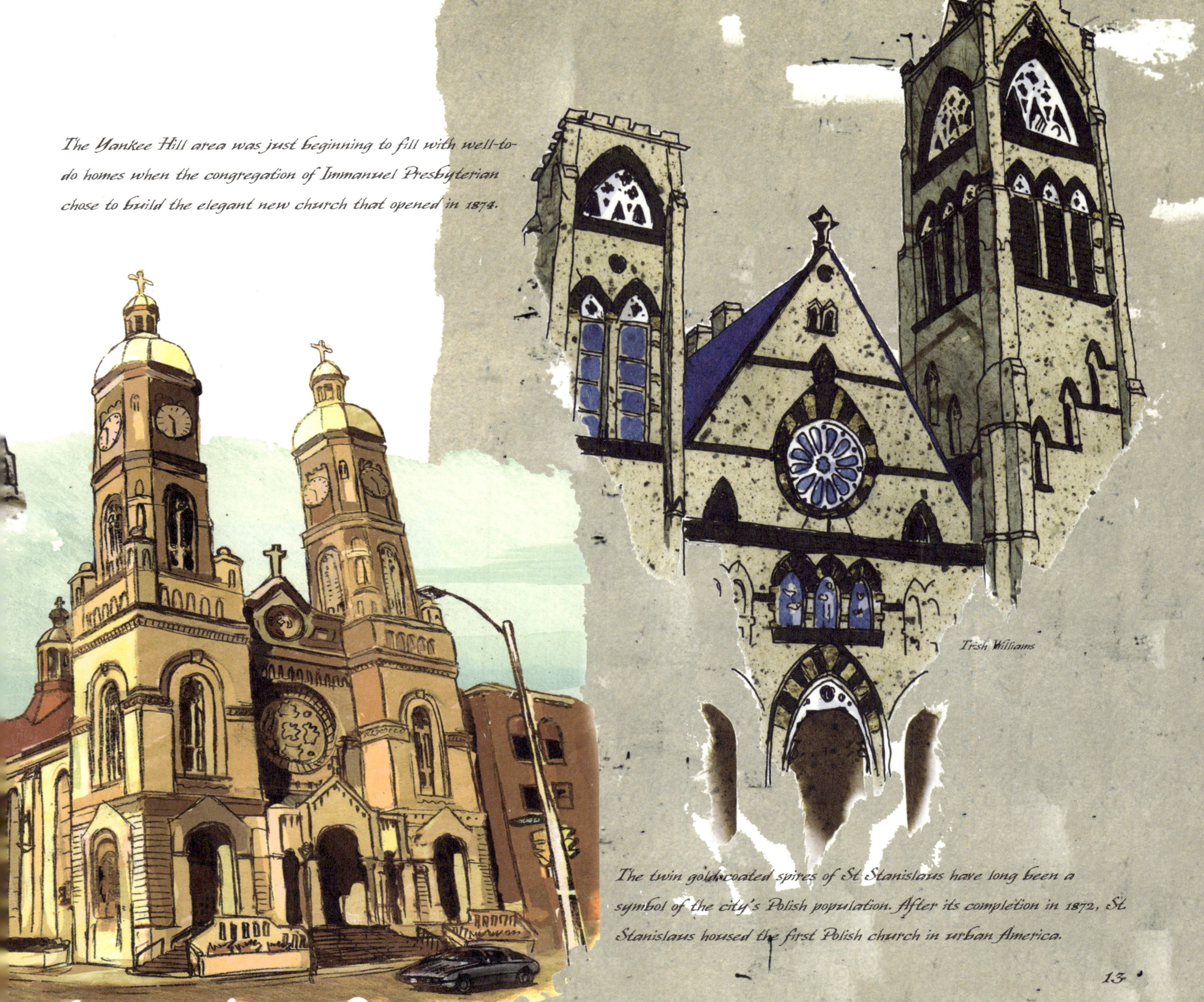

The Yankee Hill area was just beginning to fill with well-to-do homes when the congregation of Immanuel Presbyterian chose to build the elegant new church that opened in 1874.

The twin gold-coated spires of St Stanislaus have long been a symbol of the city's Polish population. After its completion in 1872, St Stanislaus housed the first Polish church in urban America.

removed, bringing new life to long stagnant waters. By then, the river had been cleaned up and was well on its way to a remarkable new life with a bustling downtown riverwalk and the conversion of scores of old factories into fancy new condominiums.

The days once enjoyed by the city's early settlers in the beer gardens that once lined the river have now returned, but in a modern new garb our ancestors could never have envisioned.

The Milwaukee River was not the only local waterway to cling to some of its past, thanks to Charles Whitnall, who for 40 years was the chief architect of Milwaukee's park system. Whitnall had grown up along the river where his father had an extensive flower and greenhouse business. He welcomed the day when Milwaukee would sprawl out into the countryside. In fact, Whitnall even designed a road map that in effect envisioned the expressways to come.

But Whitnall's real vision, released in 1923, was his plan for the system of parks and parkways that follow Milwaukee's rivers, creeks, and lakefront. Today, Milwaukeeans live near gardens and parks and commute on new highways because of Whitnall's vision which extended all across the region, making Milwaukee truly a garden city.

City Neighborhoods

Standing today looking out across the city, it is easy to see why Milwaukee became known as a city of spires and smokestacks. As each new wave of immigrants arrived and found new jobs, new churches were soon to rise as the center of their community.

Among the first was the Cathedral of St. John the Evangelist that since 1847 has stood on Jackson Street as the heart of the Catholic community.

The wide open spaces on Milwaukee's south side became a magnet for many of the Polish immigrants who longed to build tiny homes of their own near their jobs in nearby industrial plants. In 1866, St. Stanislaus became the first Polish congregation in urban America. Its twin spires, now covered in gold leaf, still welcome visitors to Mitchell Street, which for years was so popular as a shopping center that it became known as the Polish Grand Avenue.

But the gulf between rich and poor was quickly widening. Some of the more prosperous newcomers, many of them Yankees from New England, had begun settling on Milwaukee's east side in an area still known as Yankee Hill. Immanuel Presbyterian had been meeting in several other sites since 1836, when it finally built a grand home of its own on Astor Street in 1874. It was joined in the early 1900s by churches like Summerfield United Methodist. Their congregations included some of the city's most prominent names who were filling the lake bluff area with homes for the well-to-do. Until the turn of the century, Yankee Hill was the wealthiest area of the city.

The west side also had its share of wealthy mansions as meat packers, industrial barons, and financiers built their elaborate Victorian palaces on what is now the city's main street, Wisconsin Avenue. The area eventually became more a workingman's setting, thanks to the array of jobs available at nearby rail yards and breweries.

Meanwhile in 1881, a group of Jesuits opened a small college on a west side hill. As the school grew, it absorbed some of the old neighborhoods to create its present campus on Wisconsin Avenue, where in 1907 it opened schools of law and medicine and became Marquette University.

Many of the patterns established in those early days can still be traced today. Local historian John Gurda says that urban areas expand in very predictable ways, taking their identities with them as they move further away from the city's center. Thus the industries on the near south side gave birth to the more industrial flavor of the southern suburbs, while the east side continued to expand onto the more affluent north shore. The west side, originally home to the city's Germans, later attracted Irish and Jewish strongholds, then became home to the African American community of today.

It is still possible to stroll down neighborhood streets like Brady Street, on the east side, and sample the pastries, sausages, and gelato the descendants of its original Polish and Italian merchants still sell there. The street is more upscale now, with fancy shops and restaurants joining its older Italian groceries and bakeries.

On the south side, a stroll down S. Kinnickinnic and other historic streets in Bay View also feels like a step back in time. The old Bay View iron mill that once was Milwaukee's first real step toward becoming a manufacturing center is now long gone. But the small, tidy houses built by scores of the mill's workers are still lived in today.

Tourists and residents alike still gather on the west side for tours of the historic Miller Brewery that now mixes its gleaming new technology with carefully preserved memories of the old.

The city has identified nearly 100 different neighborhoods that still retain a distinctive character their residents point to with pride. Historic street signs now help to build each community's sense of identity.

That's the very nature of this place called Milwaukee. Roots run deep here, and plans for the future still take into account how the past helped create the city of today.

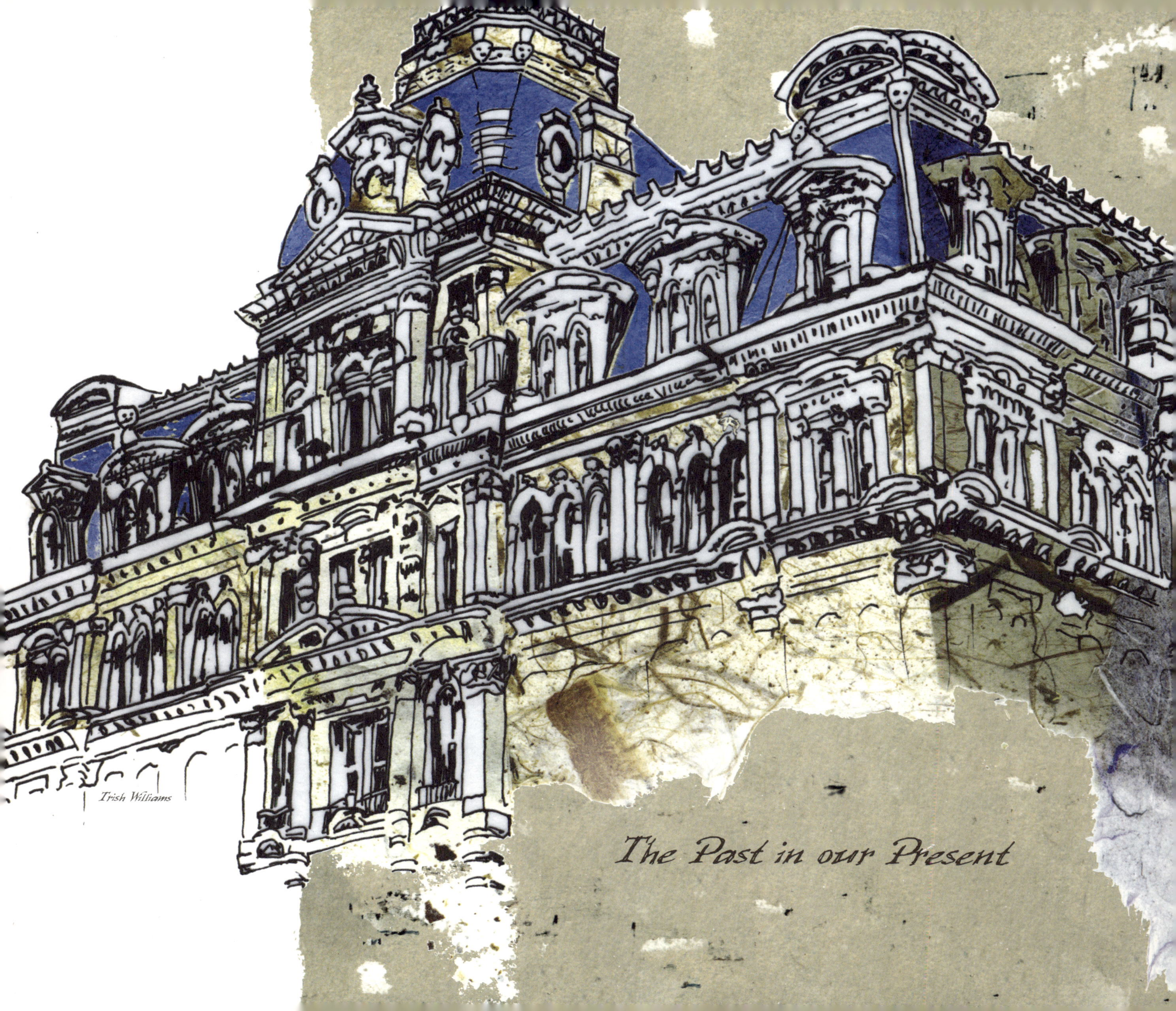
Trish Williams
The Past in our Present

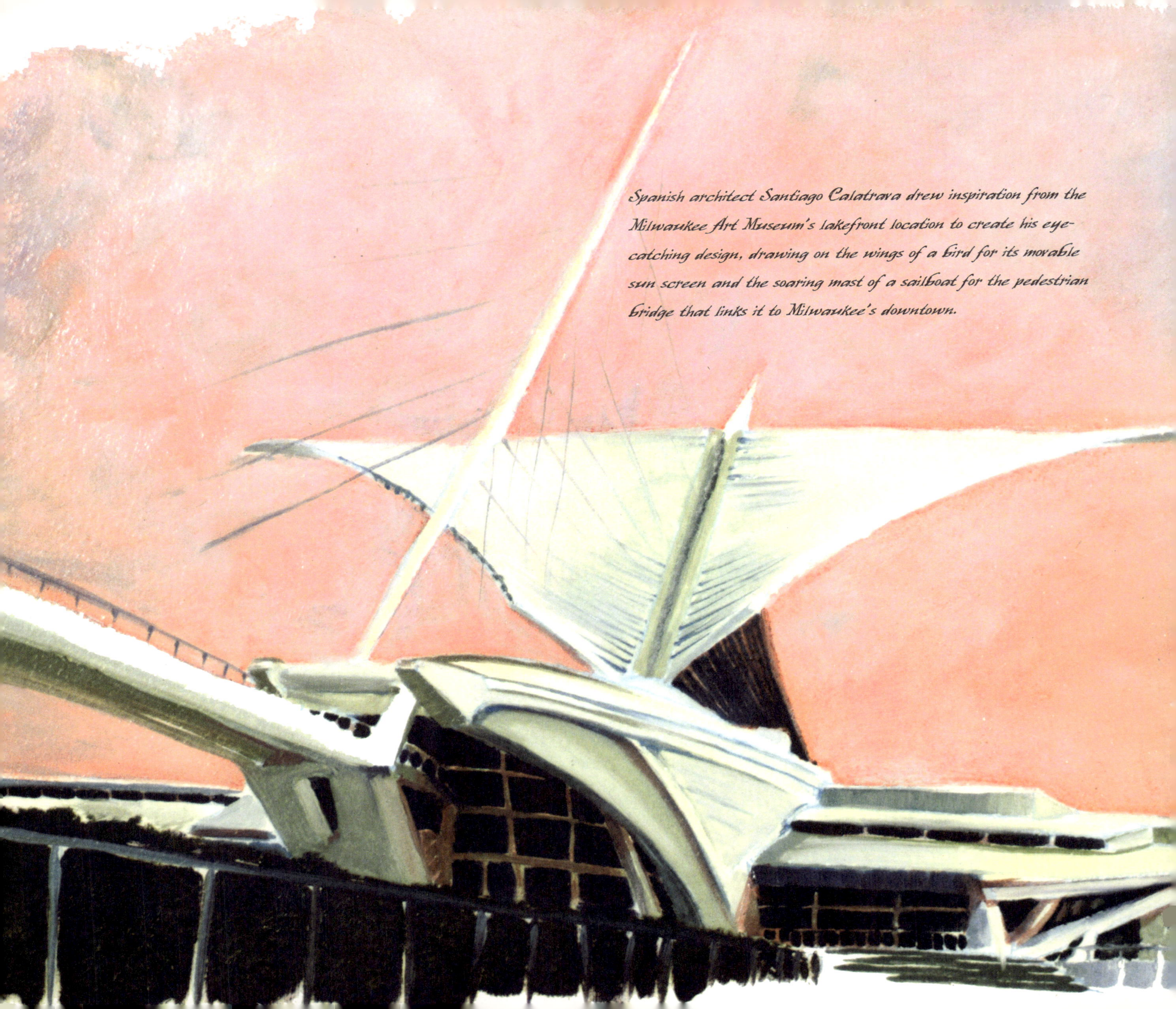

Spanish architect Santiago Calatrava drew inspiration from the Milwaukee Art Museum's lakefront location to create his eye-catching design, drawing on the wings of a bird for its movable sun screen and the soaring mast of a sailboat for the pedestrian bridge that links it to Milwaukee's downtown.

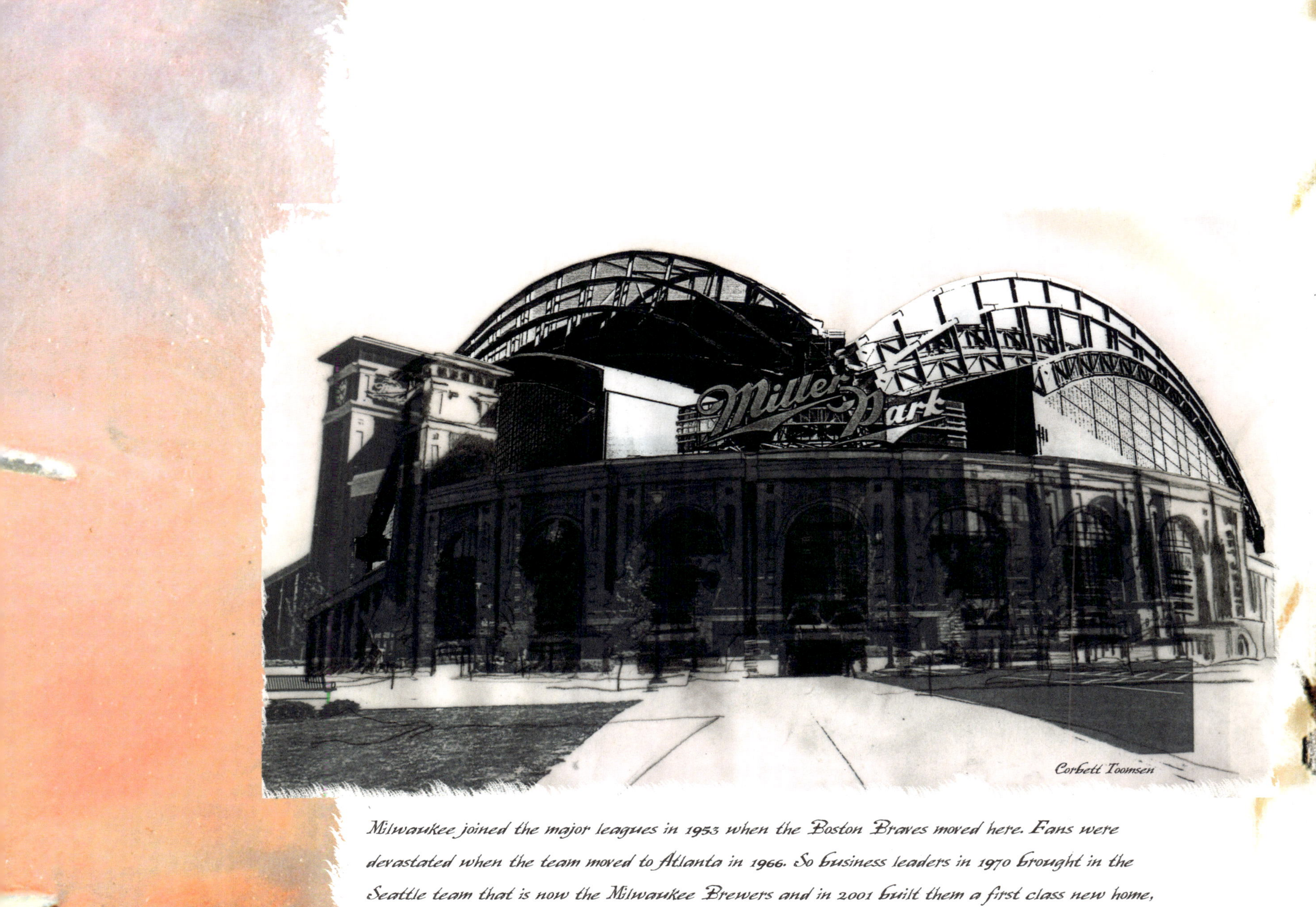

Corbett Toomsen

Denise Wallner

Milwaukee joined the major leagues in 1953 when the Boston Braves moved here. Fans were devastated when the team moved to Atlanta in 1966. So business leaders in 1970 brought in the Seattle team that is now the Milwaukee Brewers and in 2001 built them a first class new home, Miller Park.

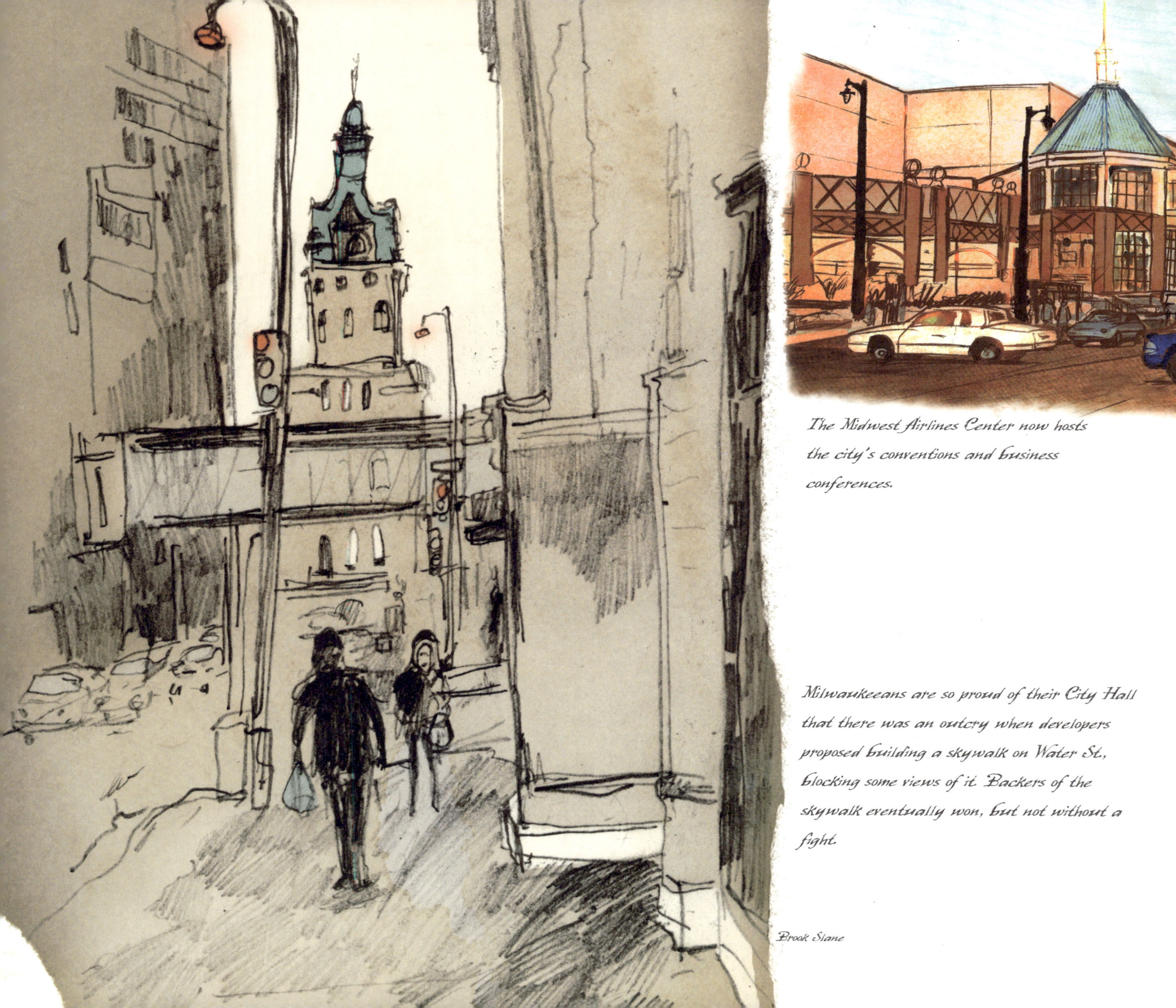

The Midwest Airlines Center now hosts the city's conventions and business conferences.

Milwaukeeans are so proud of their City Hall that there was an outcry when developers proposed building a skywalk on Water St., blocking some views of it. Backers of the skywalk eventually won, but not without a fight.

Brook Slane

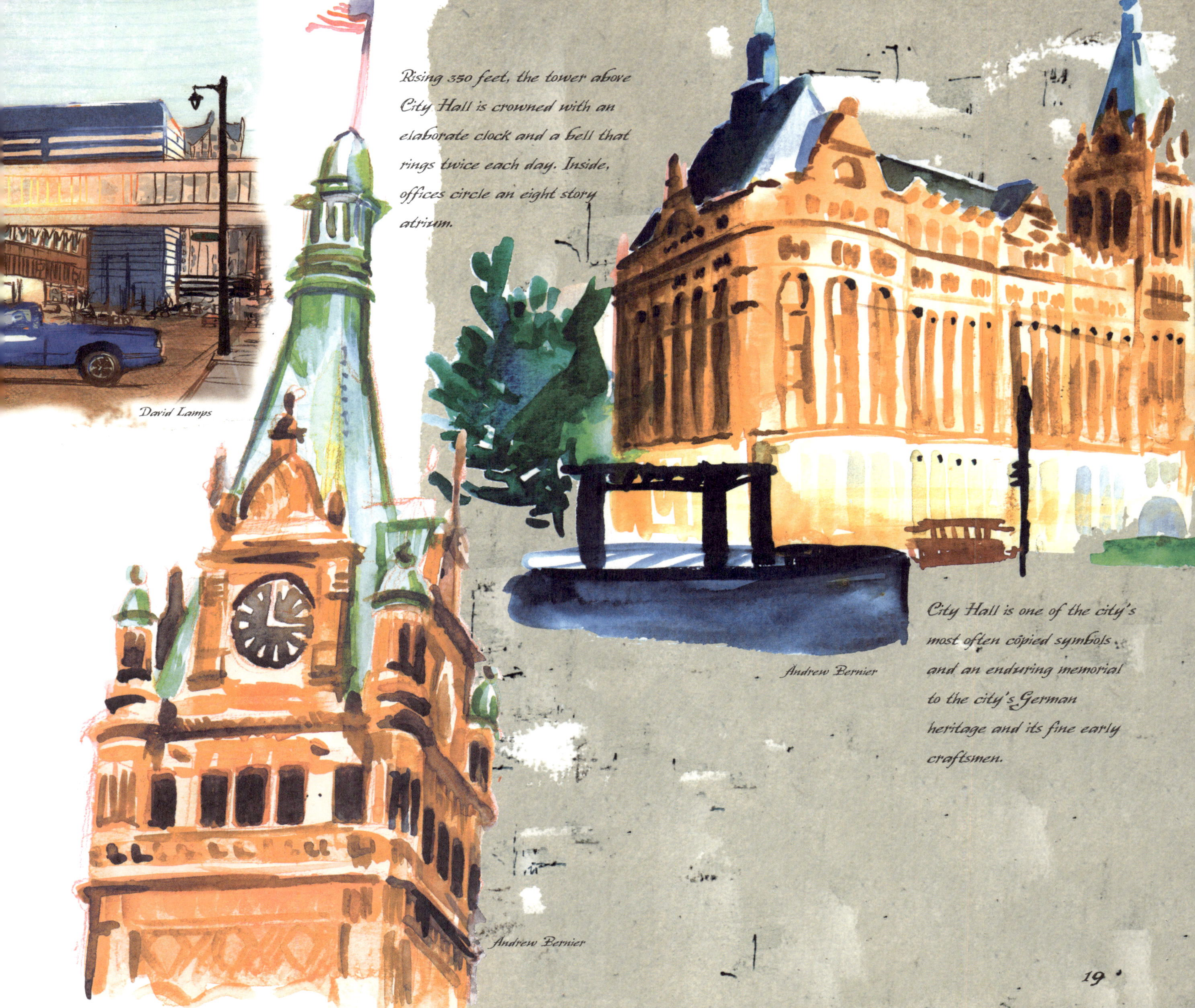

David Lamps

Rising 350 feet, the tower above City Hall is crowned with an elaborate clock and a bell that rings twice each day. Inside, offices circle an eight story atrium.

Andrew Bernier

City Hall is one of the city's most often copied symbols and an enduring memorial to the city's German heritage and its fine early craftsmen.

Andrew Bernier

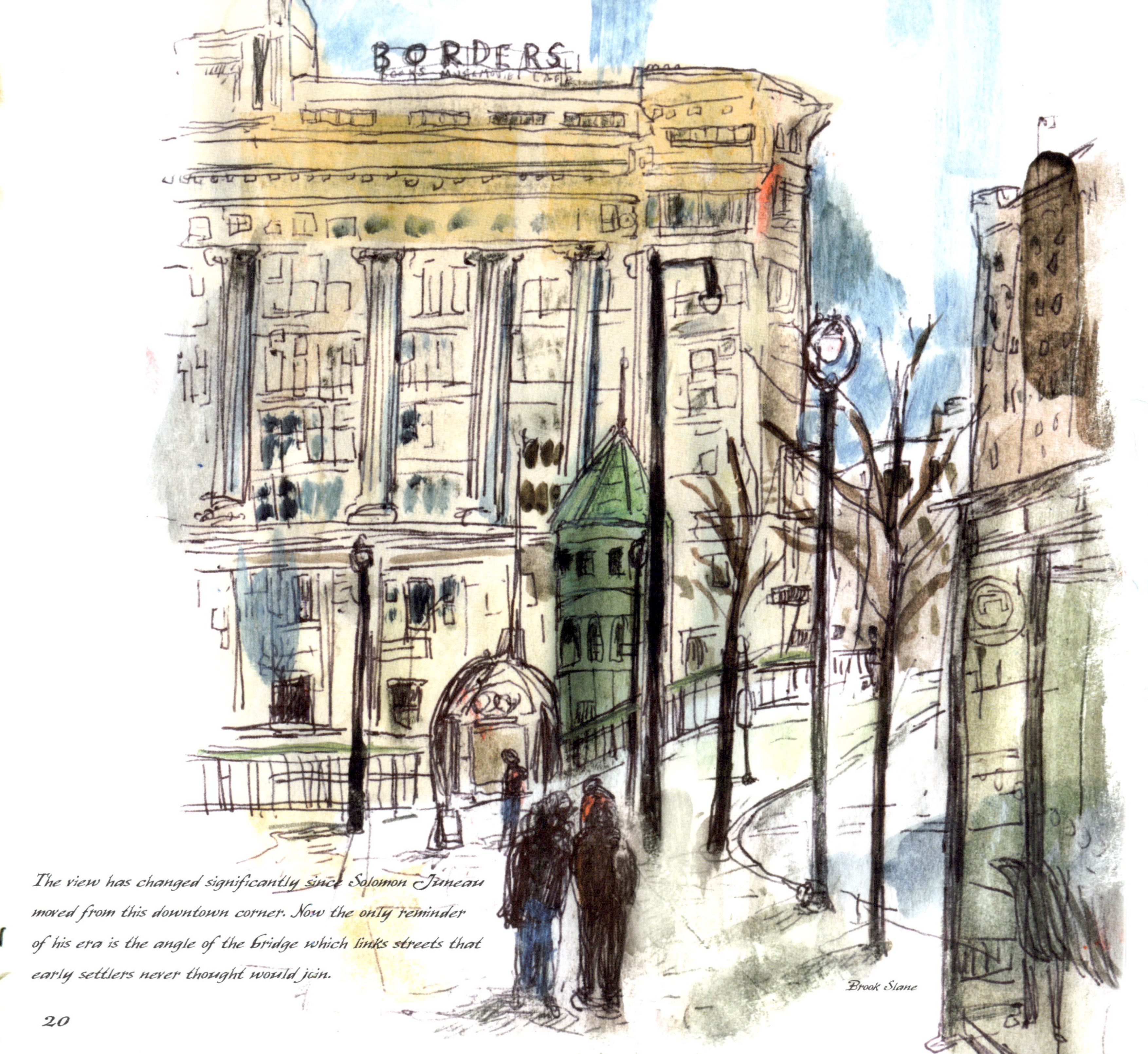

The view has changed significantly since Solomon Juneau moved from this downtown corner. Now the only reminder of his era is the angle of the bridge which links streets that early settlers never thought would join.

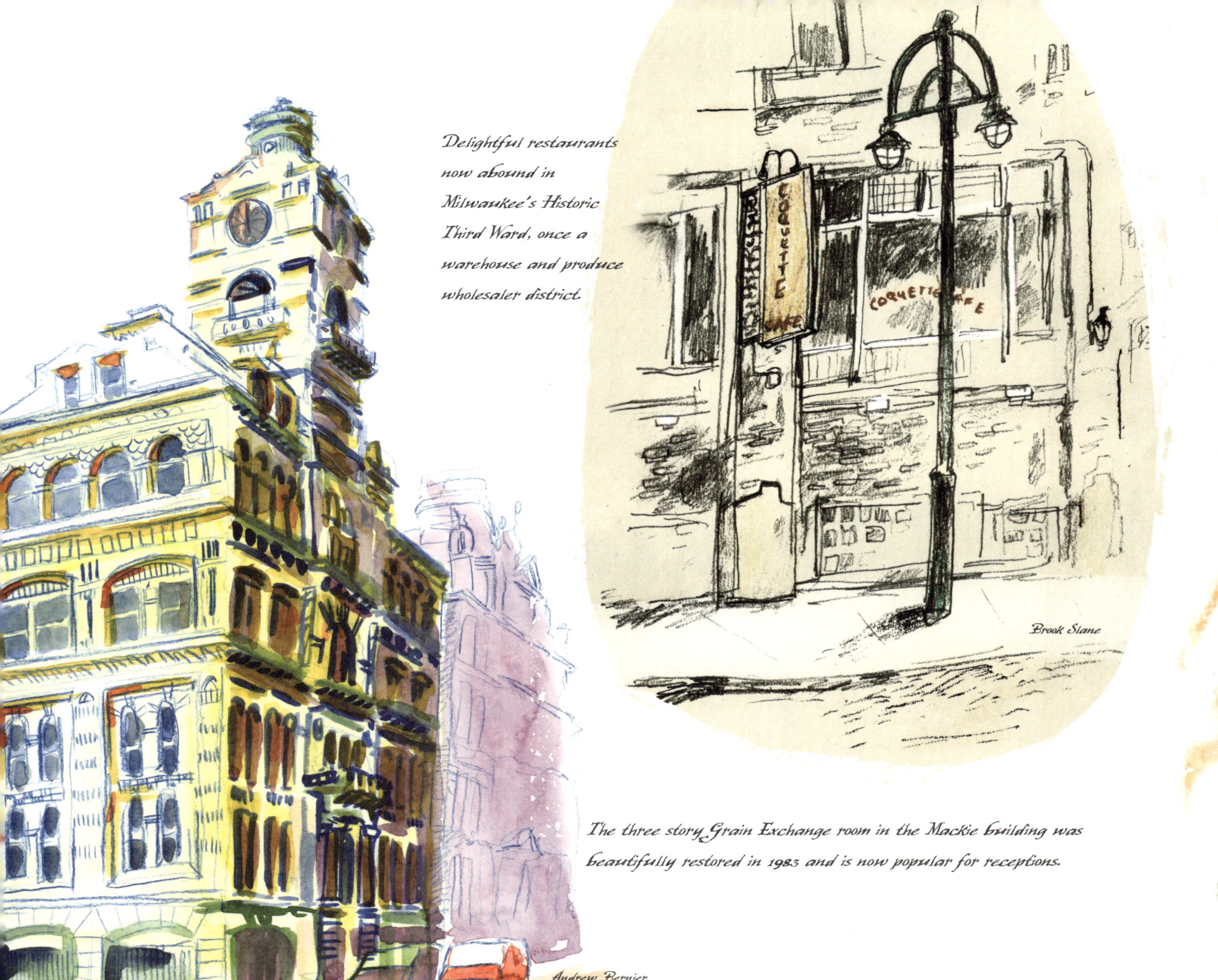

Delightful restaurants now abound in Milwaukee's Historic Third Ward, once a warehouse and produce wholesaler district.

Brook Slane

The three story Grain Exchange room in the Mackie building was beautifully restored in 1983 and is now popular for receptions.

Andrew Bernier

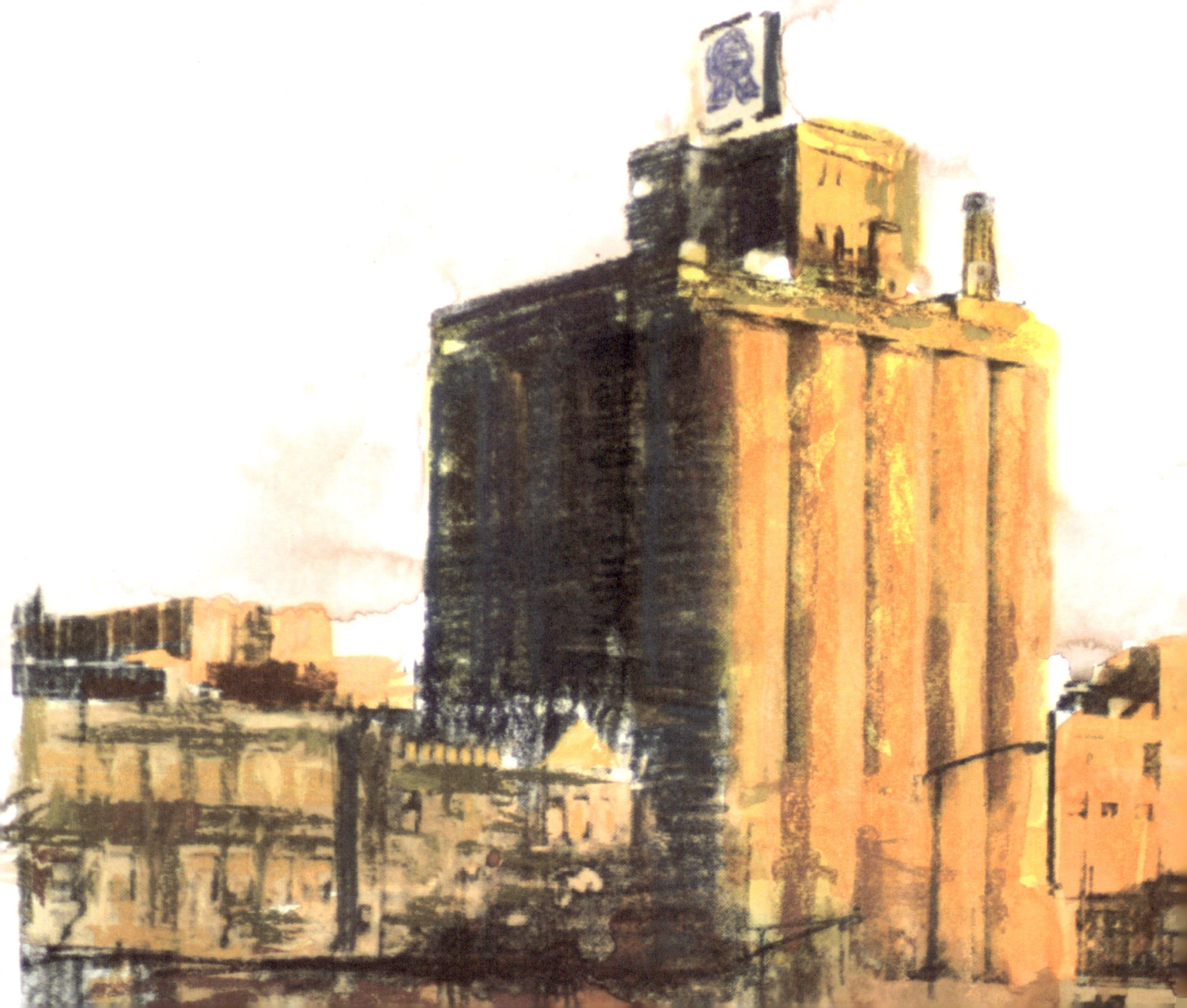

Once a key contributor to Milwaukee's reputation as the brewing capital of the world, the historic Pabst Brewing Company buildings overlook the heart of the city from their hilltop perch on downtown's western edge.

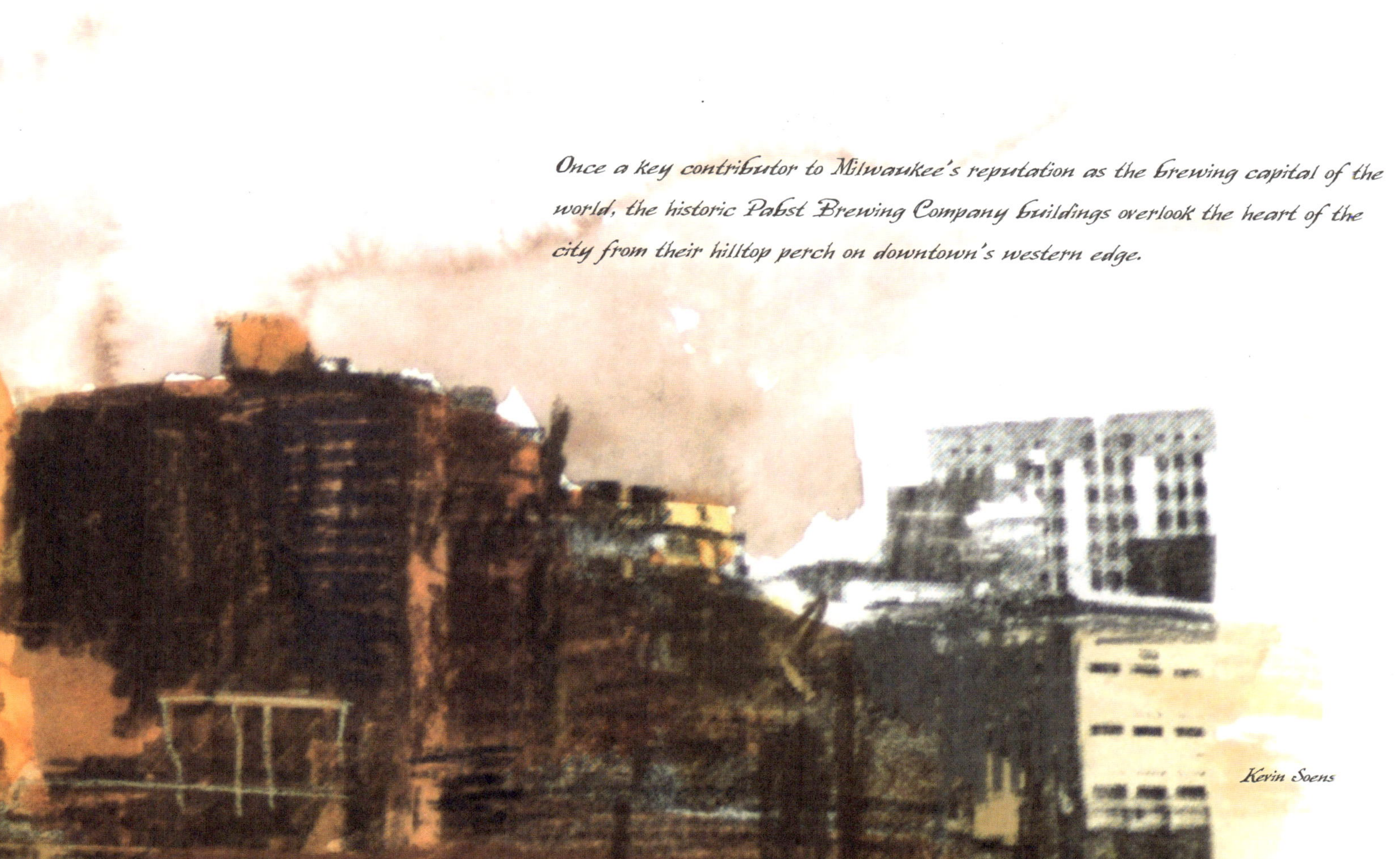

Kevin Soens

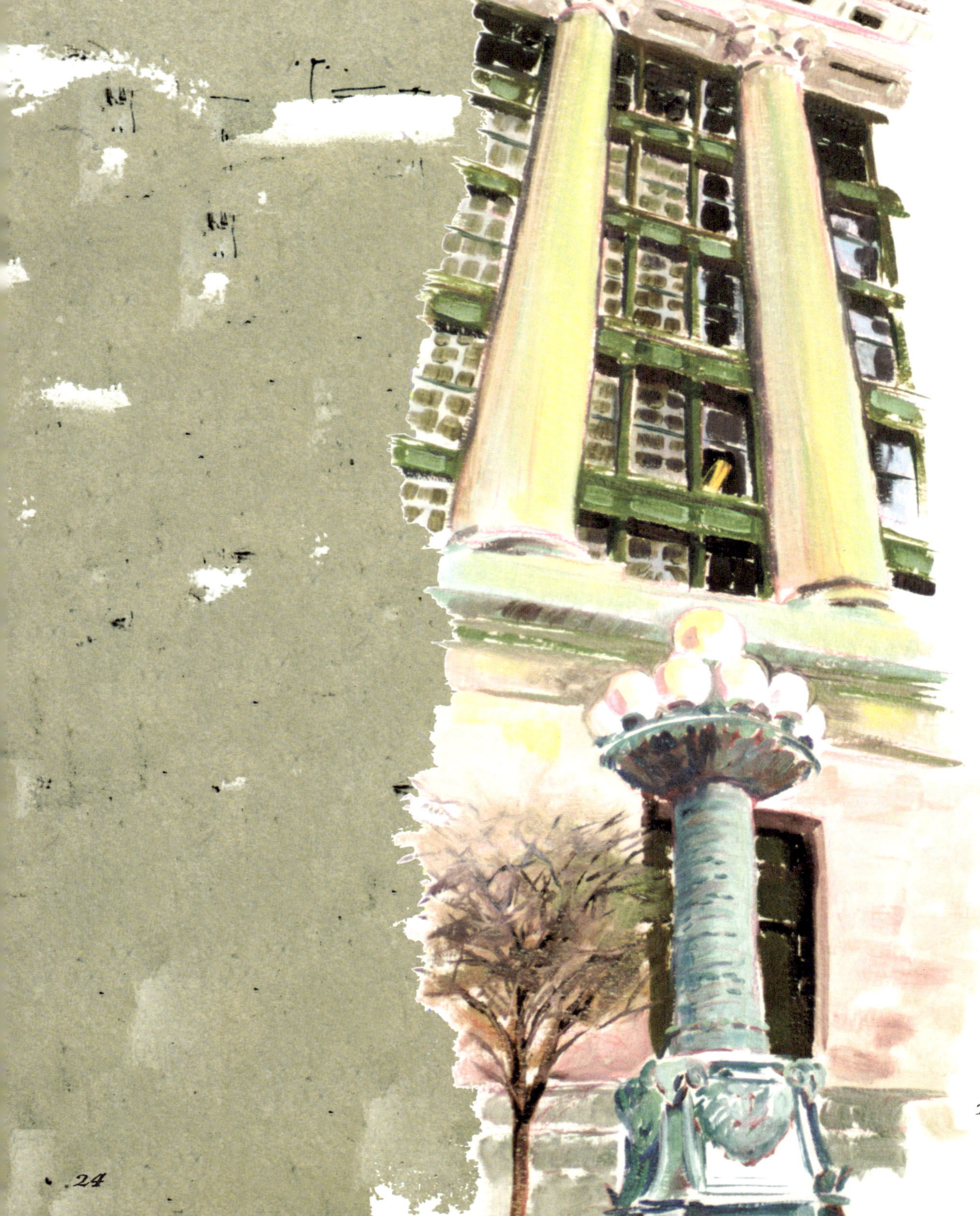

Denise Wallner

In addition to being a major insurer, Northwestern Mutual also has been a major investor in Milwaukee as well as the nation. Its massive granite headquarters building, completed in 1914, is a symbol of its success.

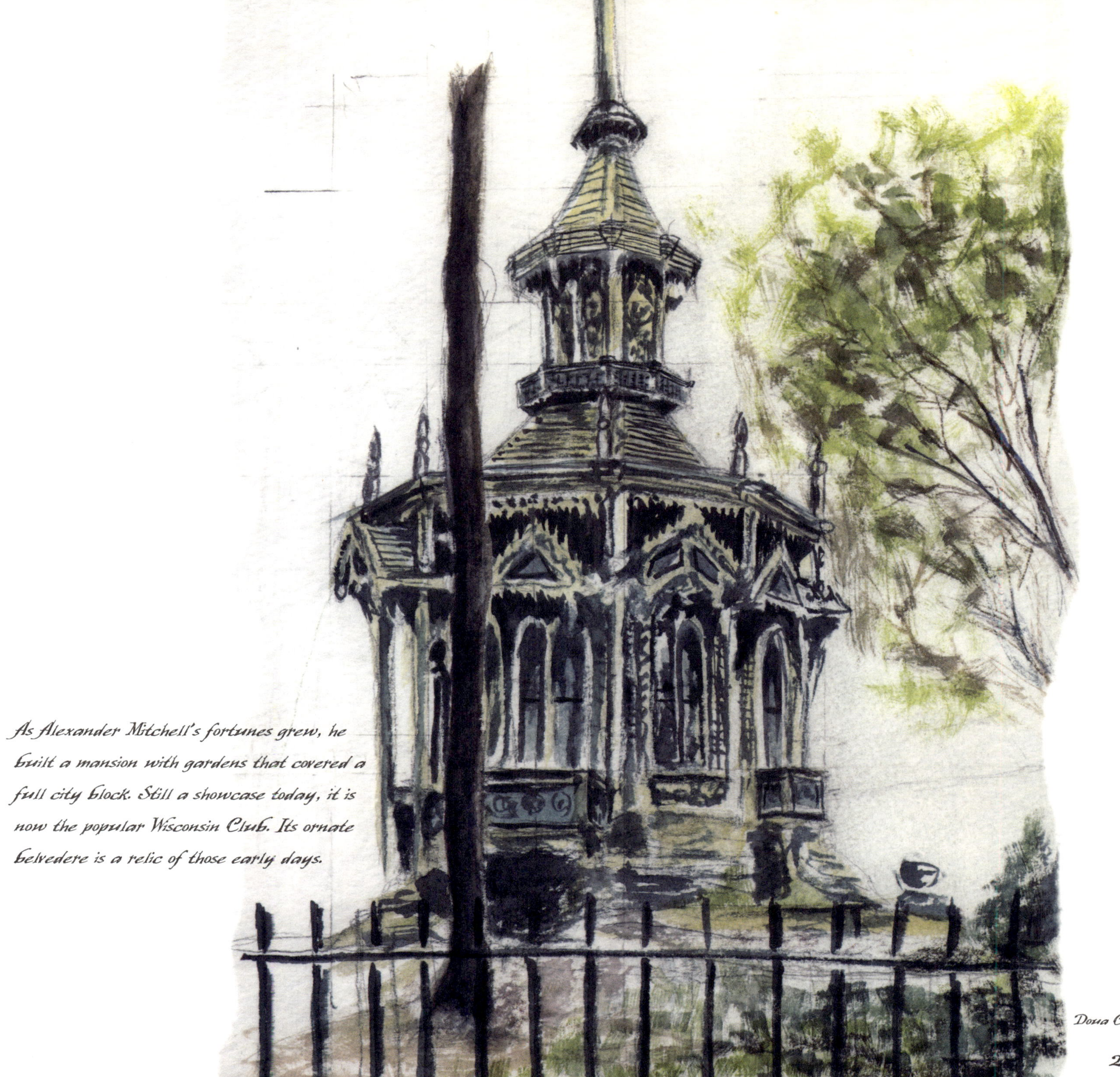

As Alexander Mitchell's fortunes grew, he built a mansion with gardens that covered a full city block. Still a showcase today, it is now the popular Wisconsin Club. Its ornate belvedere is a relic of those early days.

Doua Cheng

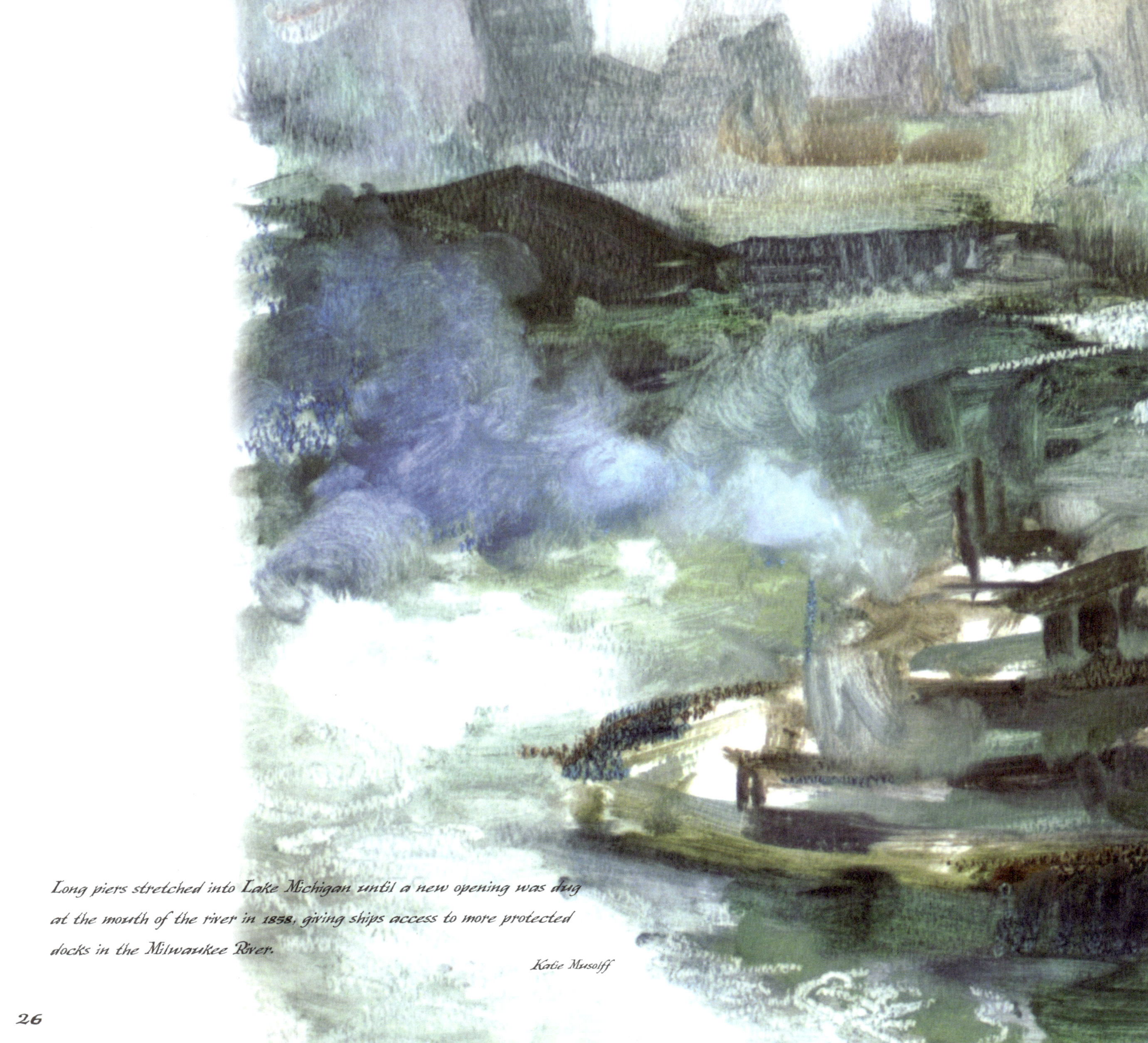

Long piers stretched into Lake Michigan until a new opening was dug at the mouth of the river in 1858, giving ships access to more protected docks in the Milwaukee River.

Katie Musolff

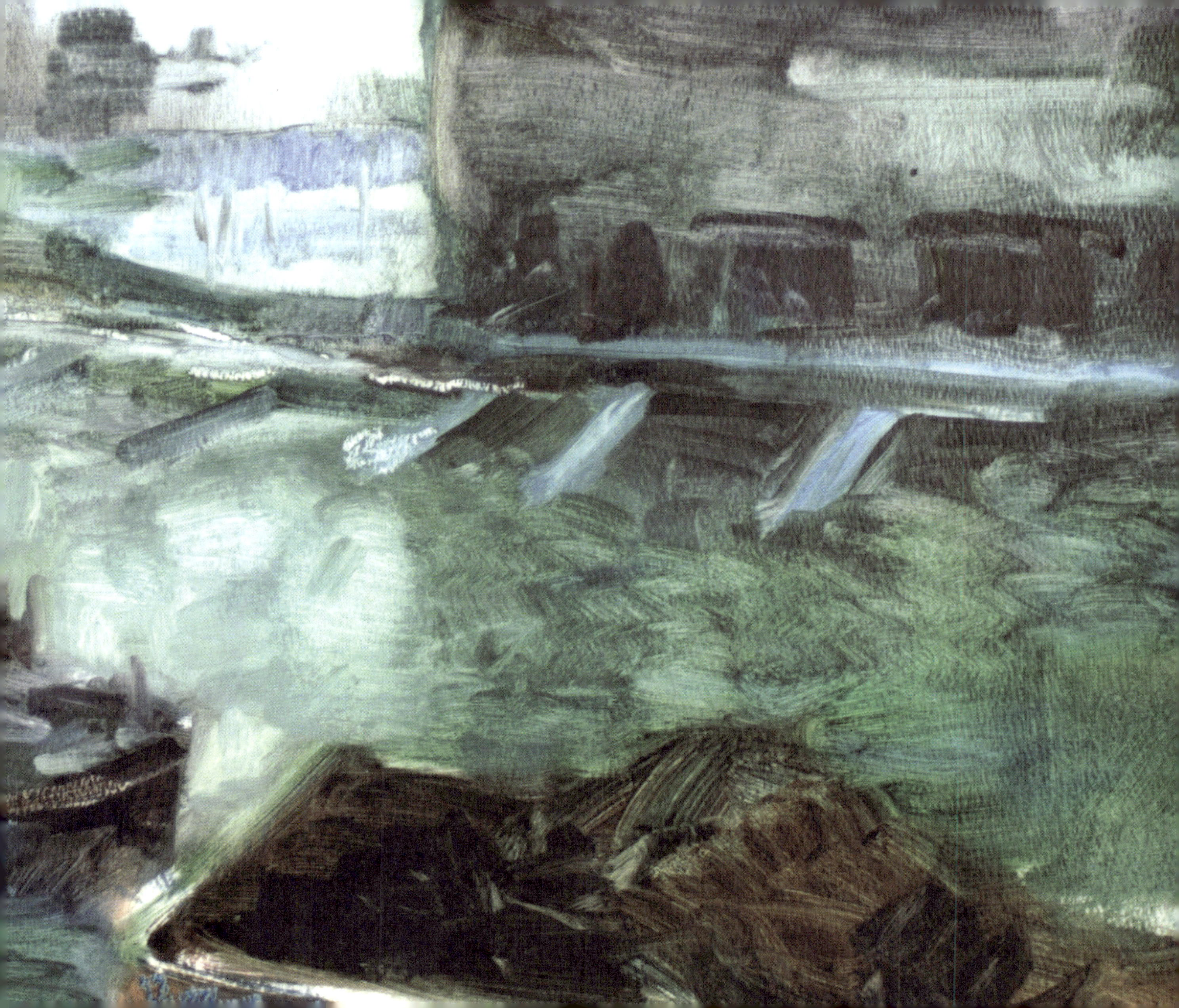

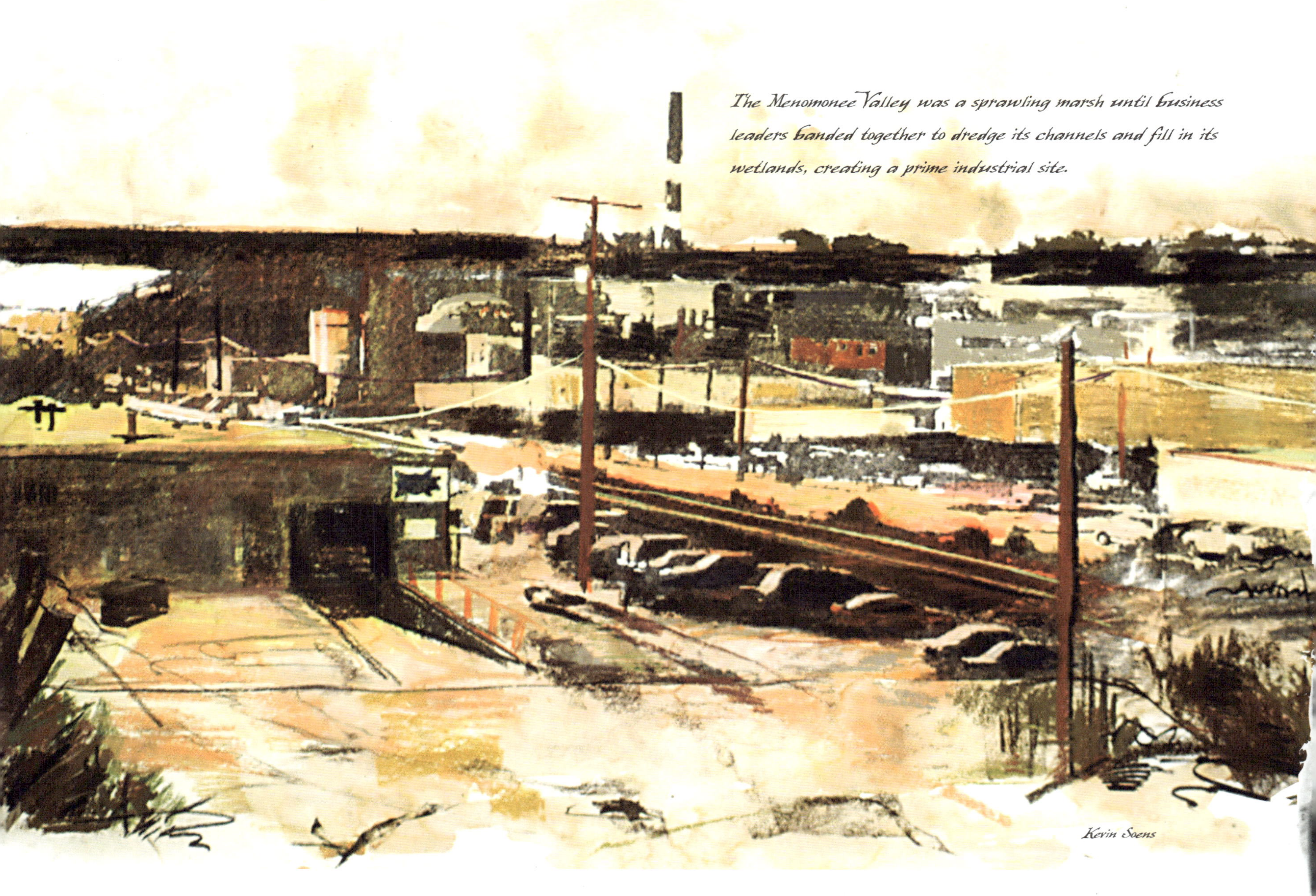

The Menomonee Valley was a sprawling marsh until business leaders banded together to dredge its channels and fill in its wetlands, creating a prime industrial site.

Kevin Soens

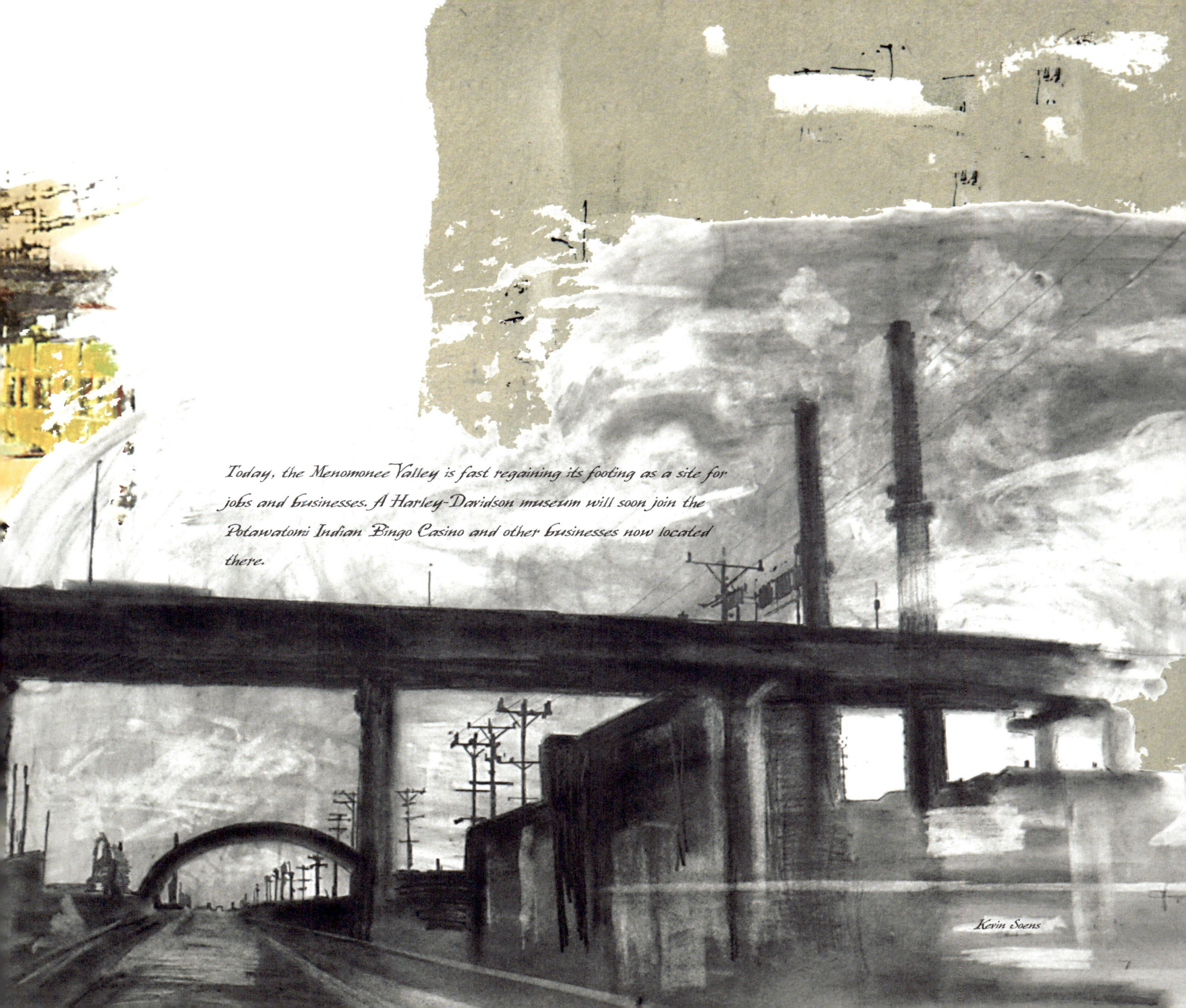

Today, the Menomonee Valley is fast regaining its footing as a site for jobs and businesses. A Harley-Davidson museum will soon join the Potawatomi Indian Bingo Casino and other businesses now located there.

Kevin Soens

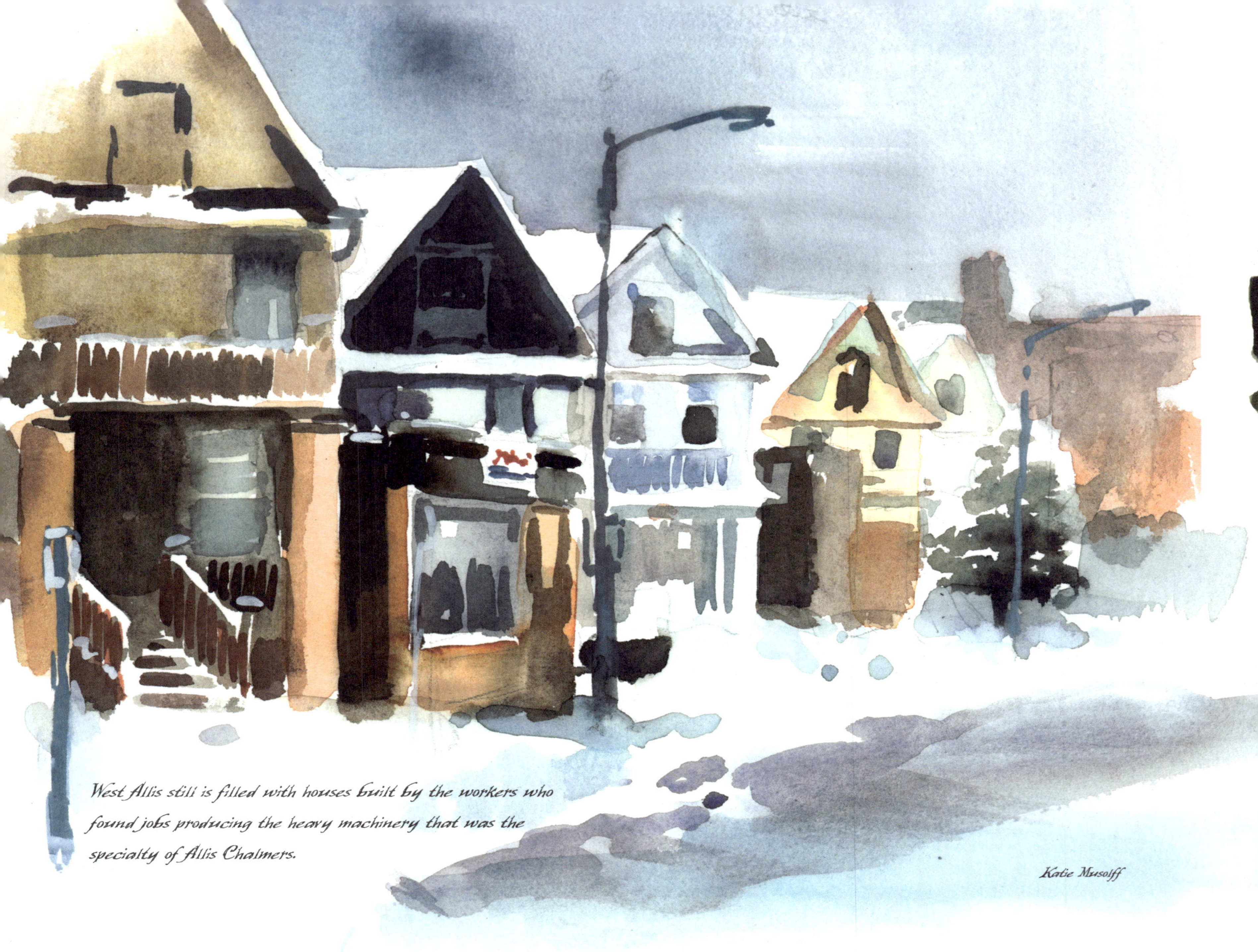

West Allis still is filled with houses built by the workers who found jobs producing the heavy machinery that was the specialty of Allis Chalmers.

Katie Musolff

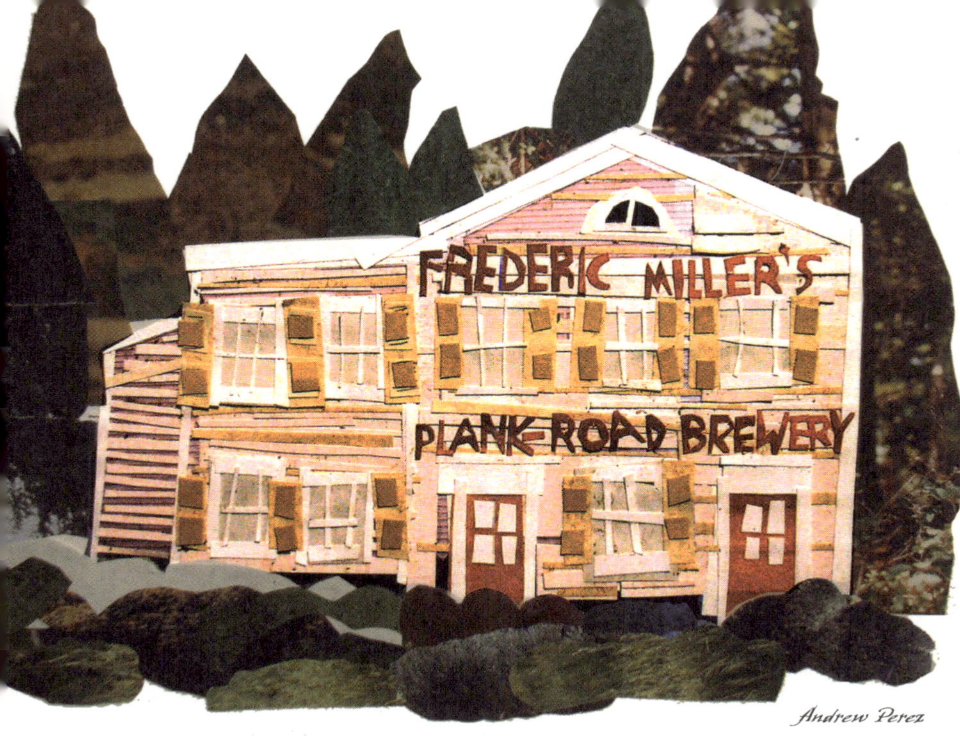

Andrew Perez

Frederick Miller arrived in Milwaukee in 1855 with enough capital to buy a small brewery on the Watertown Plank Road. The brewery is still located on what is now State St.

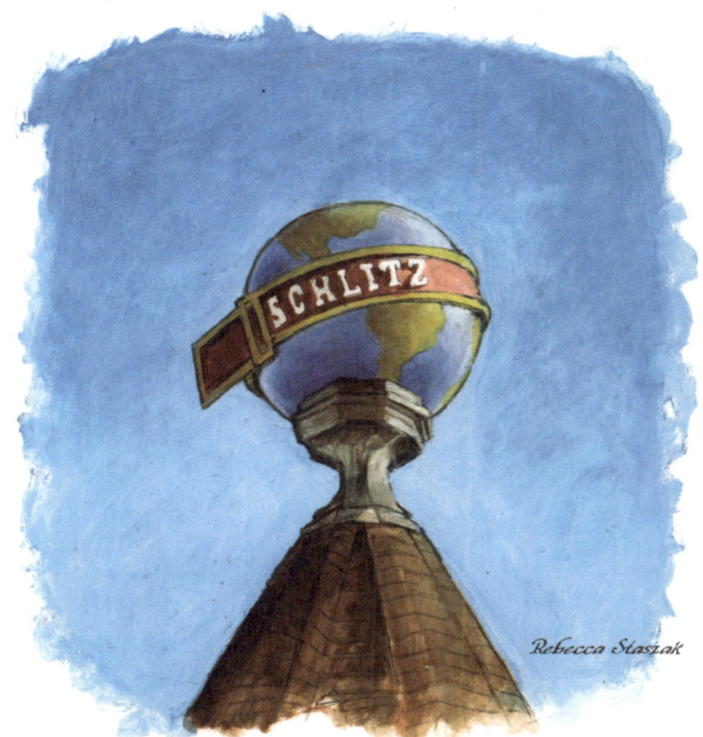

Rebecca Staszak

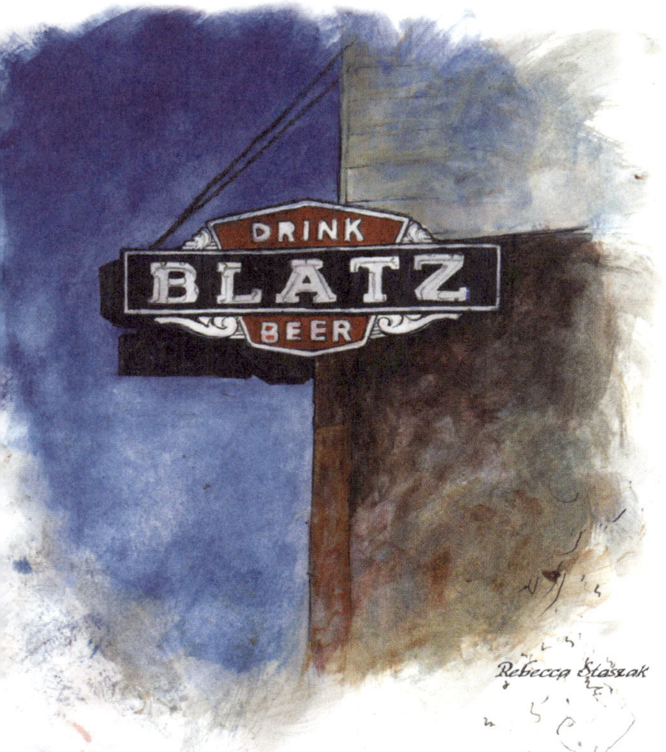

Rebecca Staszak

In the 1870s when breweries were on the rise, a Bavarian trained brew master named Valentin Blatz ran the city's third largest brewery. The brewery is only a memory and its buildings are now condominiums.

In the 1870s Joseph Schlitz turned his brewery into one of the city's leaders. Like other local brewers, Schlitz had its own taverns that only poured its brand. This sign atop a local bar is one of the last remaining examples of how Schlitz advertised its beers.

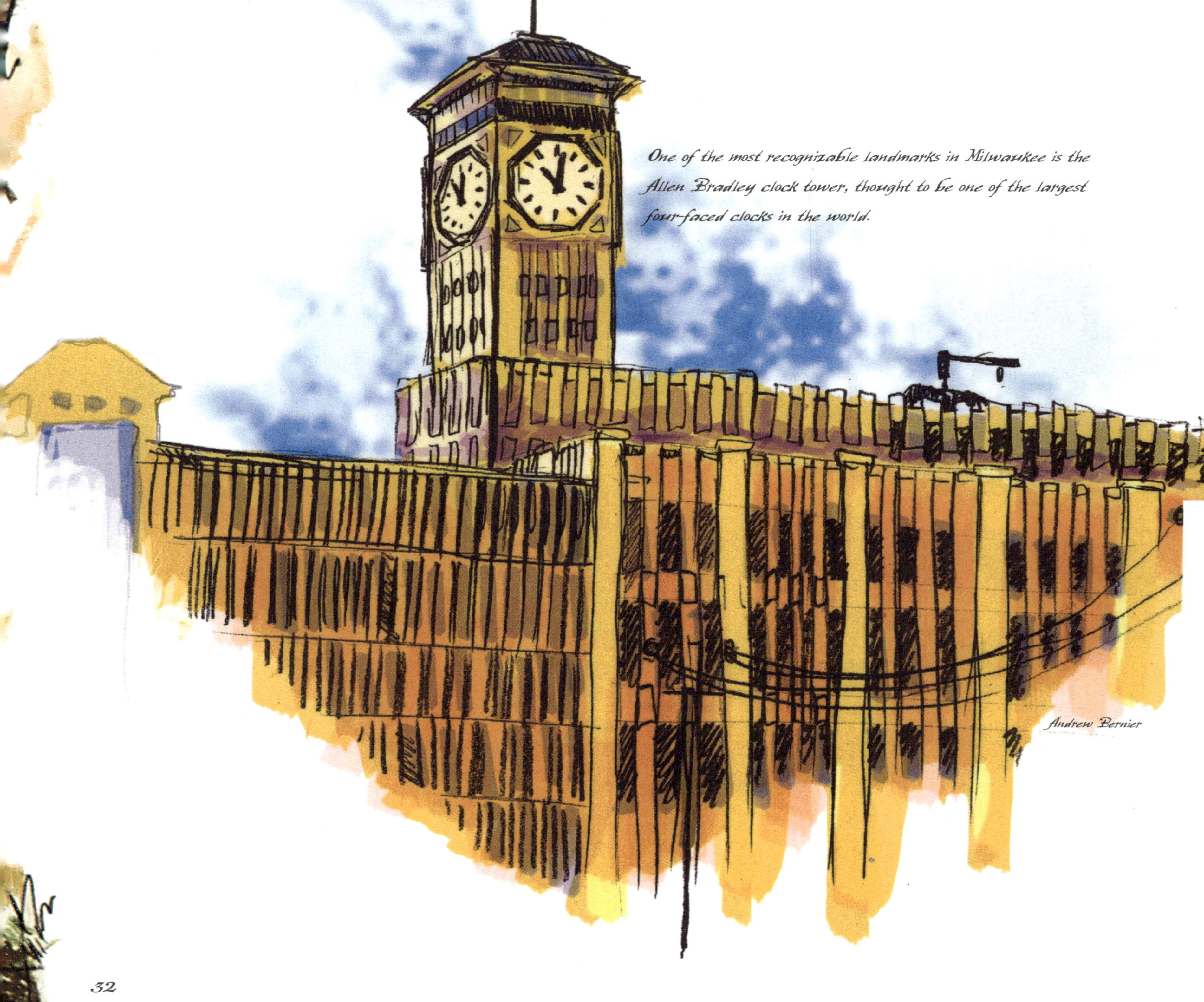

One of the most recognizable landmarks in Milwaukee is the Allen Bradley clock tower, thought to be one of the largest four-faced clocks in the world.

Andrew Bernier

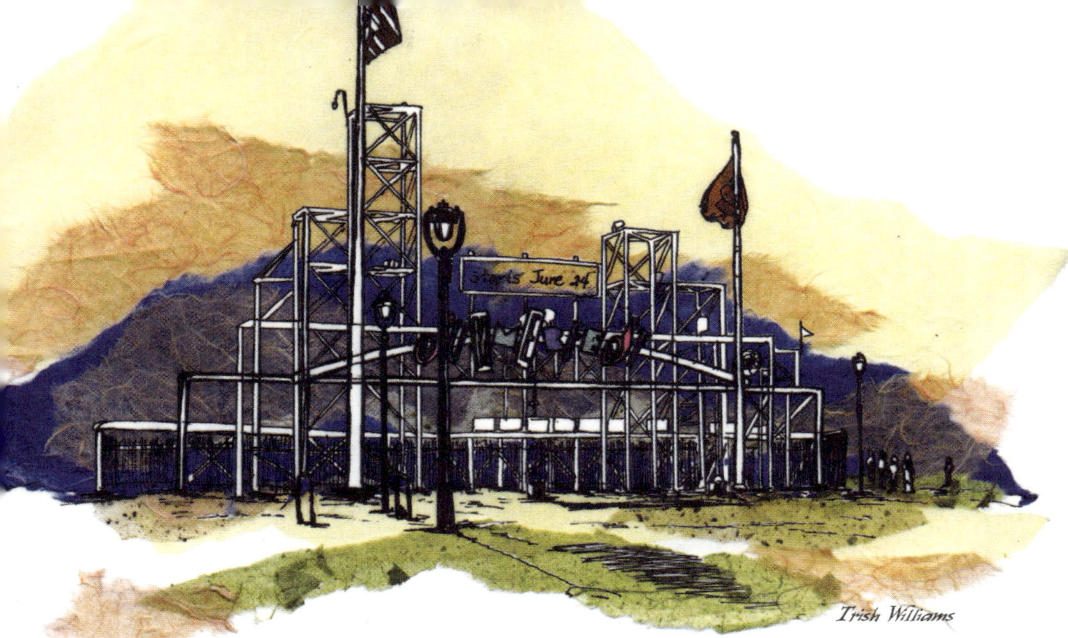

Trish Williams

Summerfest has become one of the nation's most popular music festivals. Its annual 11-day gig regularly attracts nearly a million people.

Briana MacWilliam

There's nothing quite like riding the sky glider above Summerfest grounds to cool off and enjoy the music and the crowds.

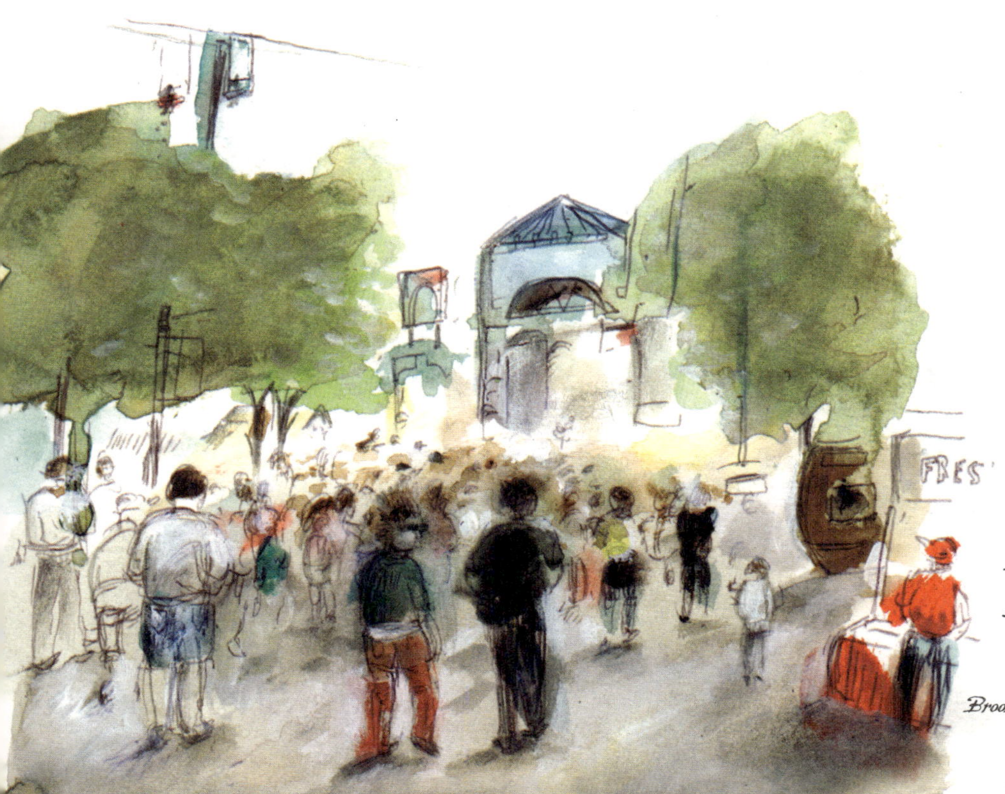

Maier Festival Park hosts both Summerfest and a series of ethnic festivals.

Brook Slane

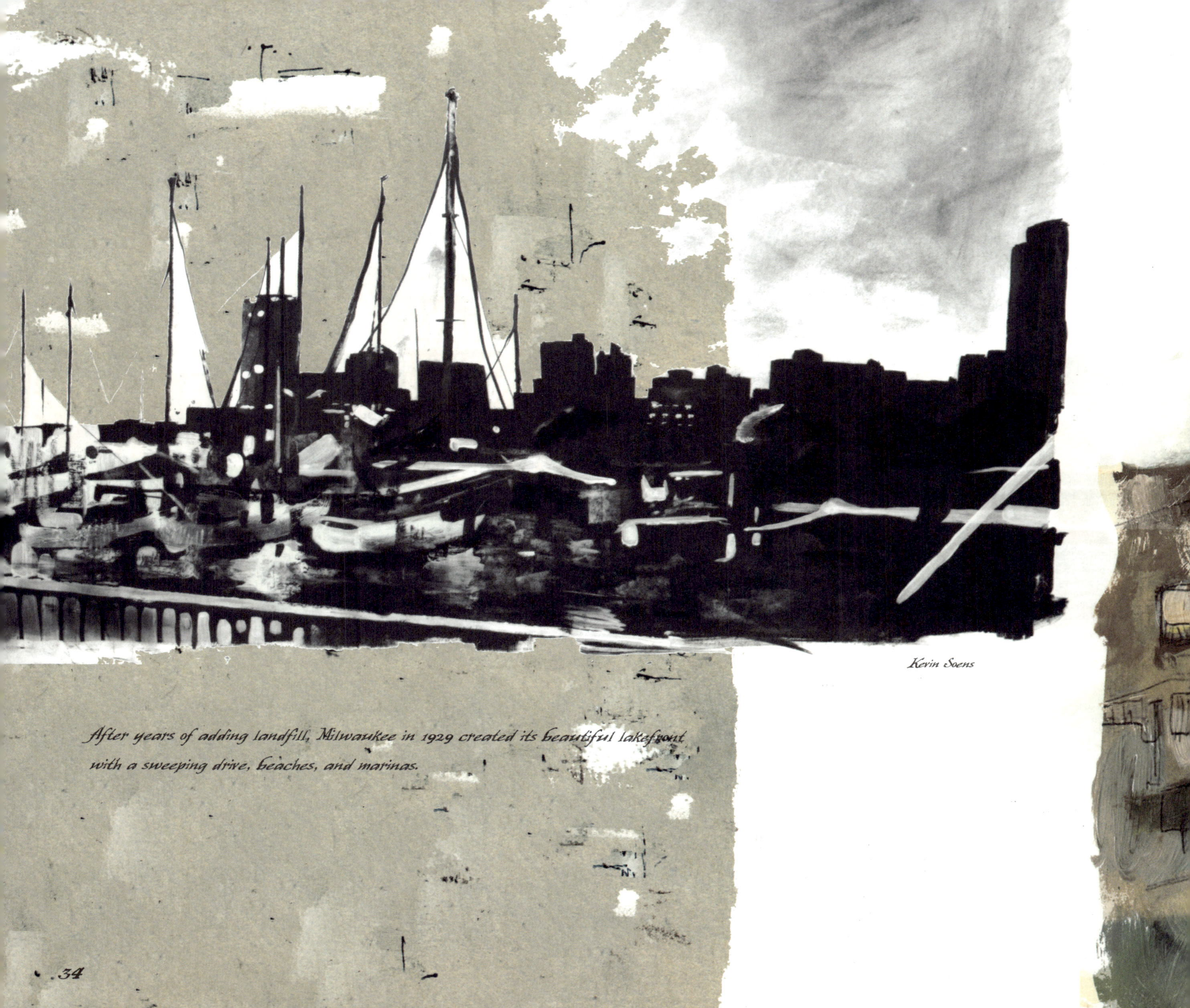

After years of adding landfill, Milwaukee in 1929 created its beautiful lakefront with a sweeping drive, beaches, and marinas.

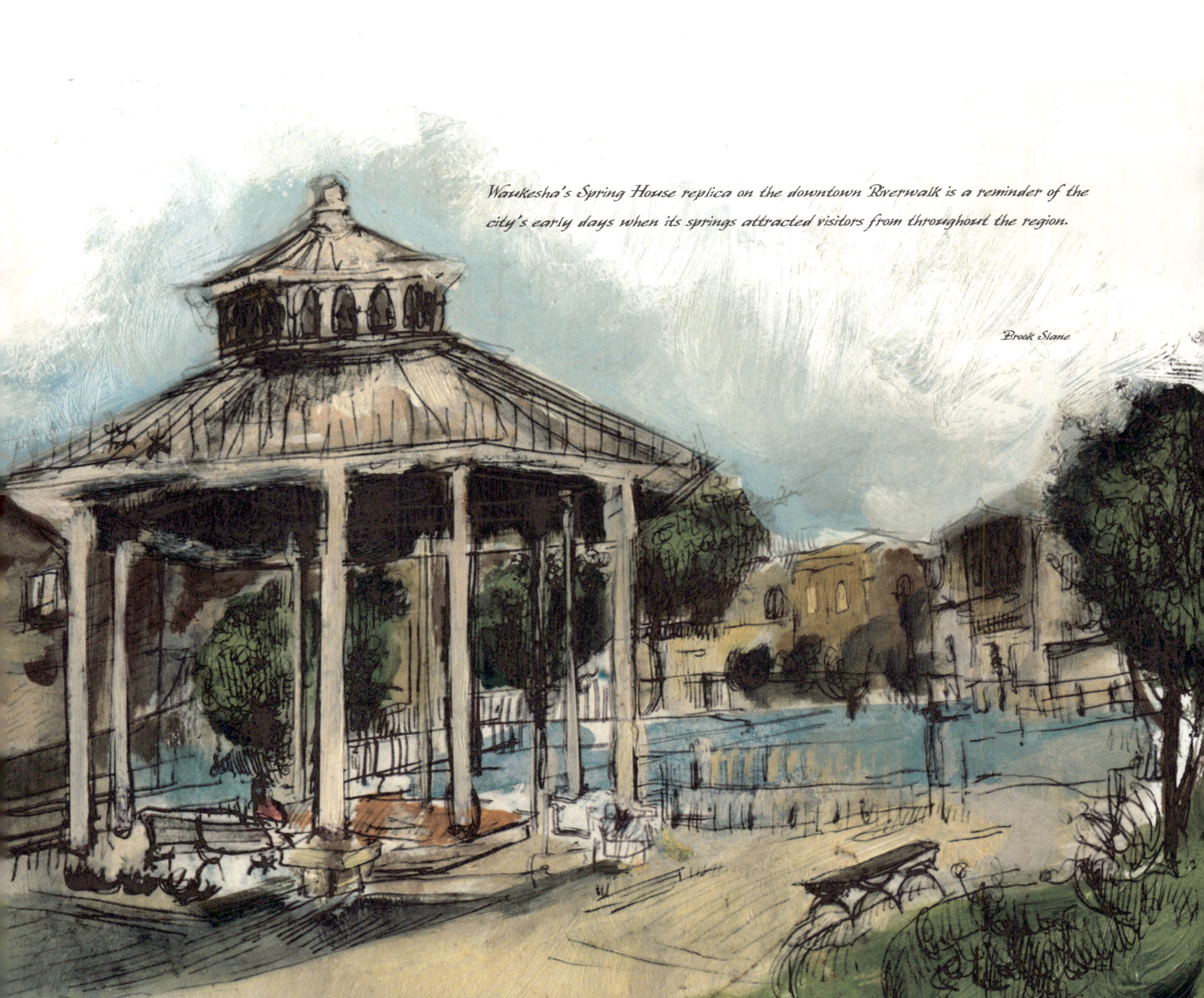

Waukesha's Spring House replica on the downtown Riverwalk is a reminder of the city's early days when its springs attracted visitors from throughout the region.

Brook Slane

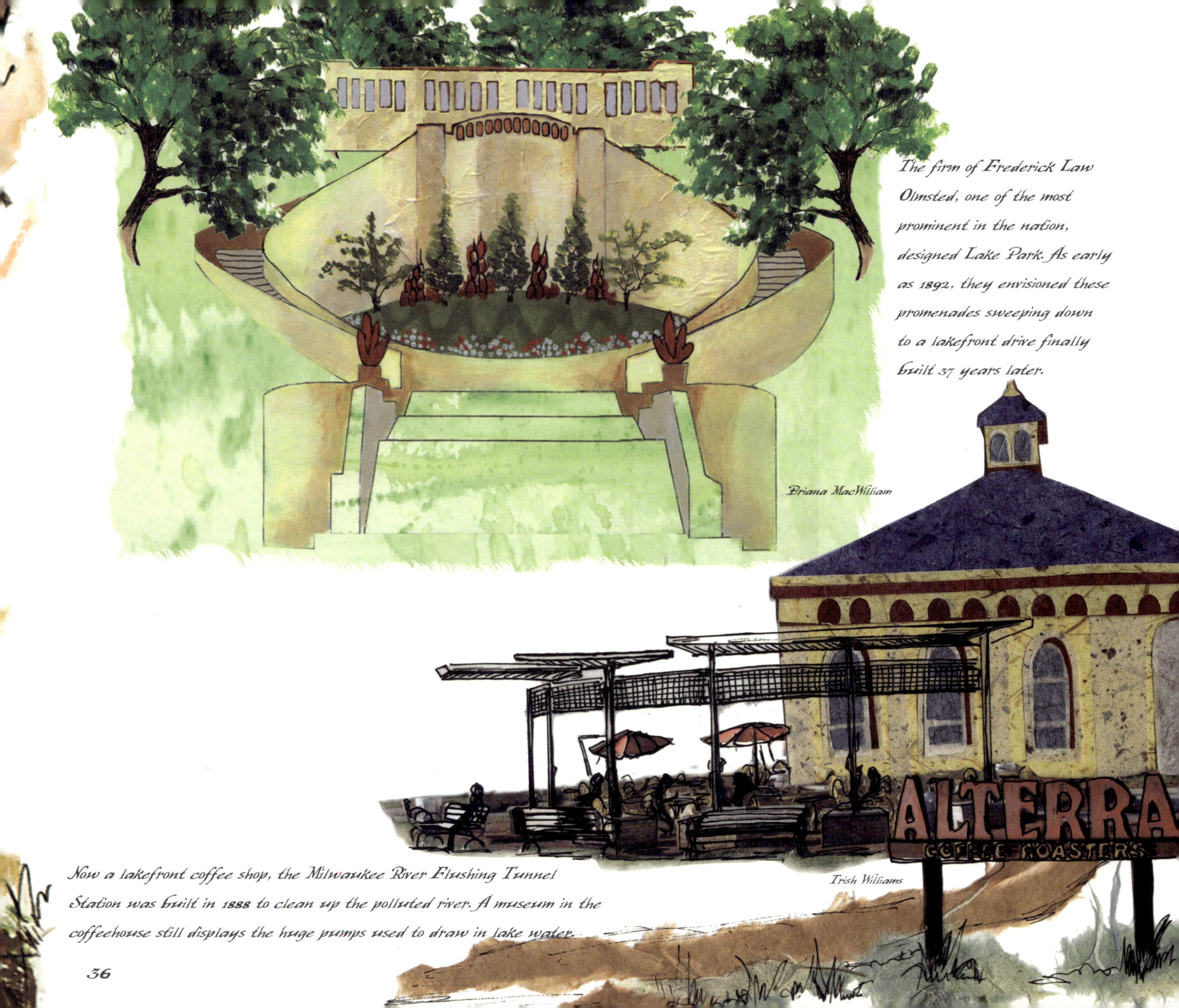

The firm of Frederick Law Olmsted, one of the most prominent in the nation, designed Lake Park. As early as 1892, they envisioned these promenades sweeping down to a lakefront drive finally built 37 years later.

Briana MacWilliam

Now a lakefront coffee shop, the Milwaukee River Flushing Tunnel Station was built in 1888 to clean up the polluted river. A museum in the coffeehouse still displays the huge pumps used to draw in lake water.

Trish Williams

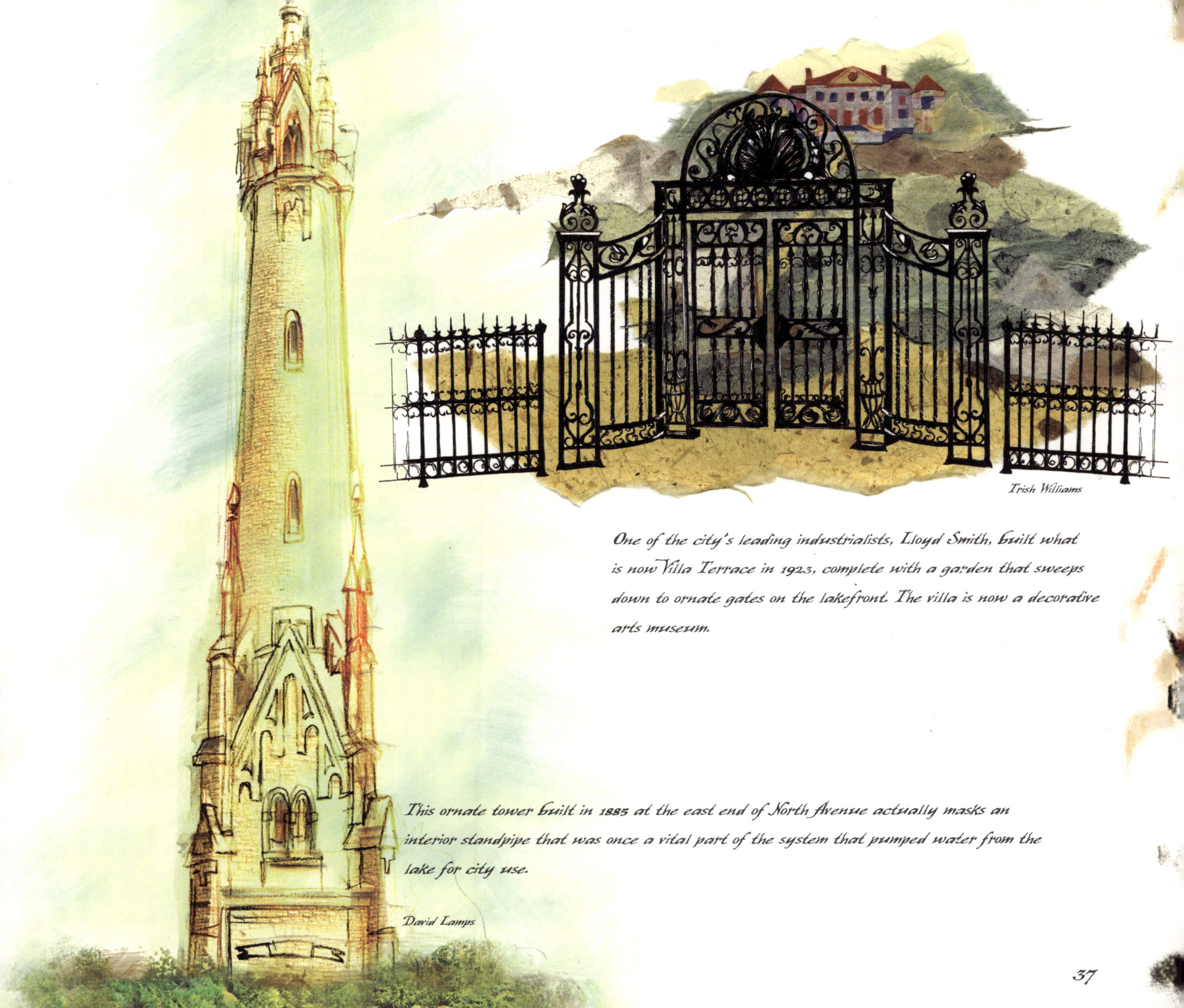

One of the city's leading industrialists, Lloyd Smith, built what is now Villa Terrace in 1923, complete with a garden that sweeps down to ornate gates on the lakefront. The villa is now a decorative arts museum.

This ornate tower built in 1885 at the east end of North Avenue actually masks an interior standpipe that was once a vital part of the system that pumped water from the lake for city use.

Milwaukee became known as a "city of steeples" because so many of its early immigrant families built churches that became the center of their social and religious lives.

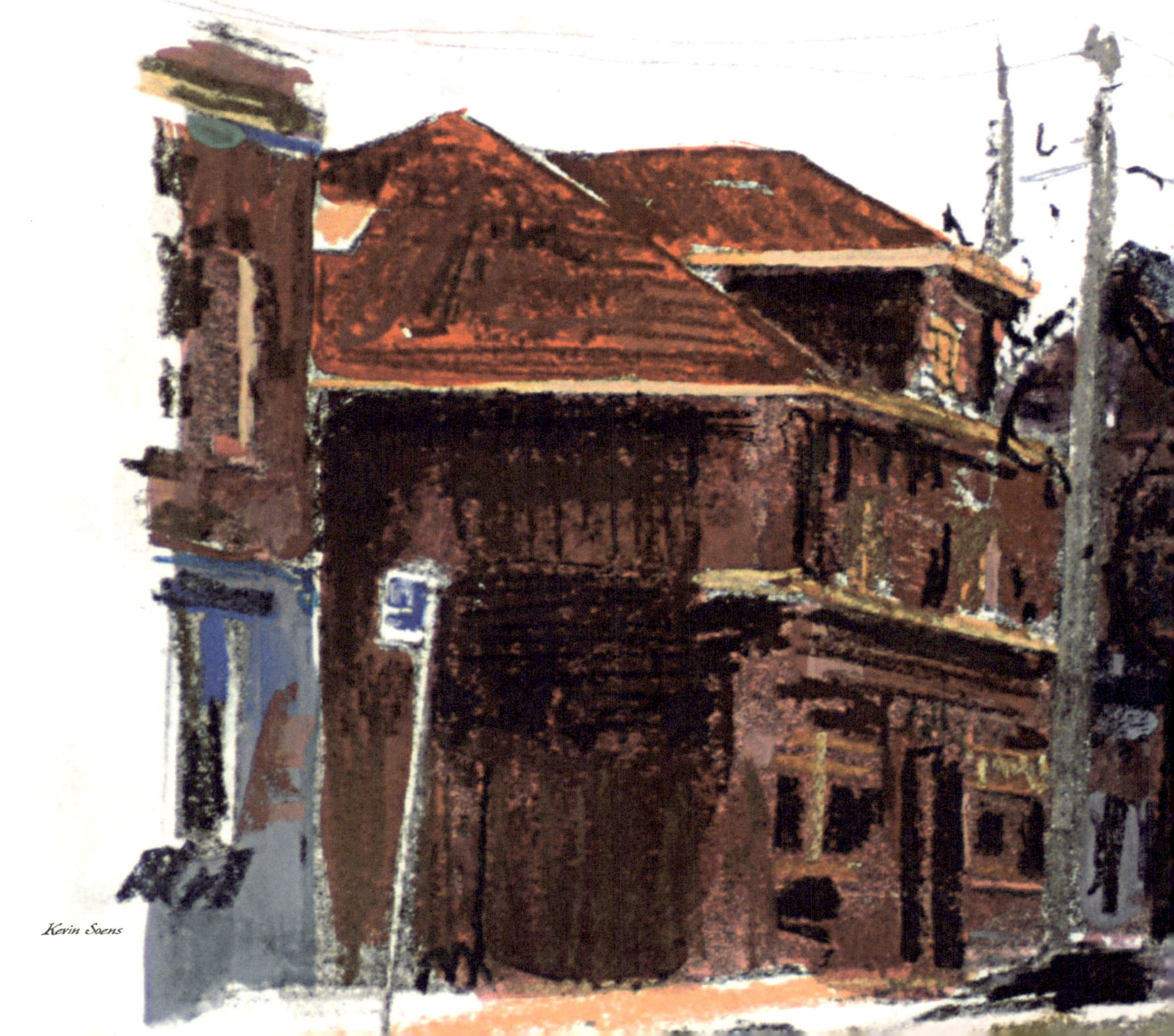

Kevin Soens

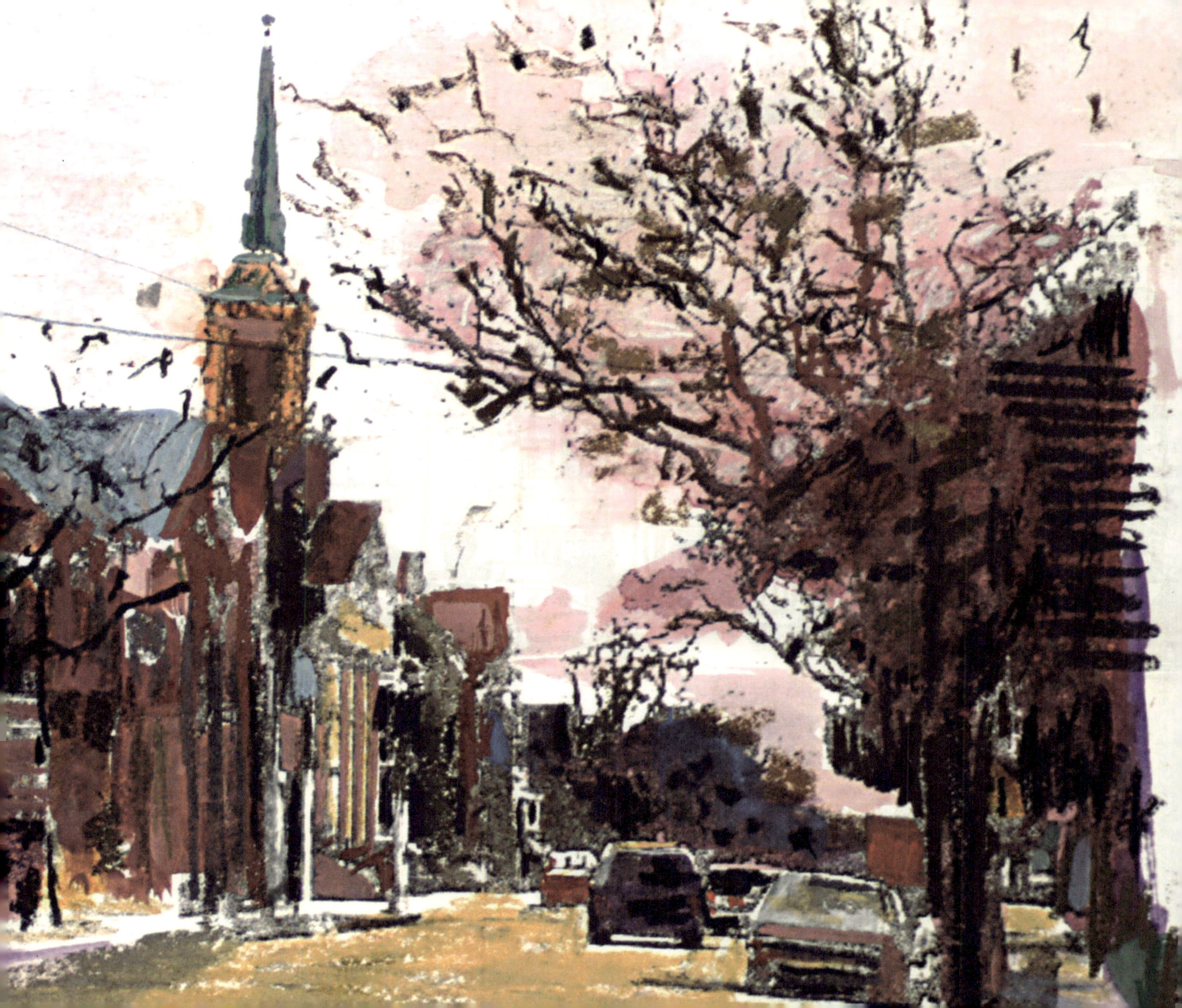

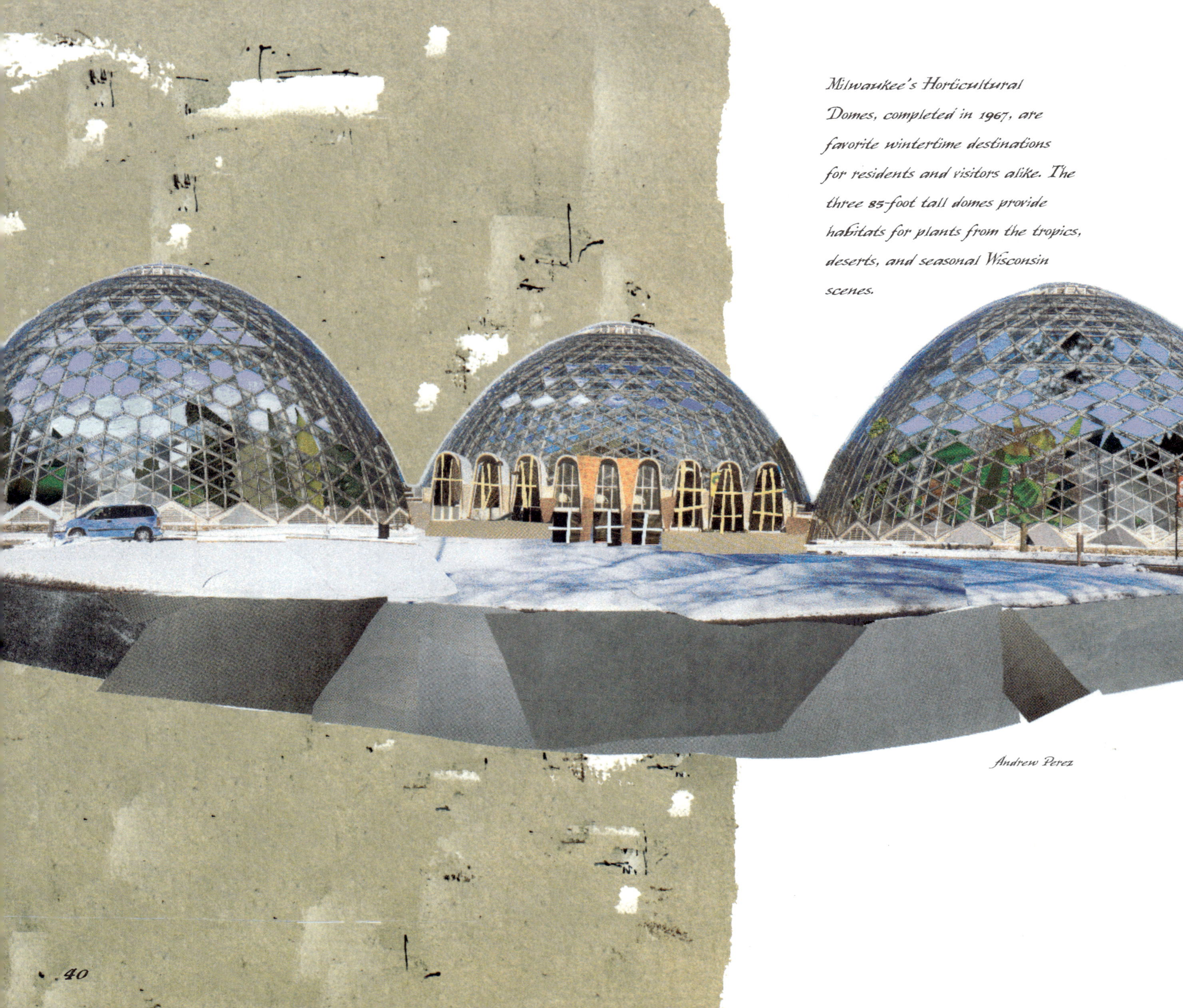

Milwaukee's Horticultural Domes, completed in 1967, are favorite wintertime destinations for residents and visitors alike. The three 85-foot tall domes provide habitats for plants from the tropics, deserts, and seasonal Wisconsin scenes.

Andrew Perez

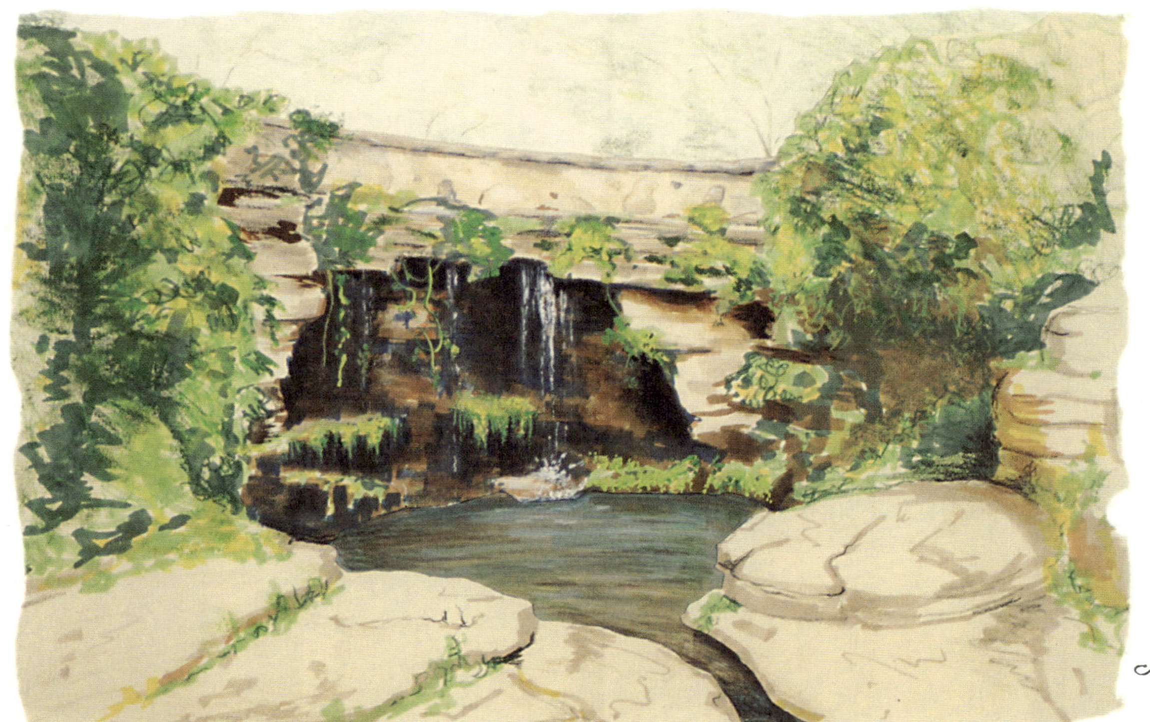

Jessica Case

Whitnall Park became the largest in the county during the Depression in the 1930s when relief workers turned it into a showplace with a chain of lagoons and waterfalls.

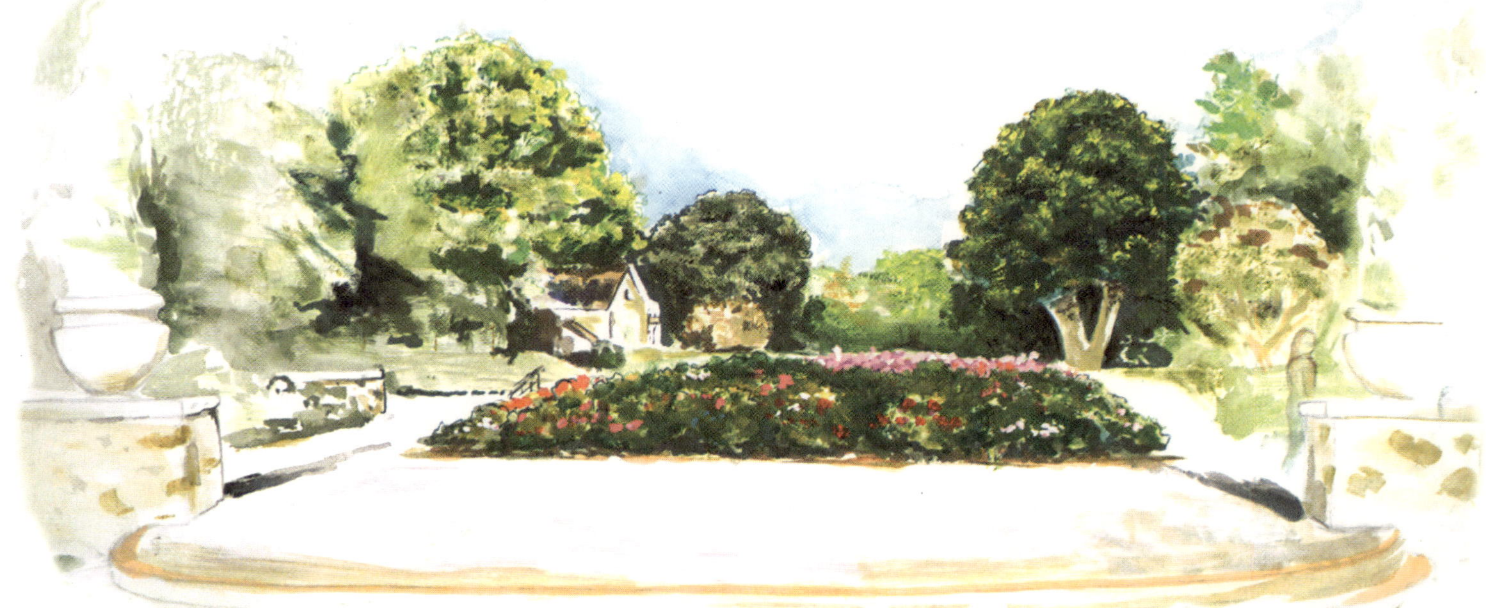

Jessica Case

Boener Botanical Gardens in Whitnall Park remain one of Milwaukee's favorite destinations.

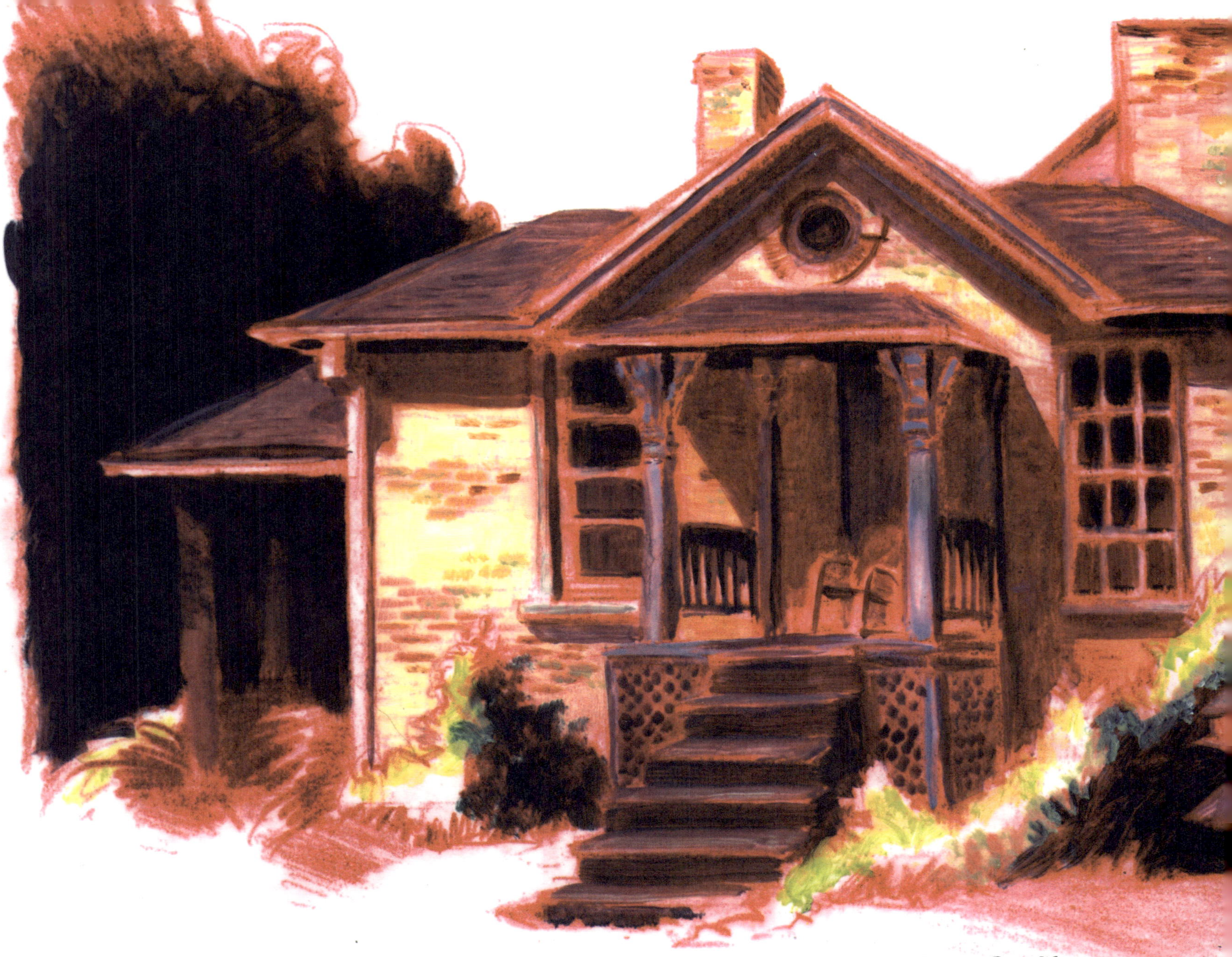

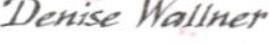

The farmhouse in which Charles Whitnall was raised on Locust Street is still lived in today, and part of the family's gardens is now Gordon Park.

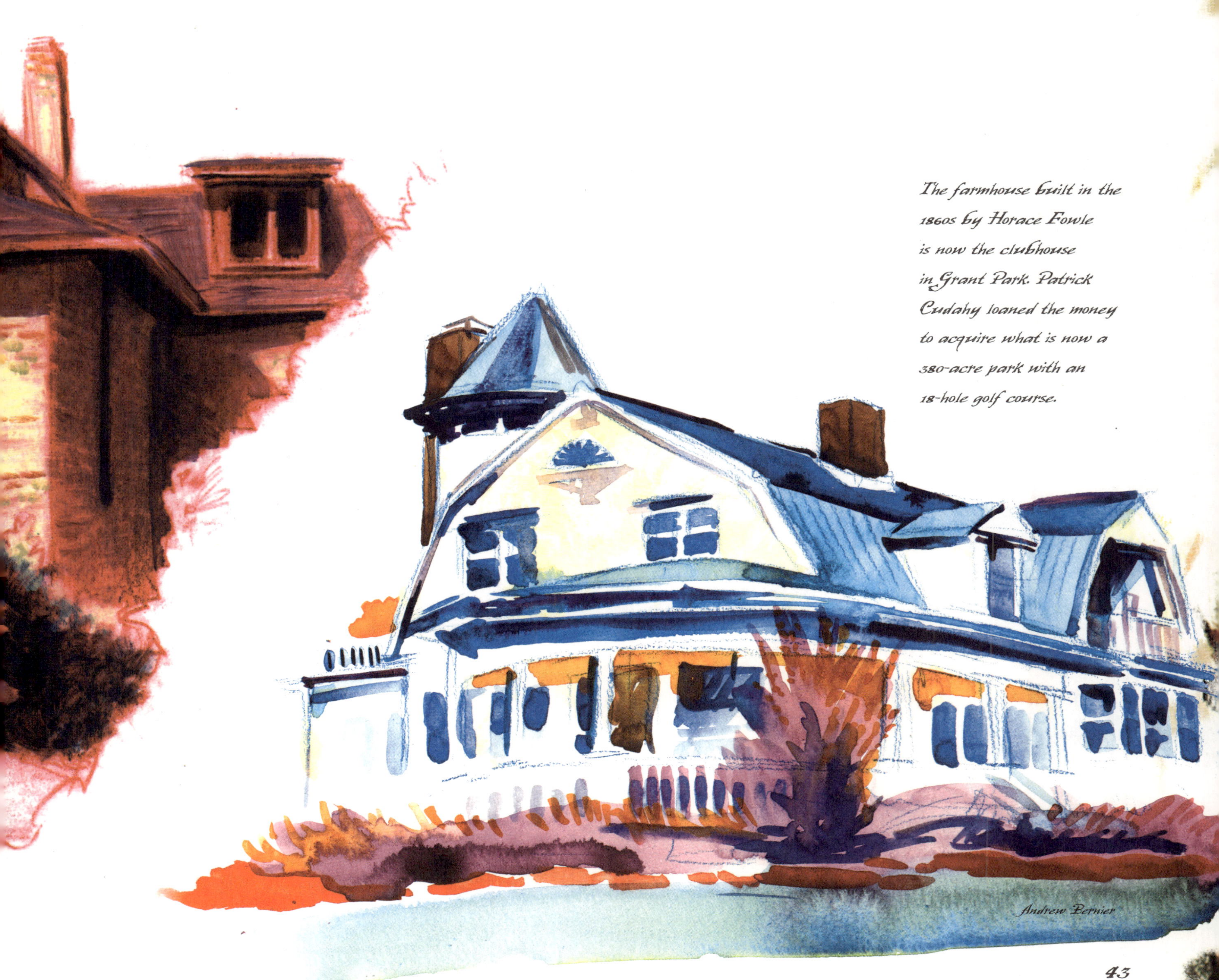

The farmhouse built in the 1860s by Horace Fowle is now the clubhouse in Grant Park. Patrick Cudahy loaned the money to acquire what is now a 380-acre park with an 18-hole golf course.

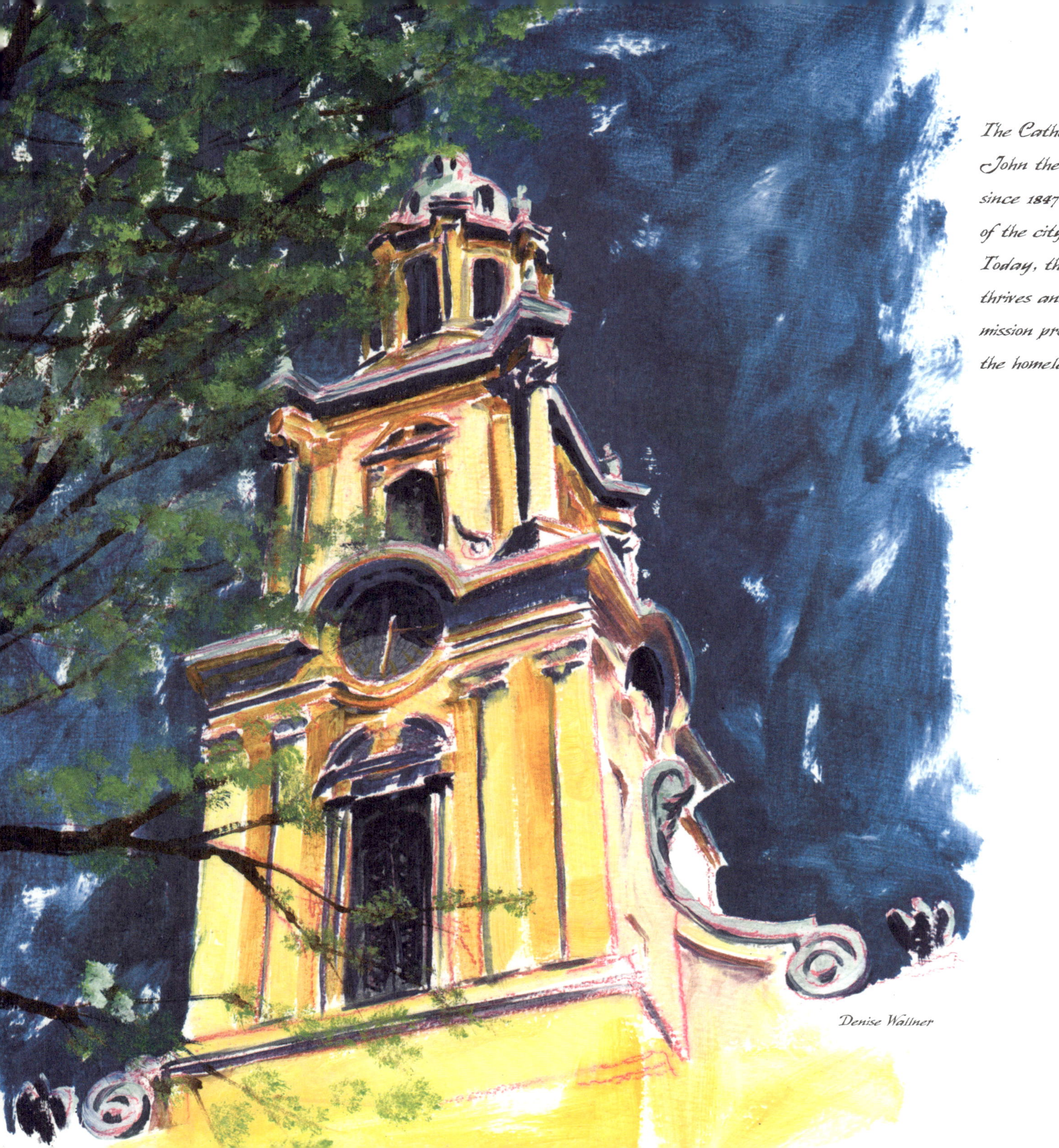

The Cathedral of St. John the Evangelist has since 1847 been the hub of the city's Catholic life. Today, the church still thrives and as part of its mission provides shelter for the homeless.

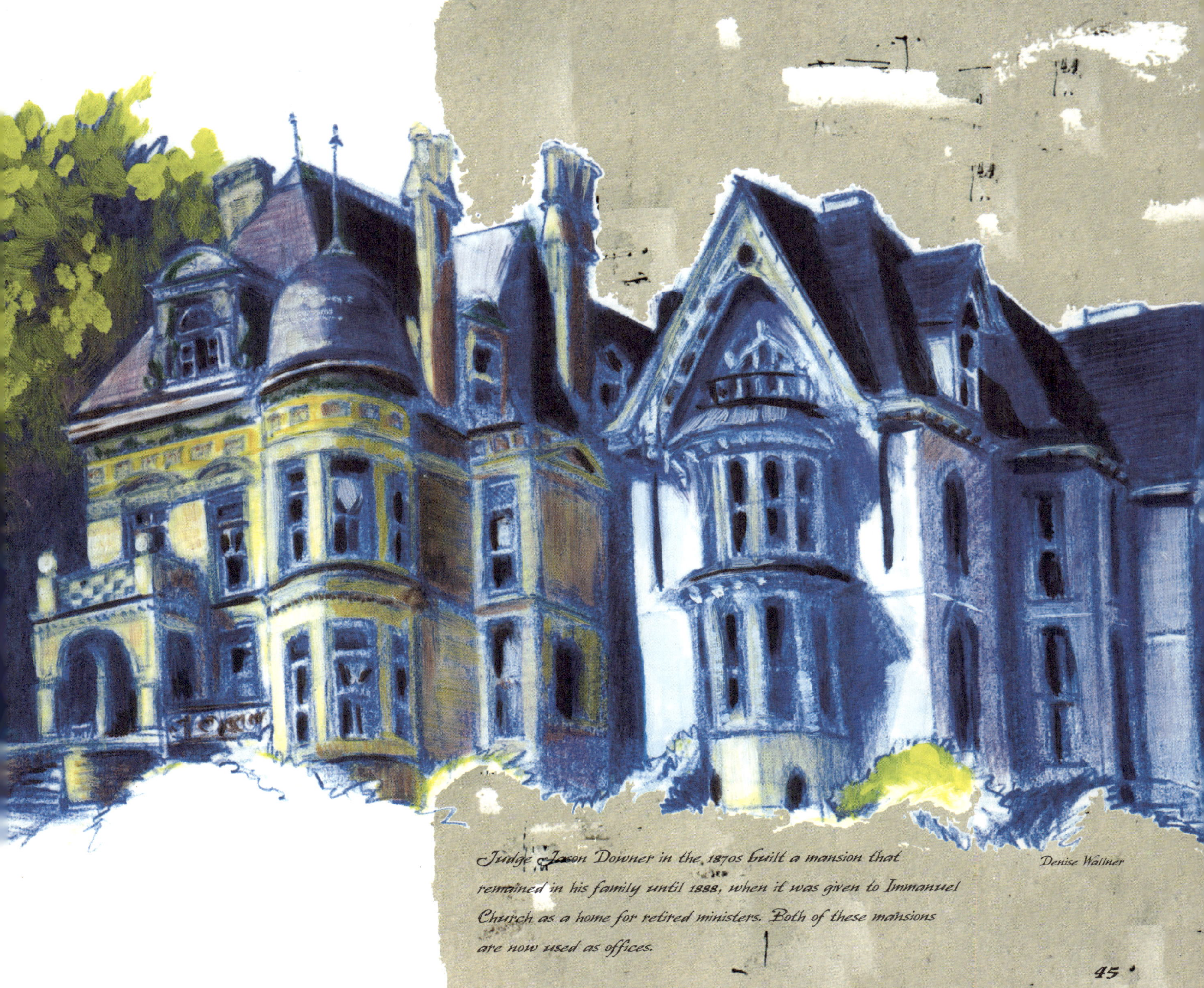

Judge Jason Downer in the 1870s built a mansion that remained in his family until 1888, when it was given to Immanuel Church as a home for retired ministers. Both of these mansions are now used as offices.

Denise Wallner

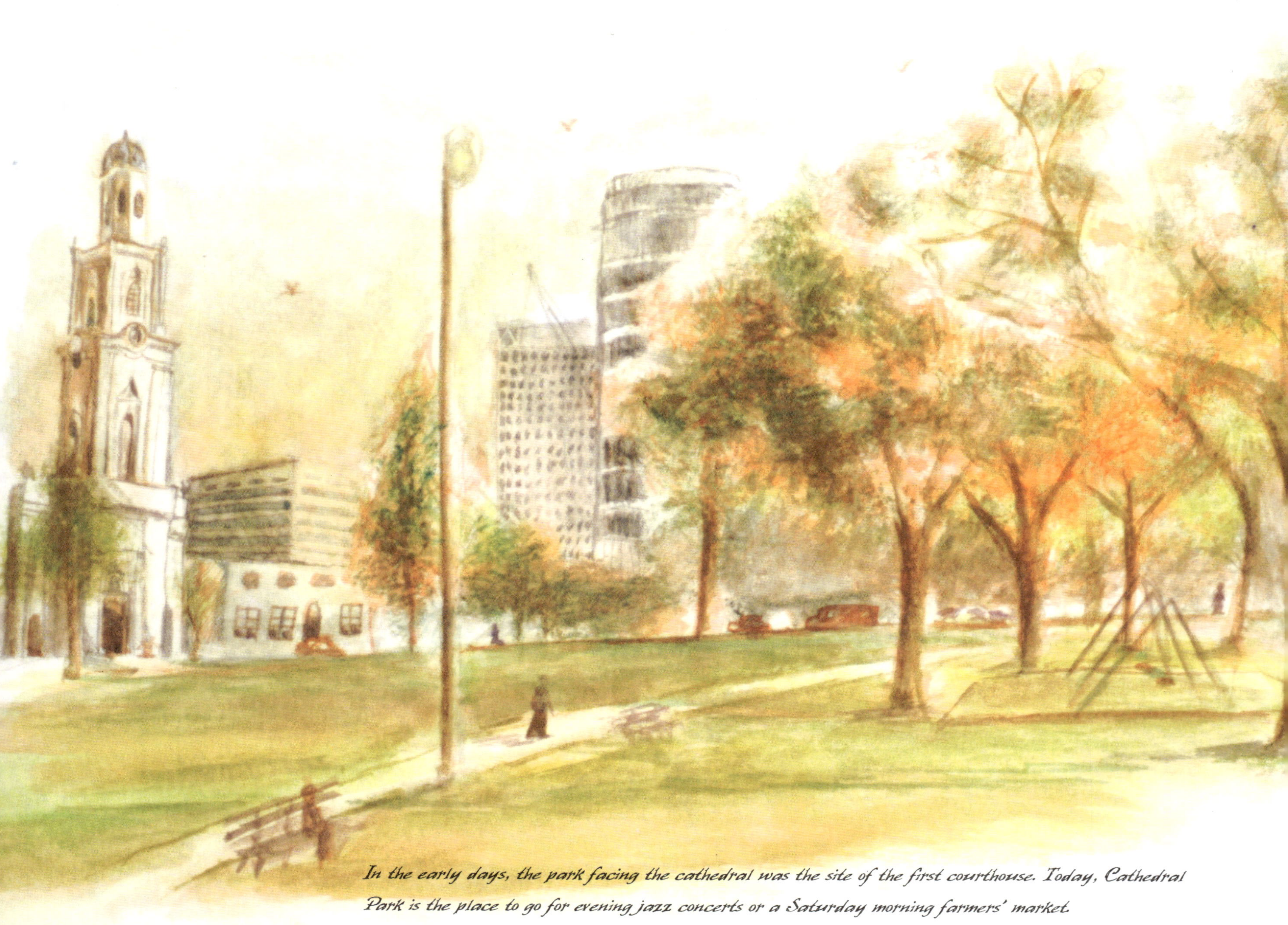

In the early days, the park facing the cathedral was the site of the first courthouse. Today, Cathedral Park is the place to go for evening jazz concerts or a Saturday morning farmers' market.

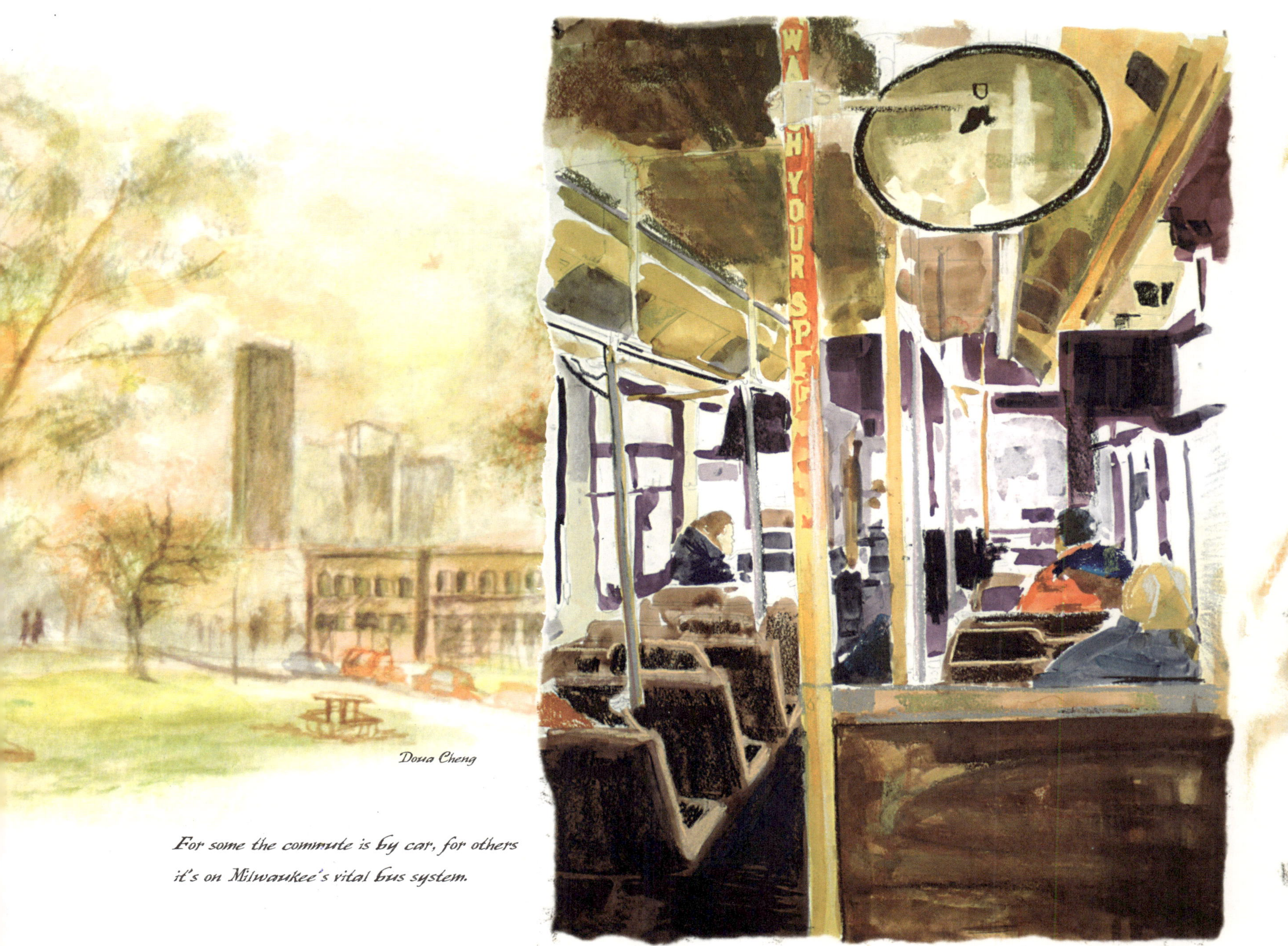

Doua Cheng

For some the commute is by car, for others it's on Milwaukee's vital bus system.

Kevin Soens

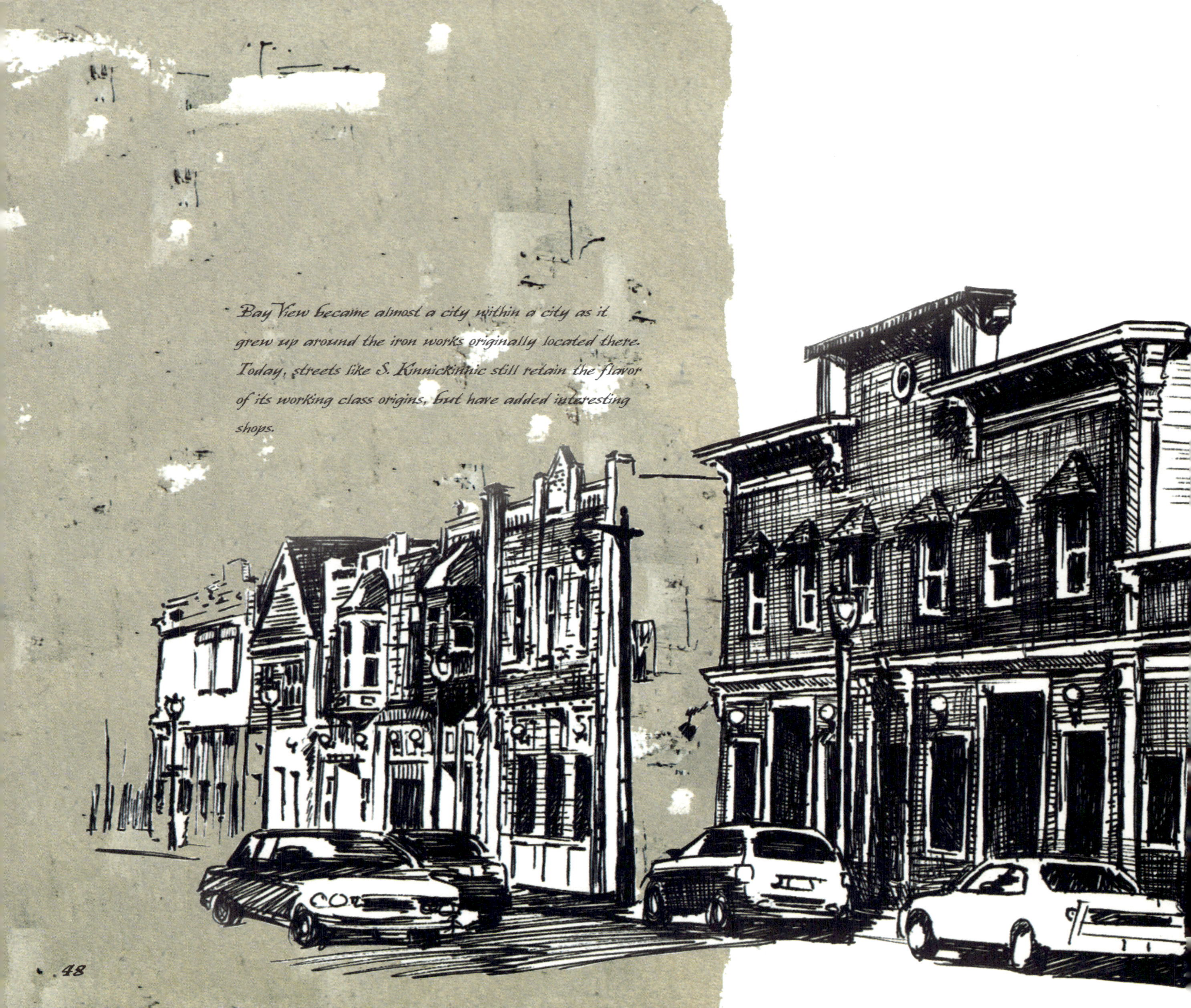

Bay View became almost a city within a city as it grew up around the iron works originally located there. Today, streets like S. Kinnickinnic still retain the flavor of its working class origins, but have added interesting shops.

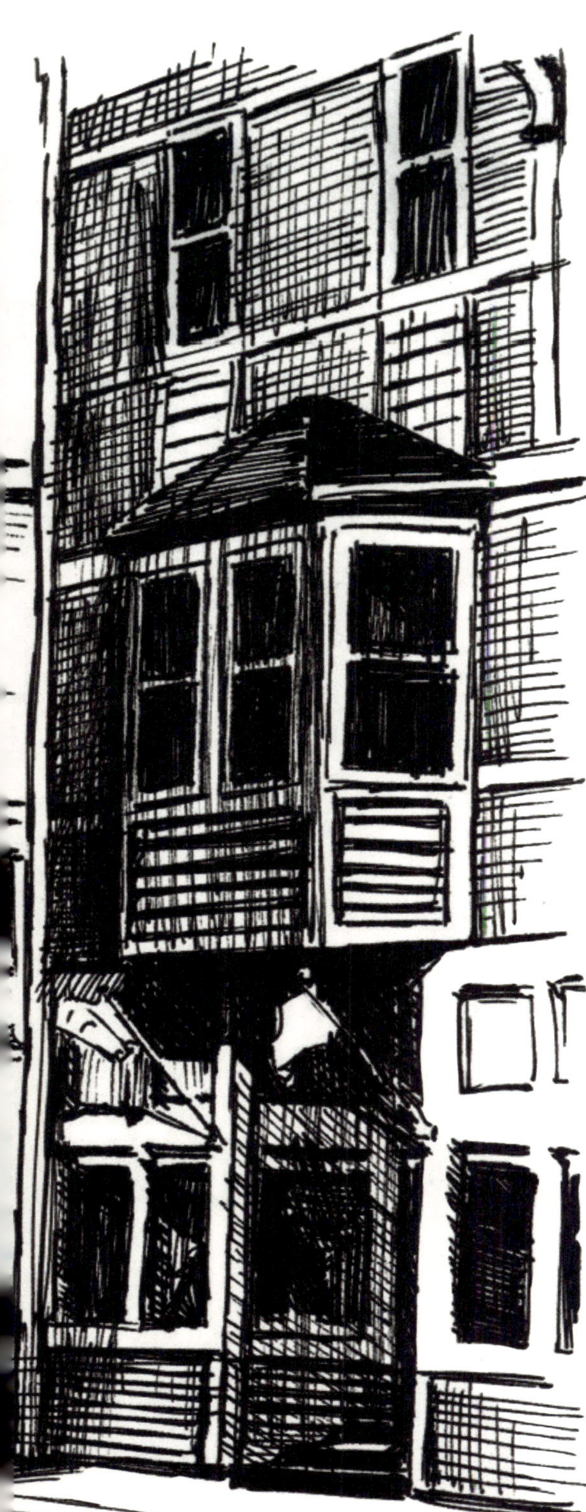

Denise Wallner

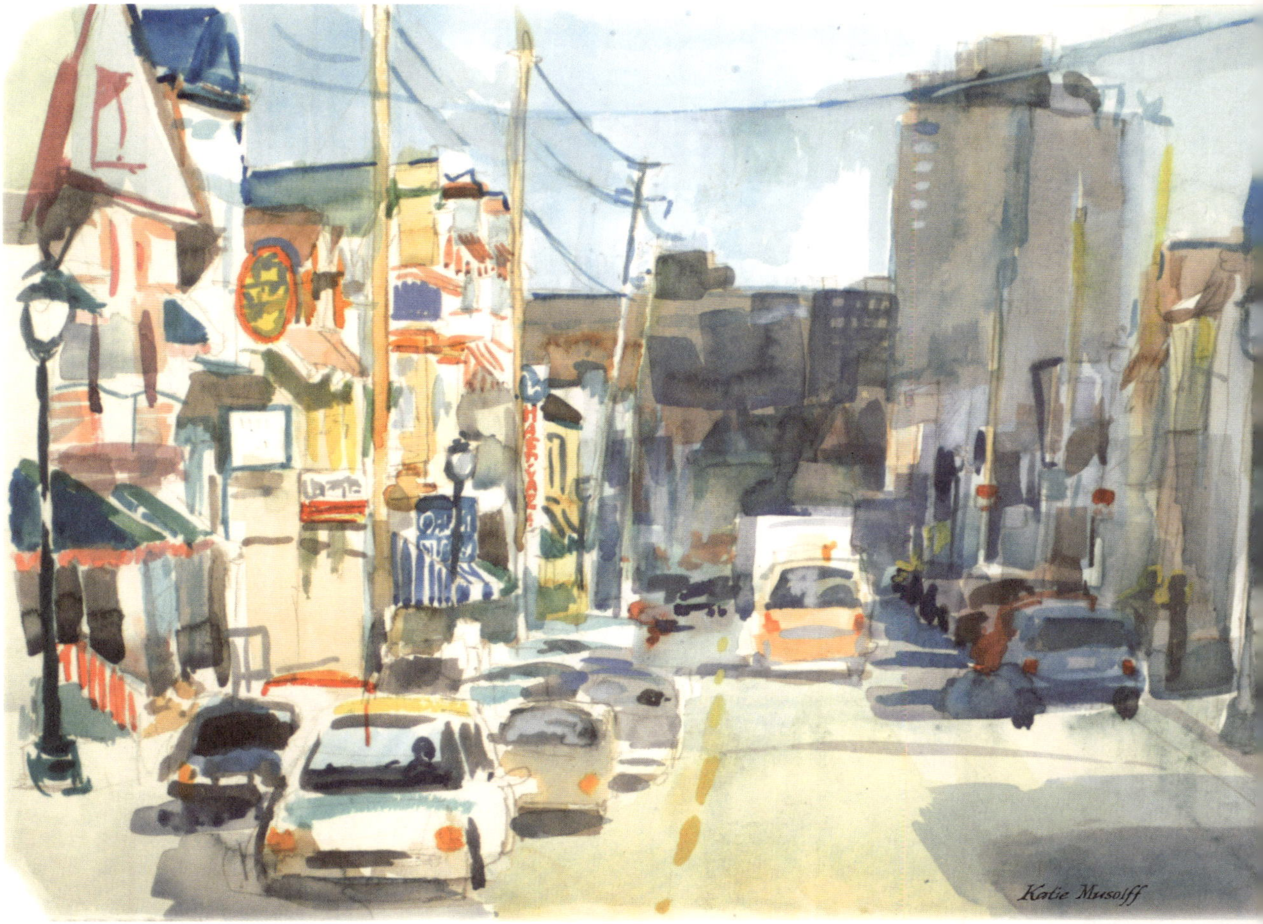

Katie Musolff

Brady St. was originally a Polish settlement, but waves of Italians moved there after being forced out of the Third Ward by freeway construction. In the 1960s, Brady became a haven for the hippie counter-culture. Now it has become a trendy place with galleries, restaurants, and shops.

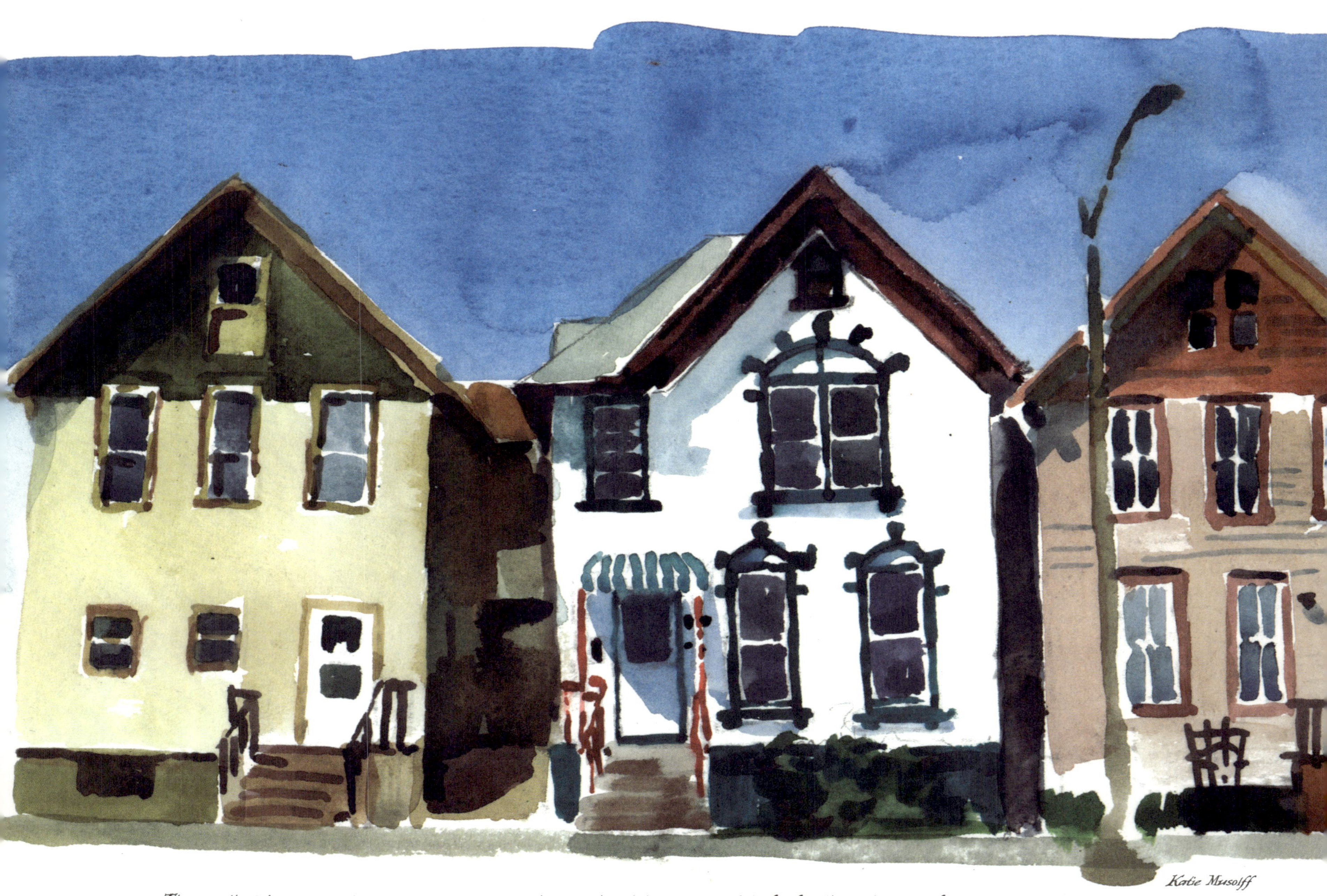

The south side grew quickly as new immigrants moved out to open land to fulfill their dreams of owning a home of their own near their jobs in local industries.

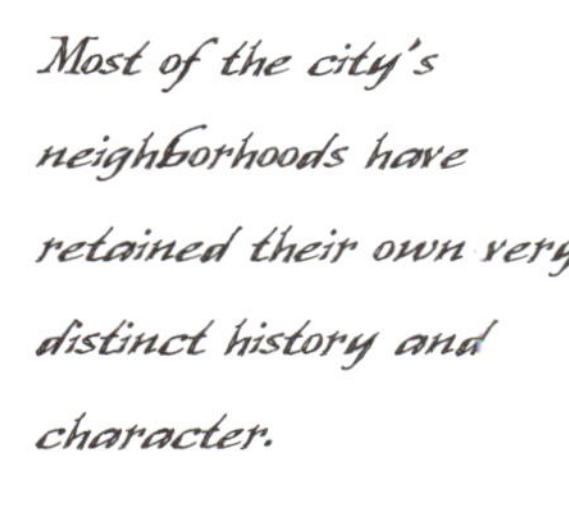

Most of the city's neighborhoods have retained their own very distinct history and character.

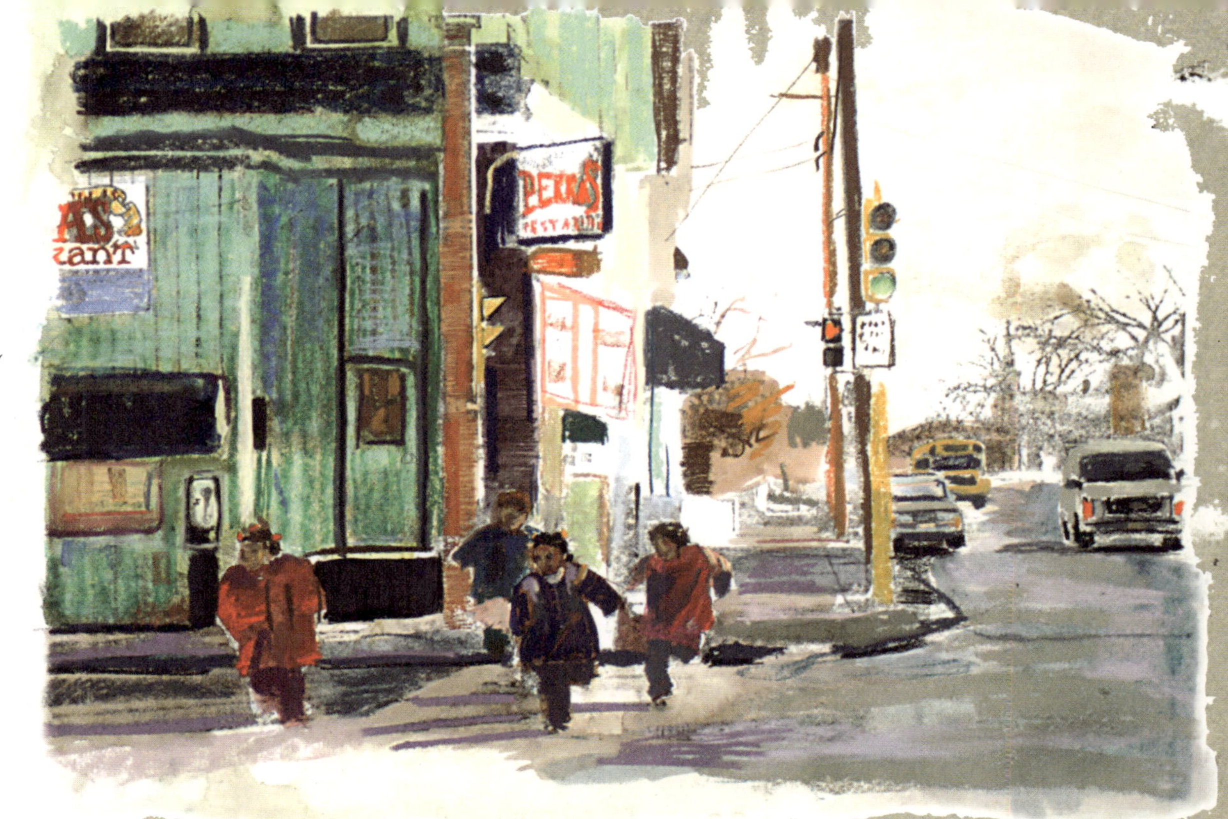

Kevin Soens

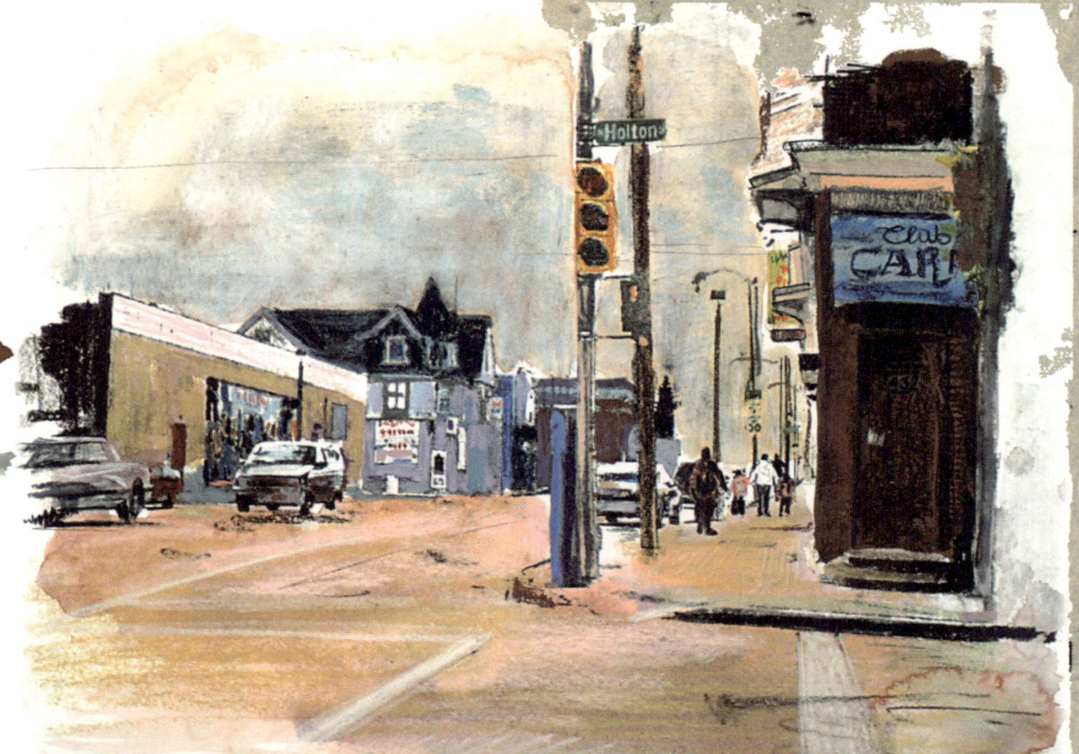

This area of Riverwest began as a playground for wealthy Germans, turned into a haven for working class Poles, then found new life as a Puerto Rican barrio and home for the counterculture and now is a lively blend of cultures, art, and entertainment—all in the span of 120 years.

Kevin Soens

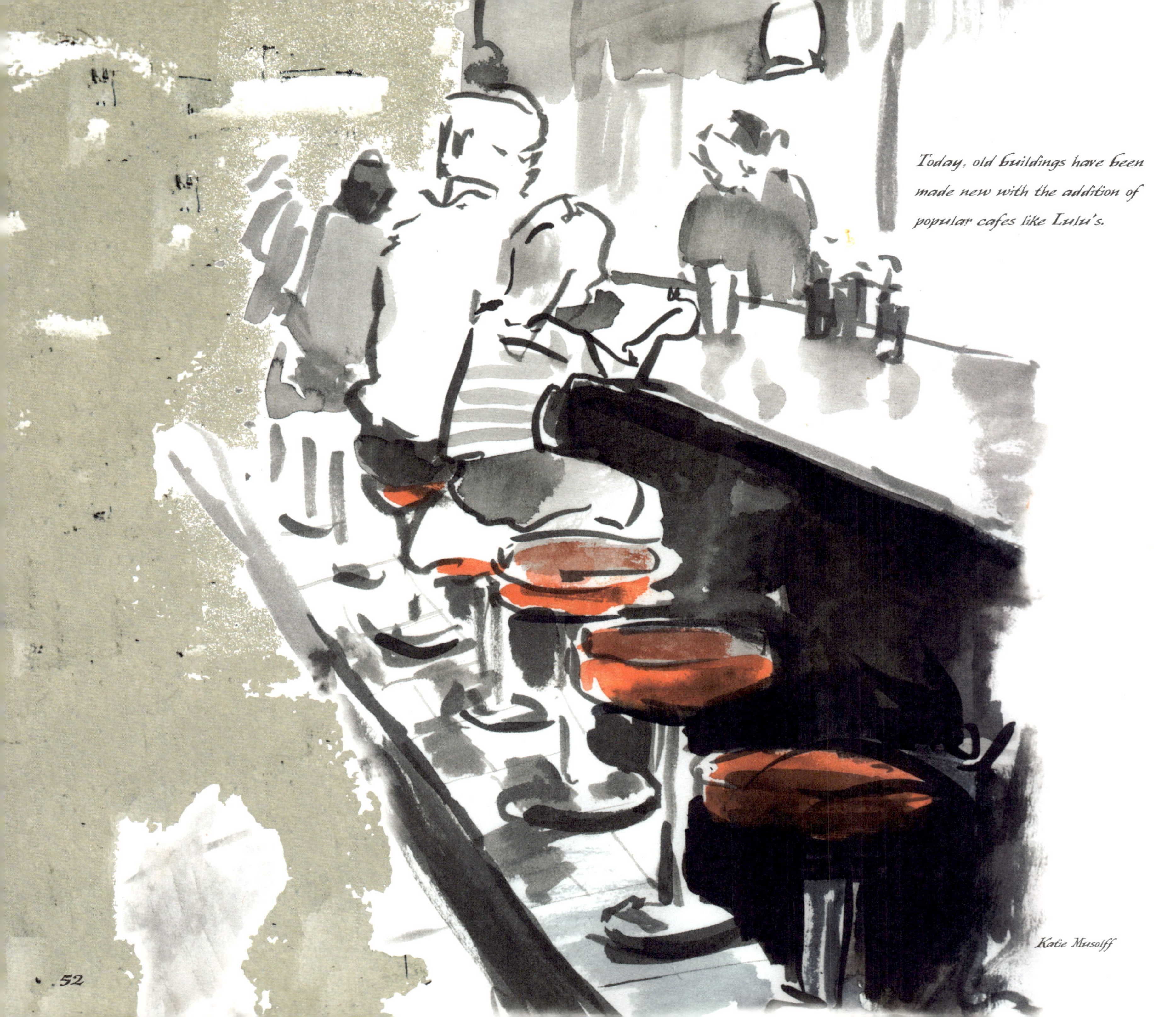

Today, old buildings have been made new with the addition of popular cafes like Lulu's.

Katie Musolff

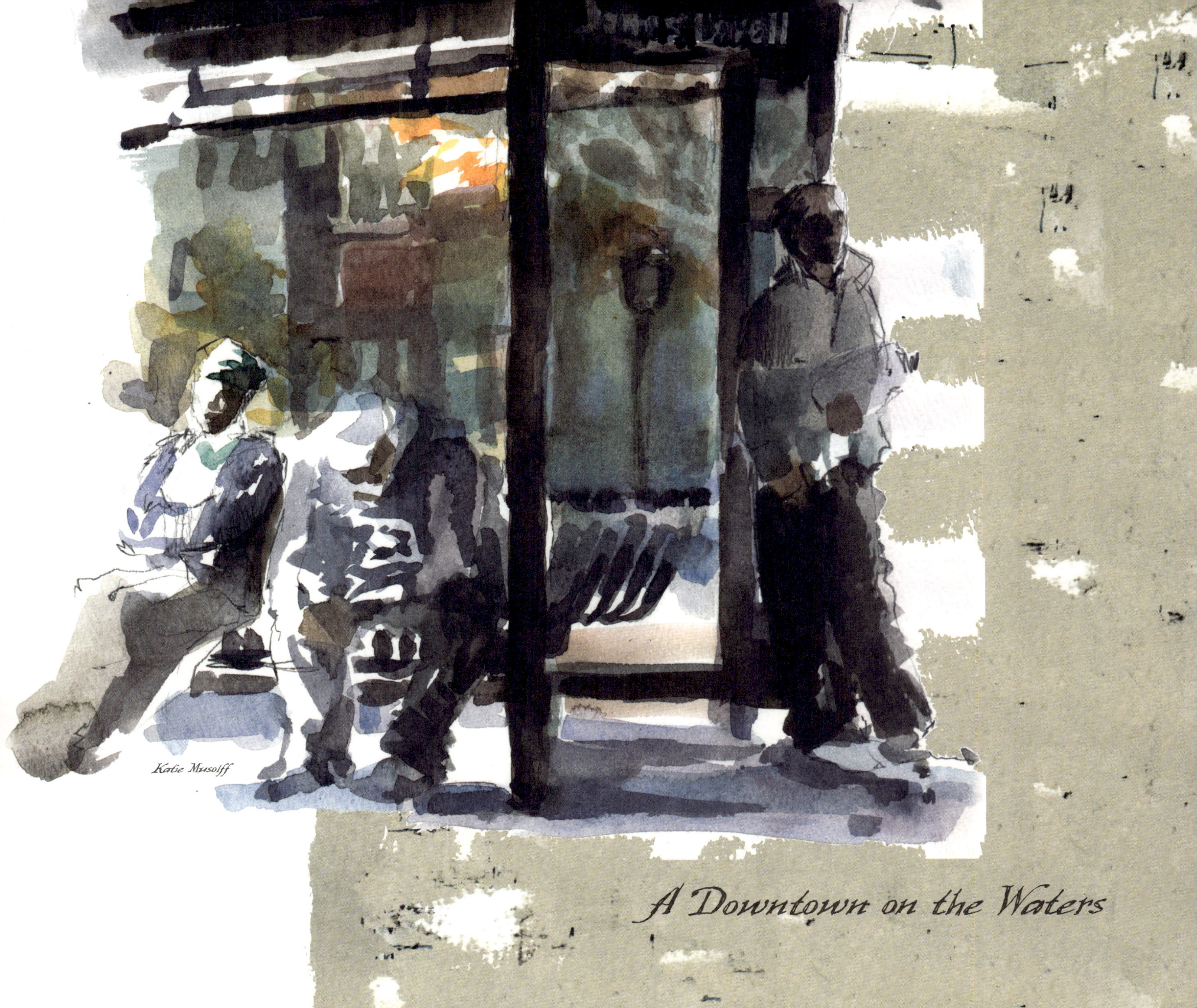

A Downtown on the Waters

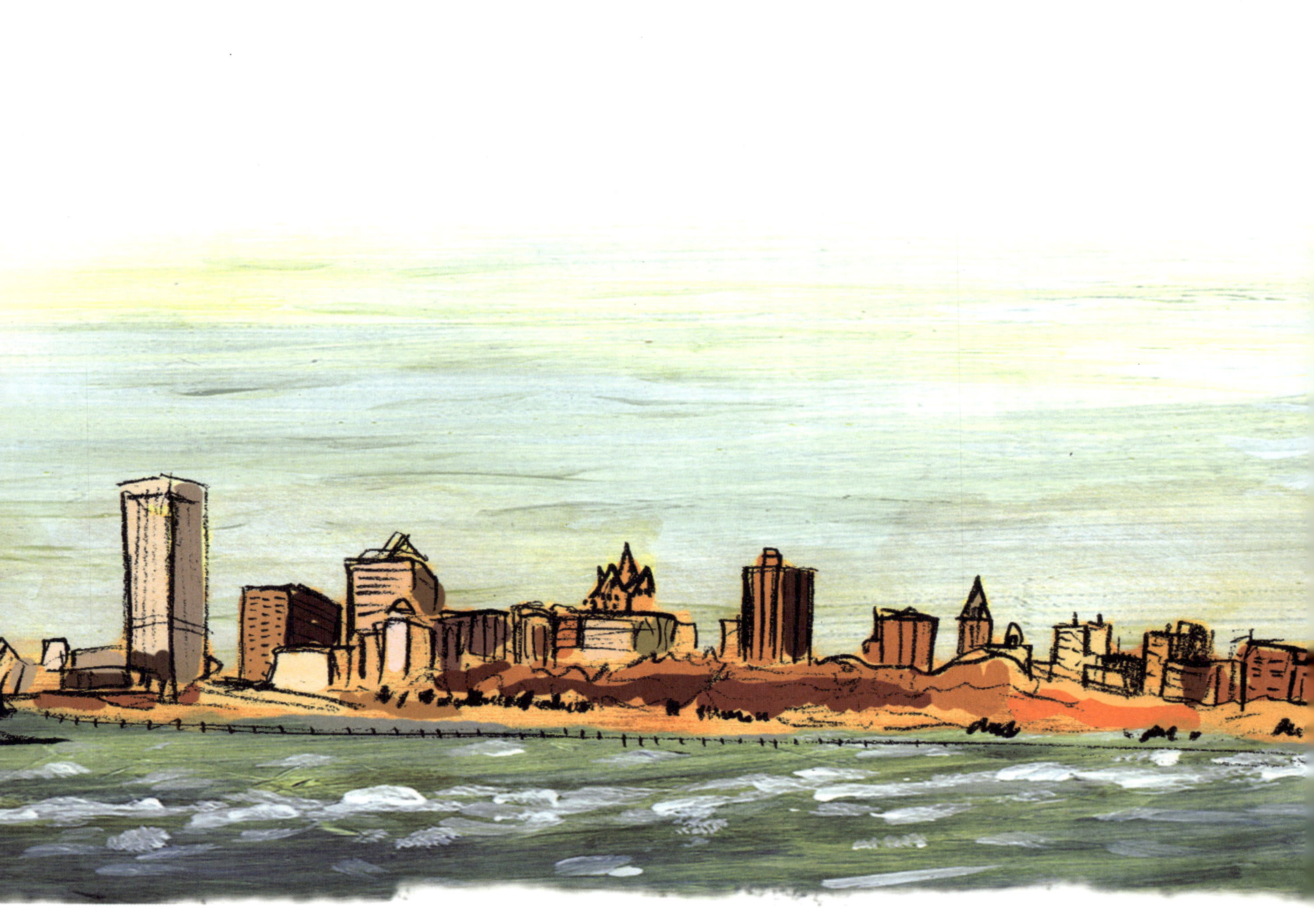

A boat ride offers one of the best views of Milwaukee's skyline.

David Lamps

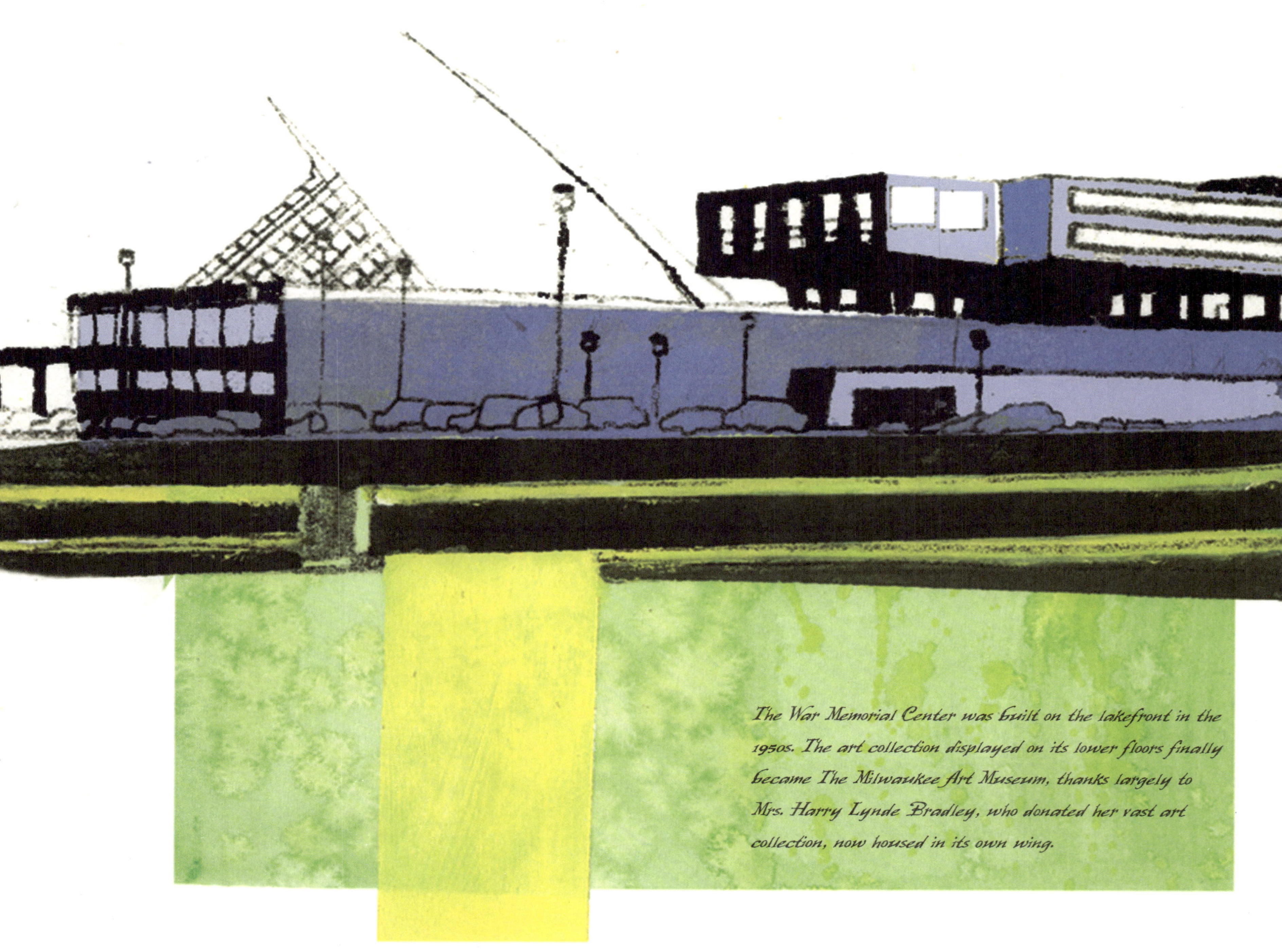

The War Memorial Center was built on the lakefront in the 1950s. The art collection displayed on its lower floors finally became The Milwaukee Art Museum, thanks largely to Mrs. Harry Lynde Bradley, who donated her vast art collection, now housed in its own wing.

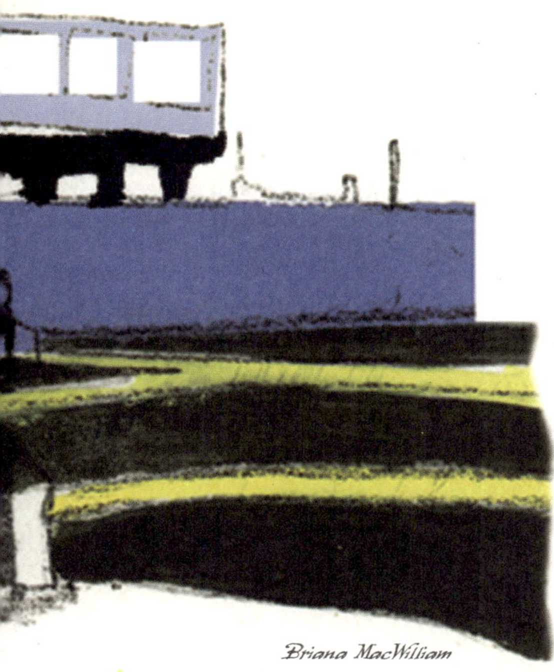

Briana MacWilliam

An anonymous donor gave Milwaukee "The Calling," the steel beamed sculpture reminiscent of a sunbeam created by sculptor Mark di Suvero. It now stands in a lake bluff park at the foot of Wisconsin Ave.

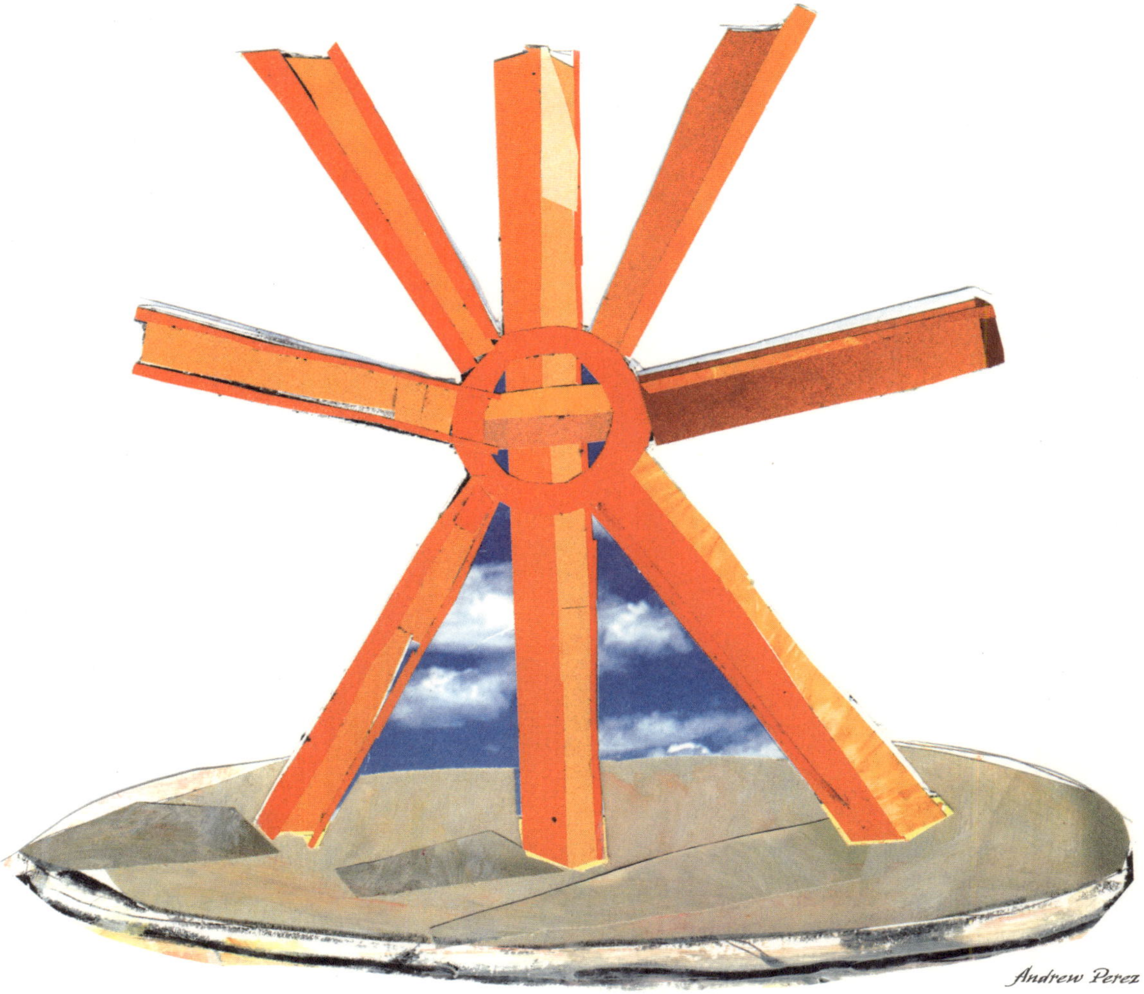

Andrew Perez

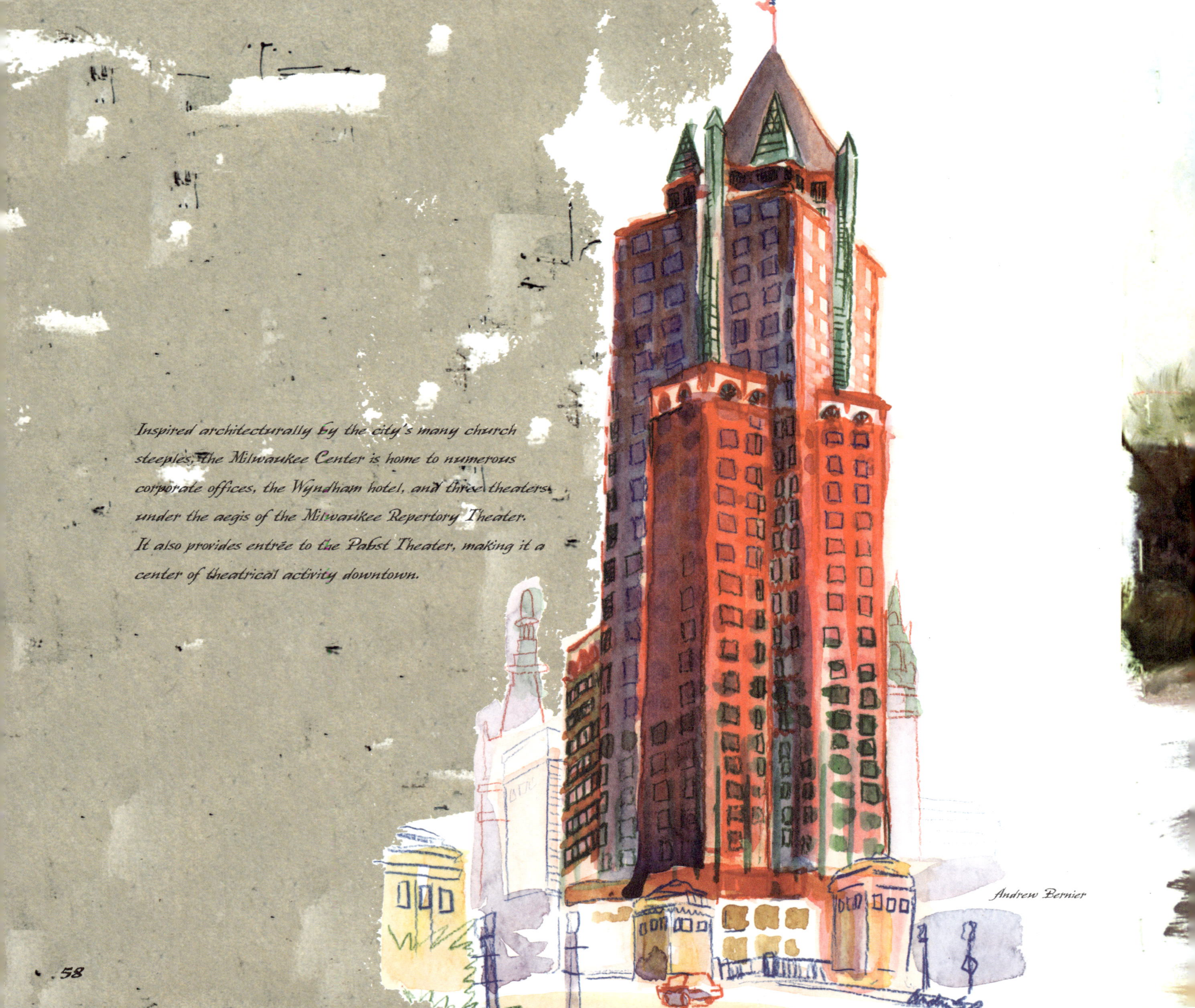

Inspired architecturally by the city's many church steeples, the Milwaukee Center is home to numerous corporate offices, the Wyndham hotel, and three theaters under the aegis of the Milwaukee Repertory Theater. It also provides entrée to the Pabst Theater, making it a center of theatrical activity downtown.

Andrew Bernier

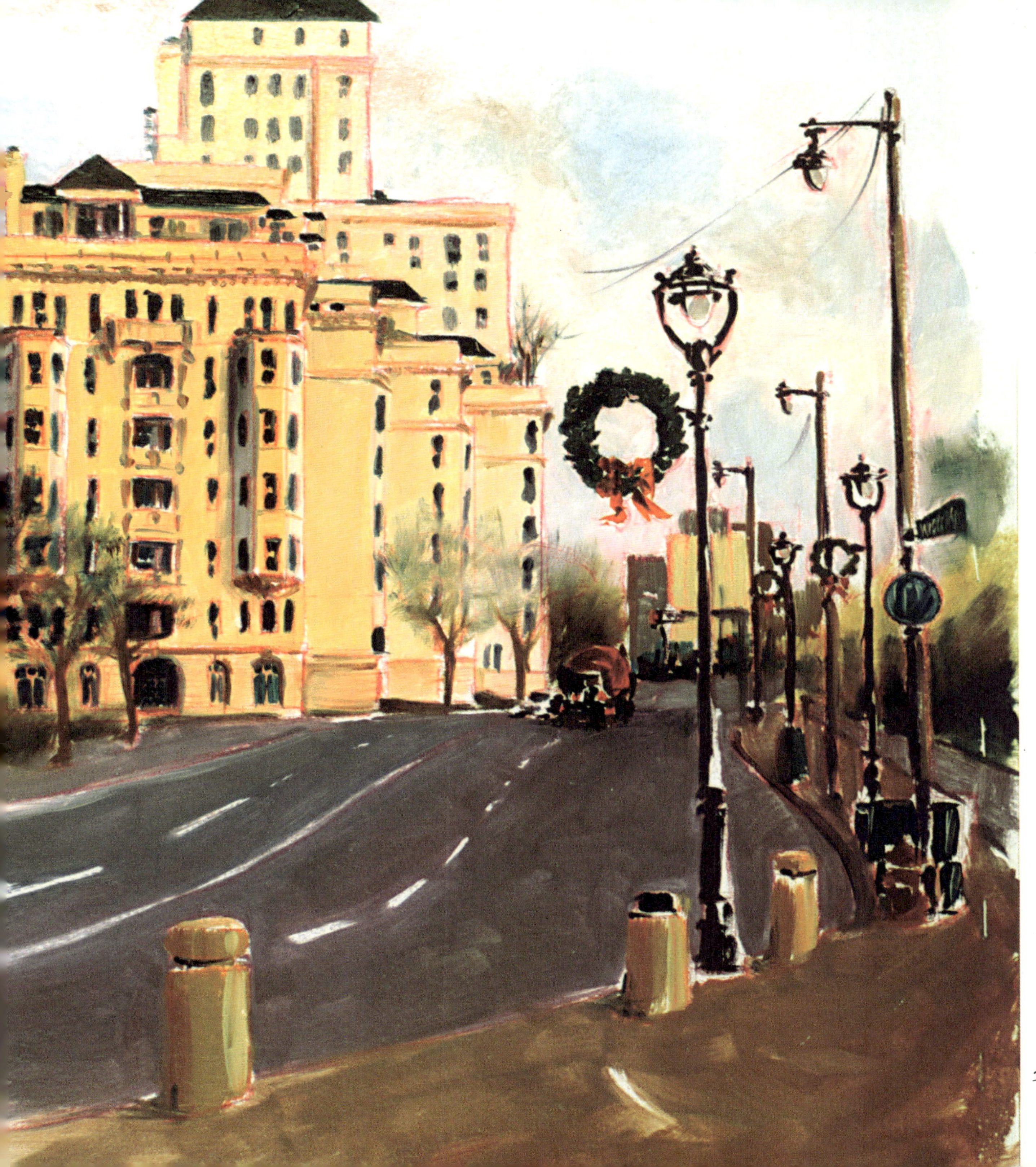

The Cudahy Tower apartments, built in the early 1900s overlooking the lakefront, remained in Patrick Cudahy's family for decades until industrialist Michael Cudahy finally bought out his fellow heirs and remodeled them in the 1980s, turning a portion into condominiums.

Denise Wallner

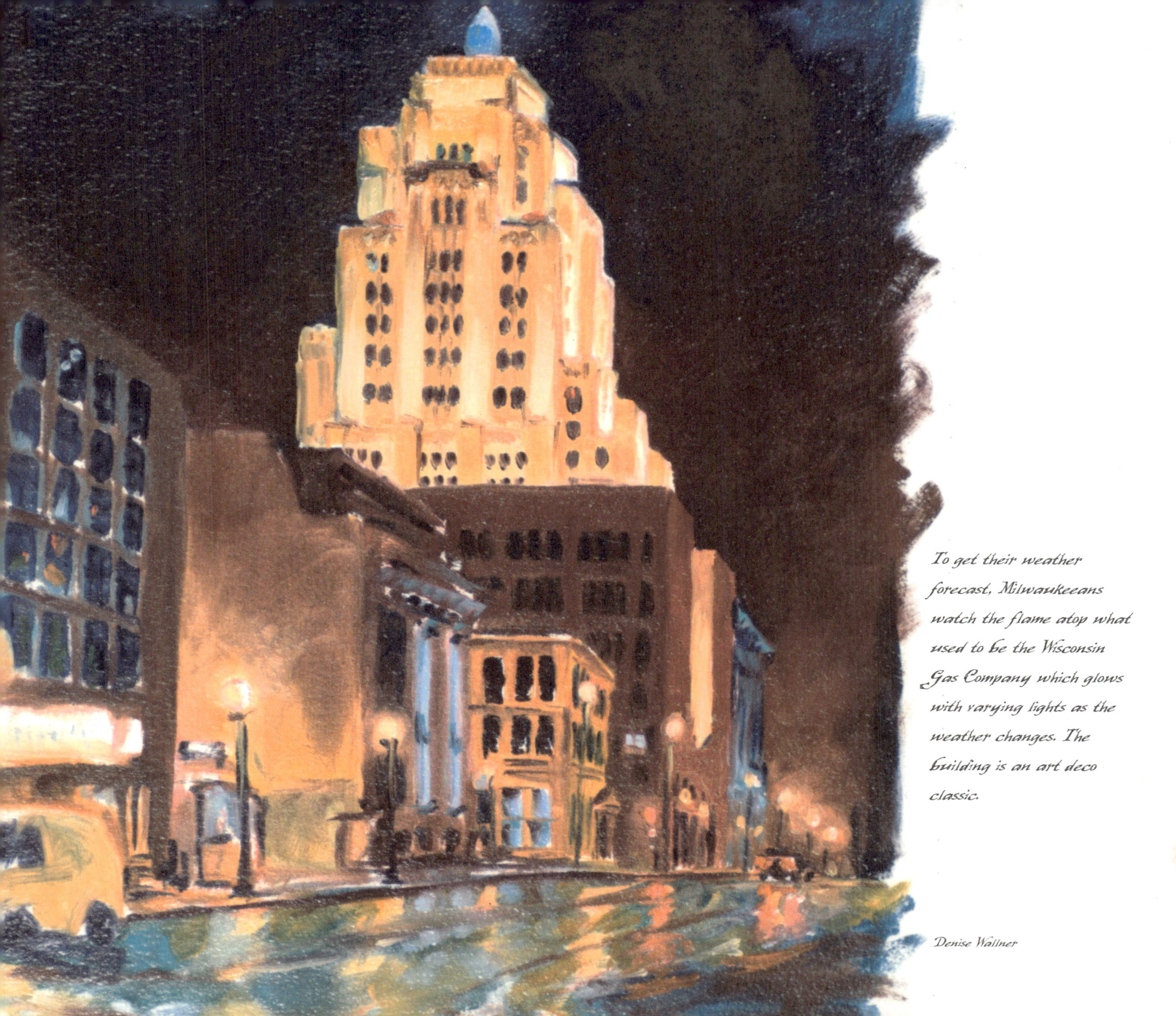

To get their weather forecast, Milwaukeeans watch the flame atop what used to be the Wisconsin Gas Company which glows with varying lights as the weather changes. The building is an art deco classic.

Denise Wallner

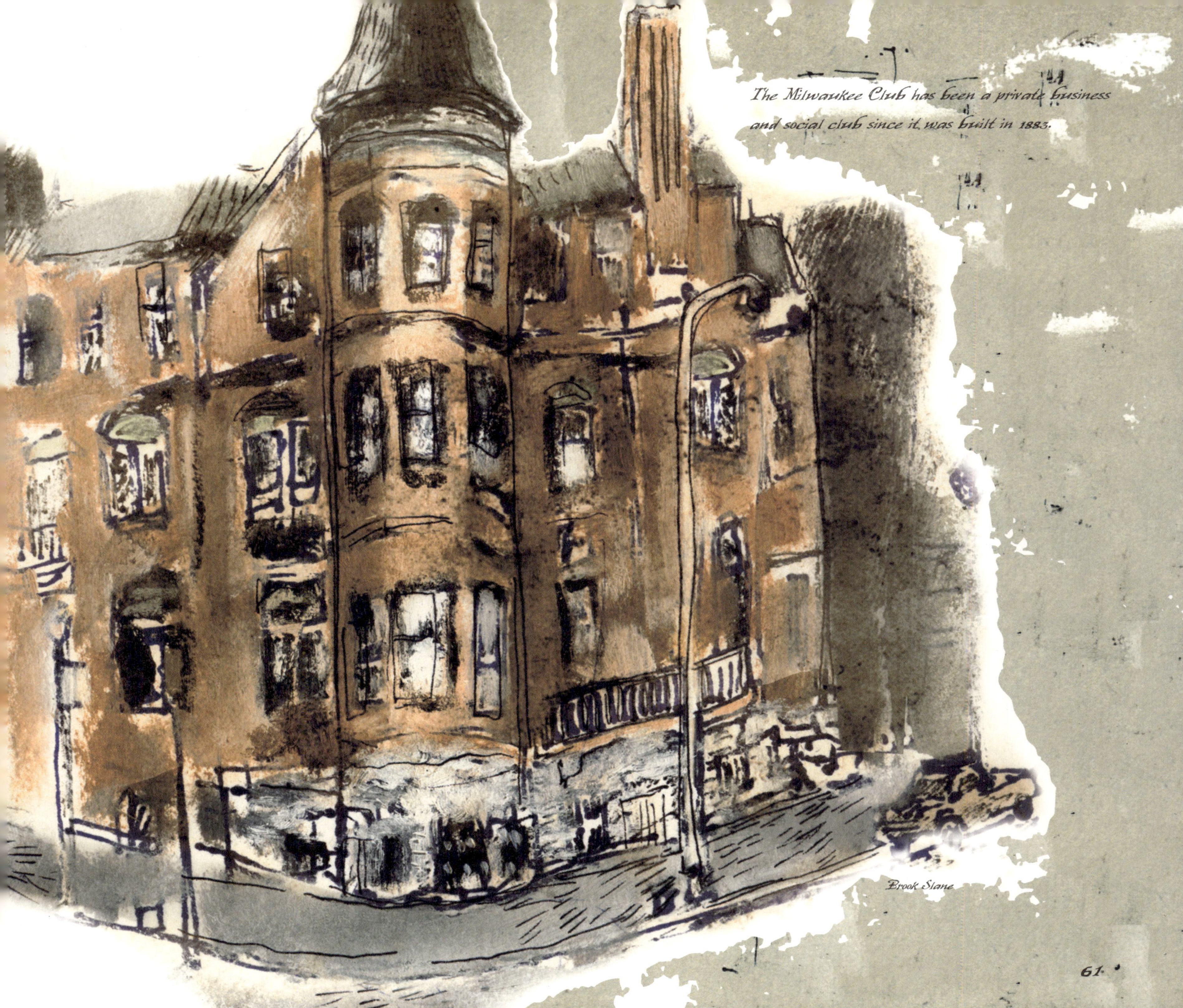

The Milwaukee Club has been a private business and social club since it was built in 1883.

Brook Slane

As early entrepreneurs like tannery owner Guido Pfister prospered, they invested their money in creating civic jewels like the elegant Pfister Hotel. Built in 1893, it quickly became the city's premiere hotel.

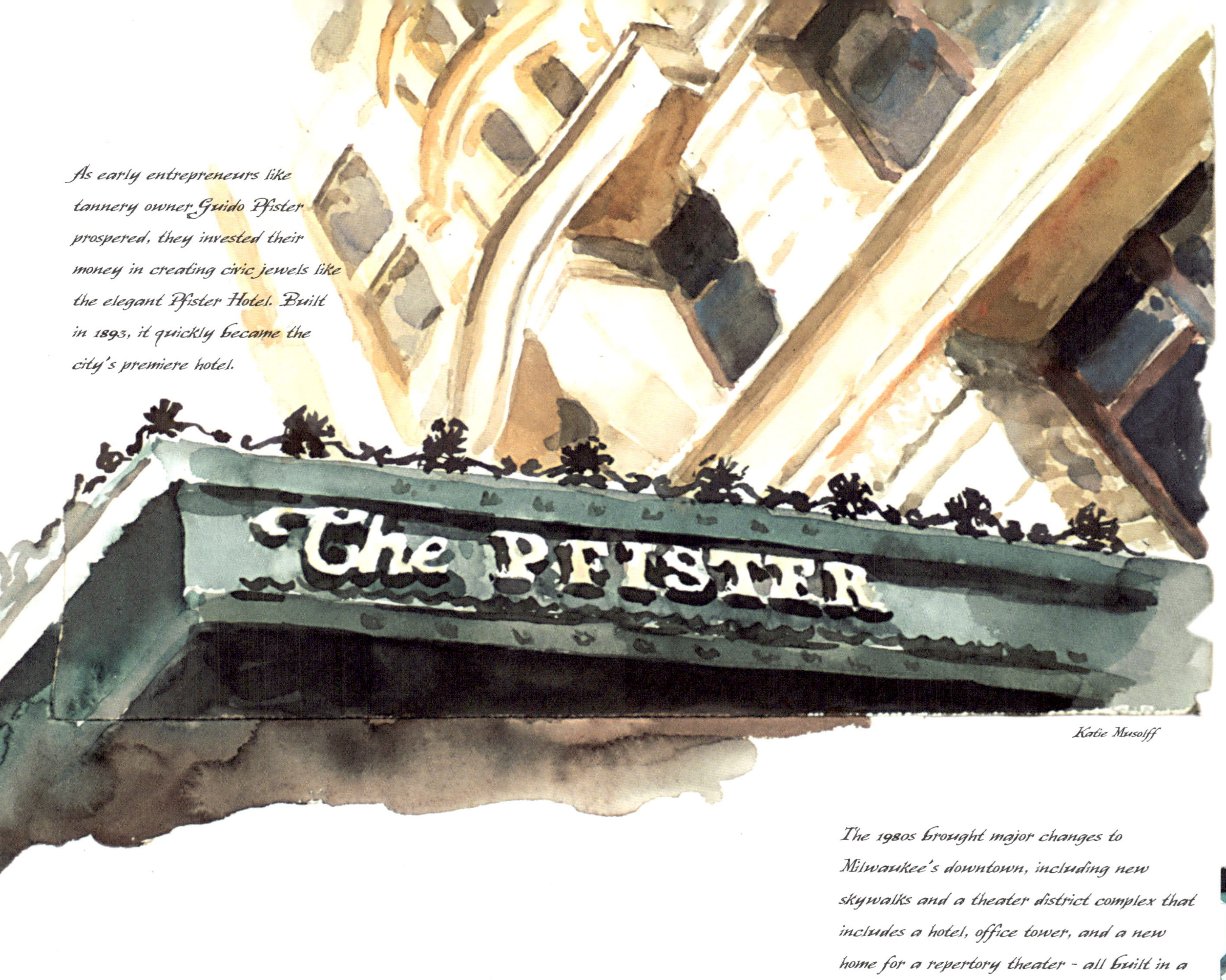

Katie Musolff

The 1980s brought major changes to Milwaukee's downtown, including new skywalks and a theater district complex that includes a hotel, office tower, and a new home for a repertory theater - all built in a style that complements its next-door neighbor, City Hall.

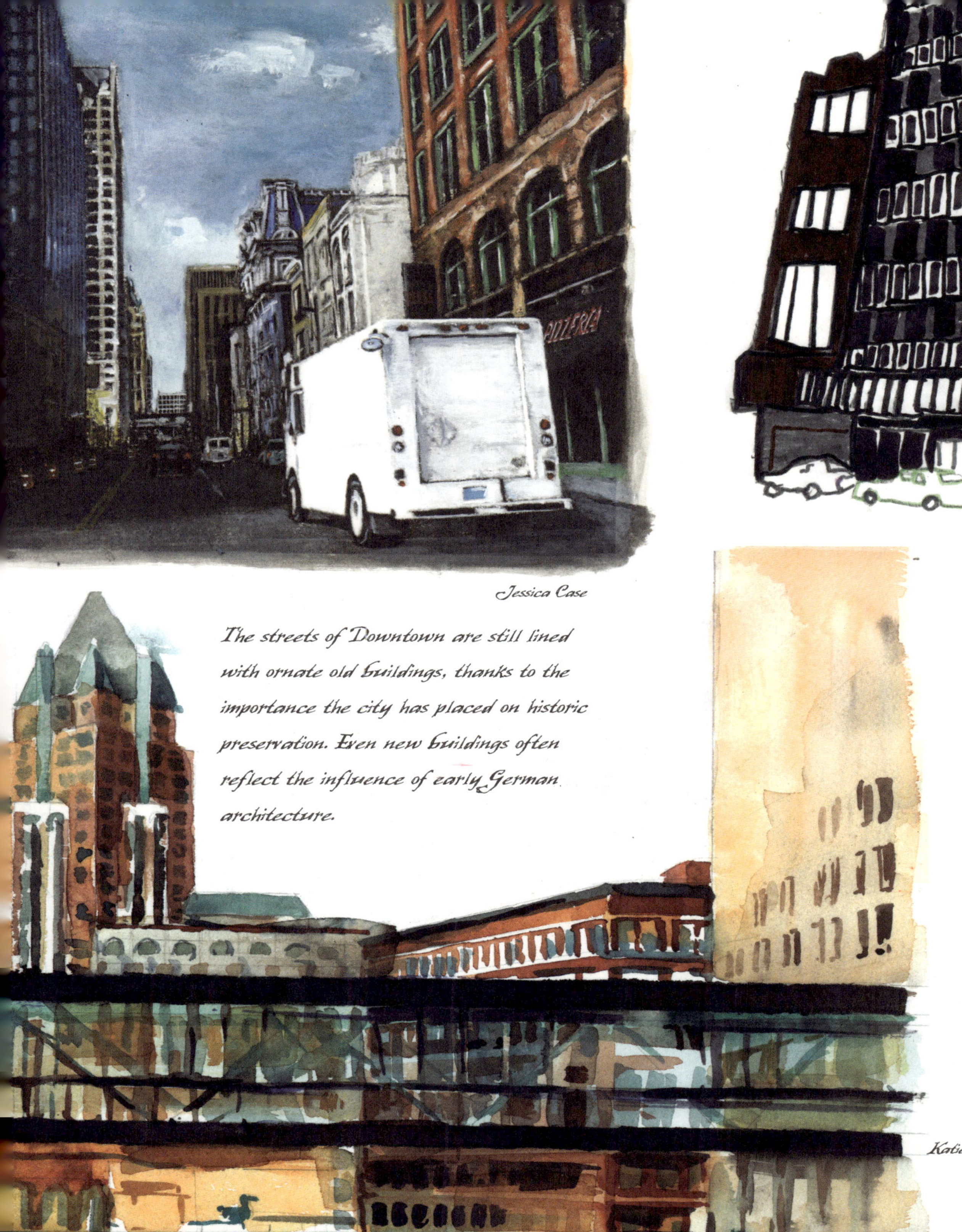

Jessica Case

Andrew Perez

The streets of Downtown are still lined with ornate old buildings, thanks to the importance the city has placed on historic preservation. Even new buildings often reflect the influence of early German architecture.

Local businessman John Burke wanted to create his own version of public art when he and his daughter Wendy hung the ladybugs on his Water St. building in 1999. Watch how they light up at night.

Katie Musolff

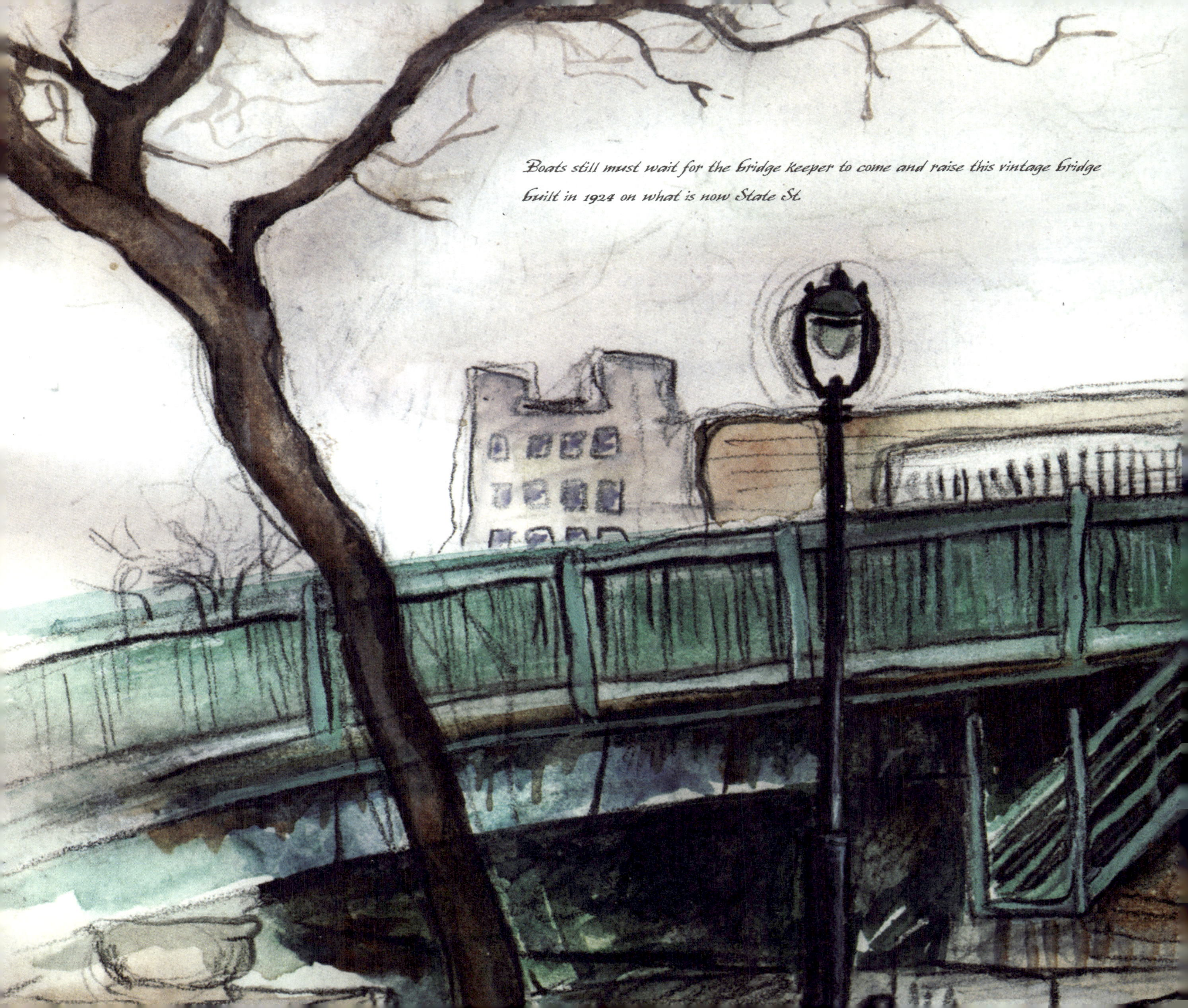

Boats still must wait for the bridge keeper to come and raise this vintage bridge built in 1924 on what is now State St.

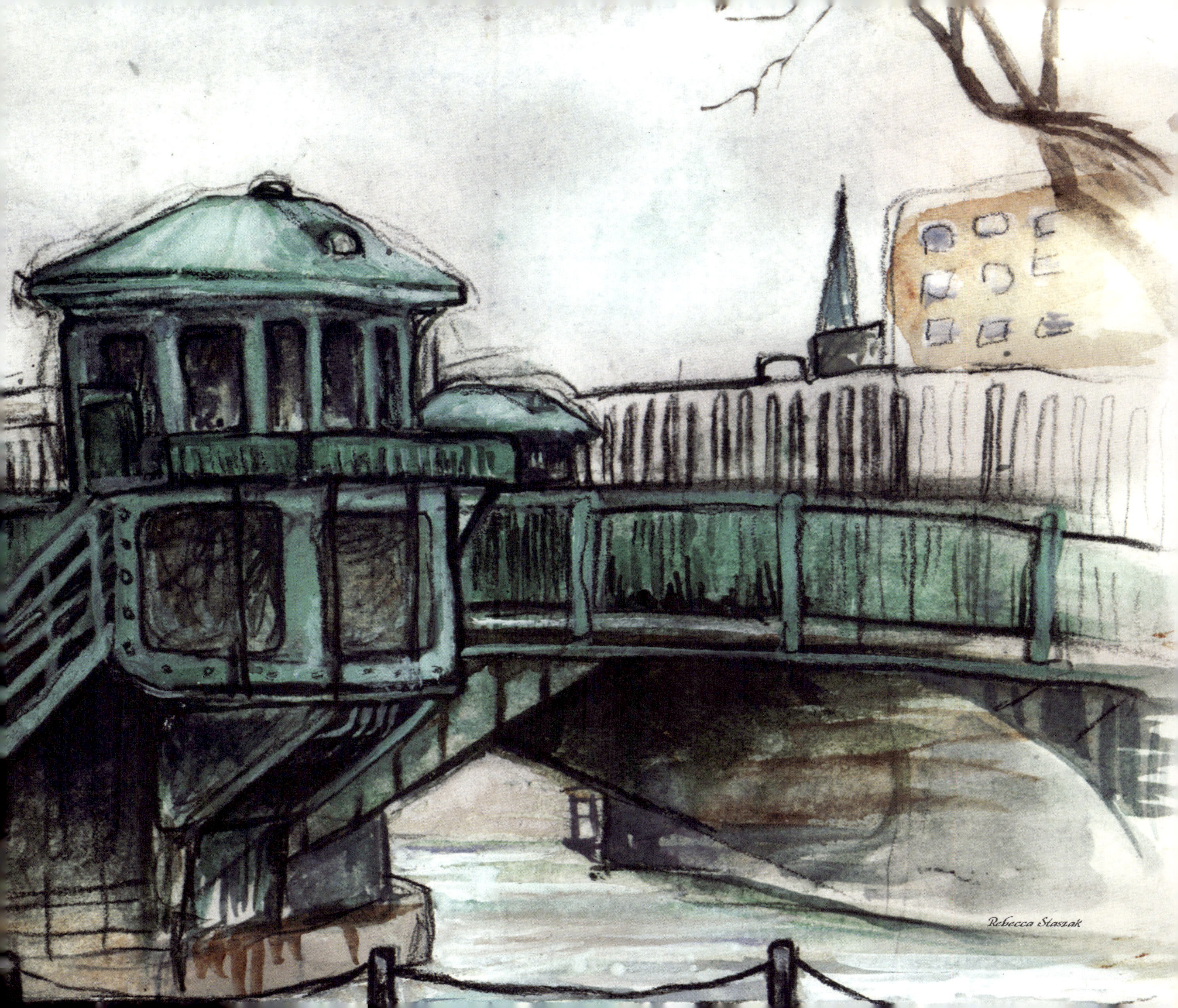
Rebecca Staszak

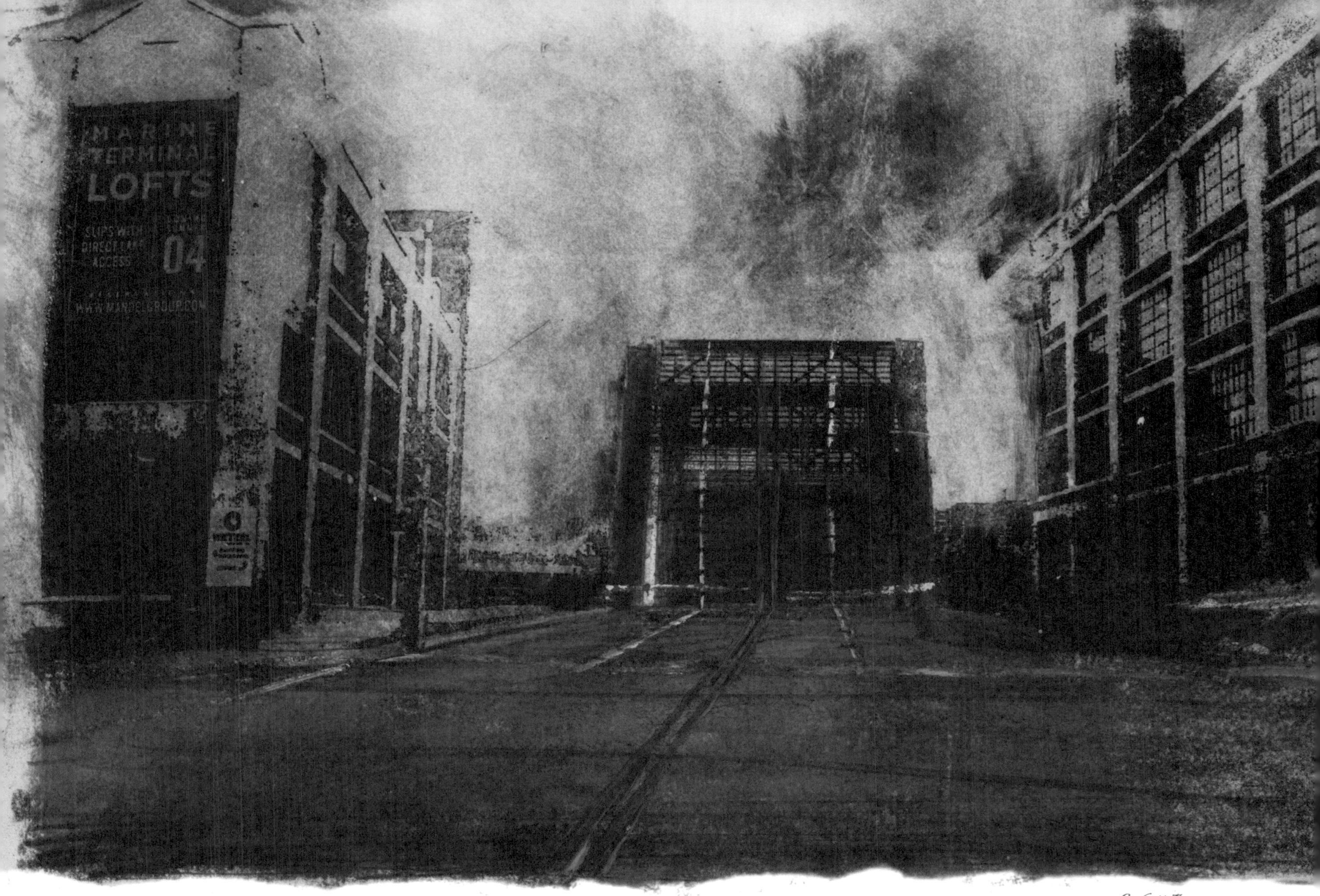

Corbett Toomsen

Traffic comes to a halt as boats chug beneath this drawbridge on their way to industrial sites in the Menomonee Valley. The bridge is a link to Walker's Point.

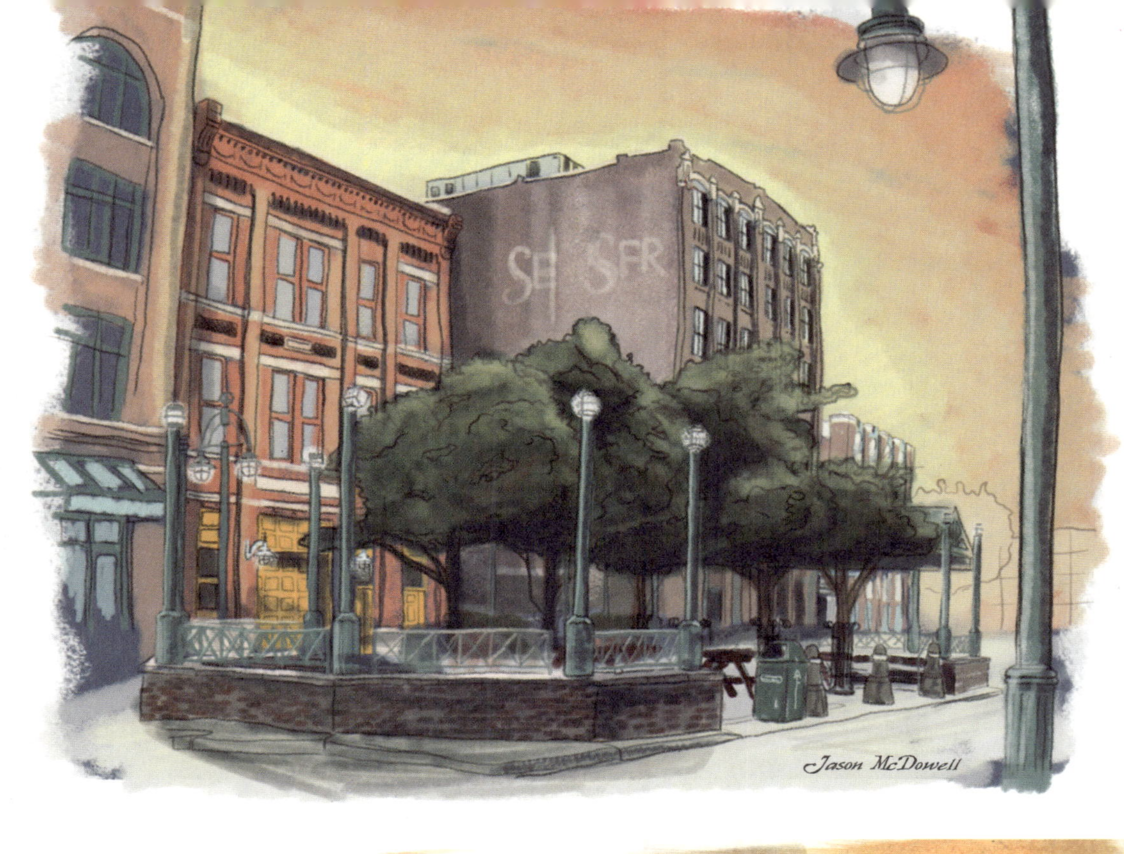

The city debated letting adult entertainment move to the Third Ward until Isabelle Polacheck threw a party in the chic loft she'd built above her factory, showing how the area could become the trendy mix of condos, businesses, and schools it is today. The imaginatively remodeled Broadway Theatre Center is shared by the Skylight Opera Theatre, Milwaukee Chamber Theatre, Bialystock & Bloom, and Renaissance Theaterworks.

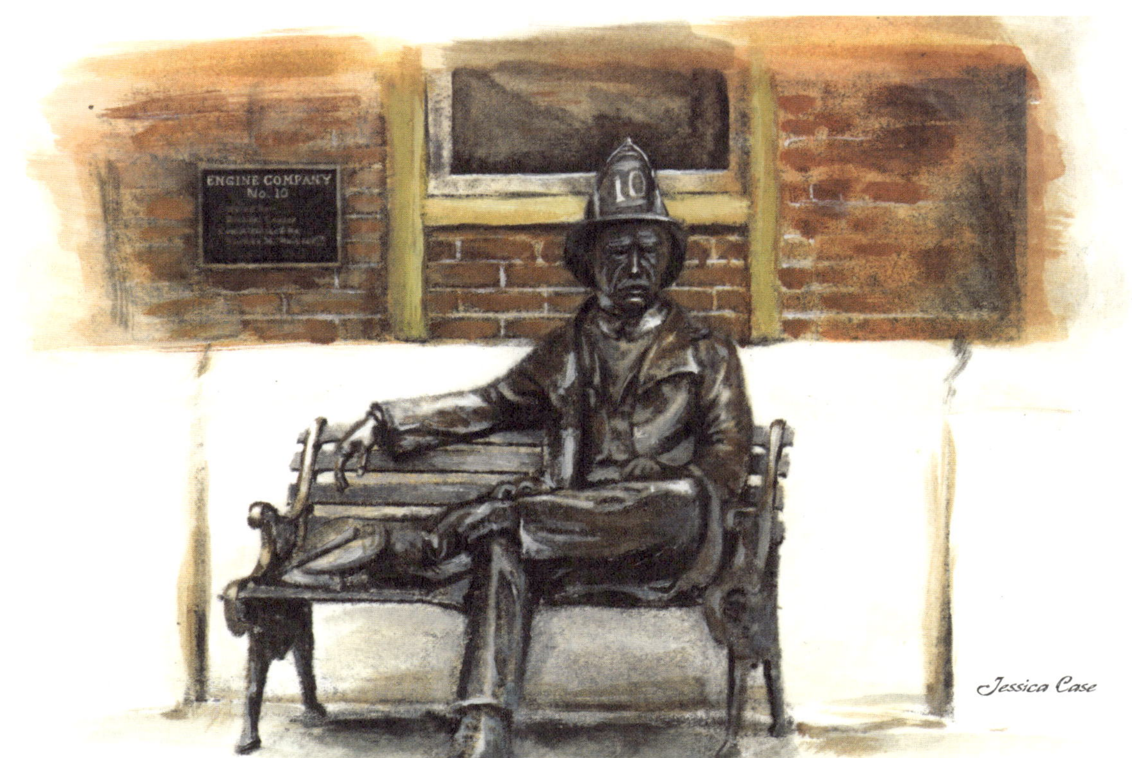

Tom Wamser, who owns an 1890s firehouse in the Third Ward, decided to add this bronze image of an old-time firefighter as a gift for everyone to enjoy. People often stop to have their picture taken with the historic figure.

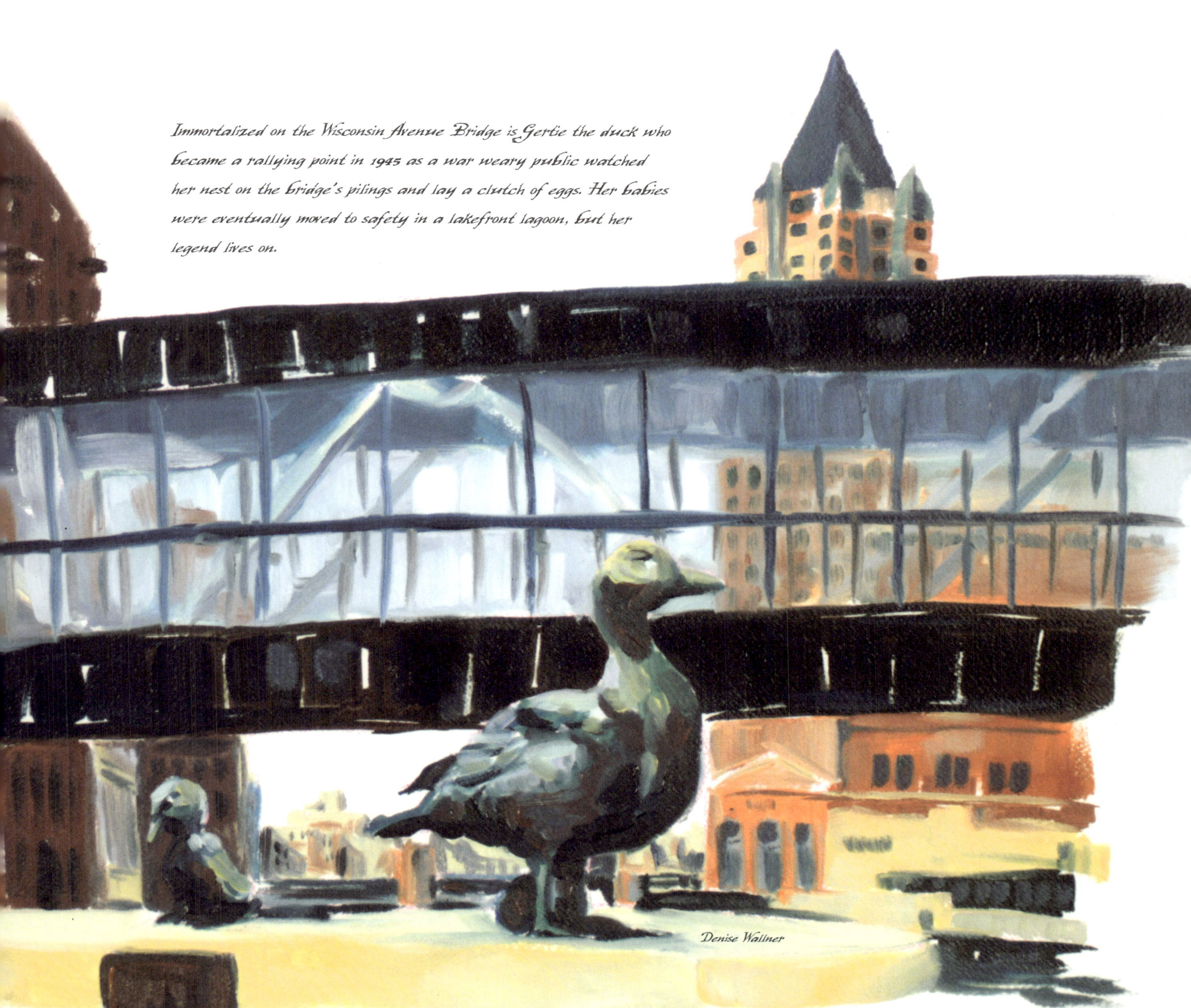

Immortalized on the Wisconsin Avenue Bridge is Gertie the duck who became a rallying point in 1945 as a war weary public watched her nest on the bridge's pilings and lay a clutch of eggs. Her babies were eventually moved to safety in a lakefront lagoon, but her legend lives on.

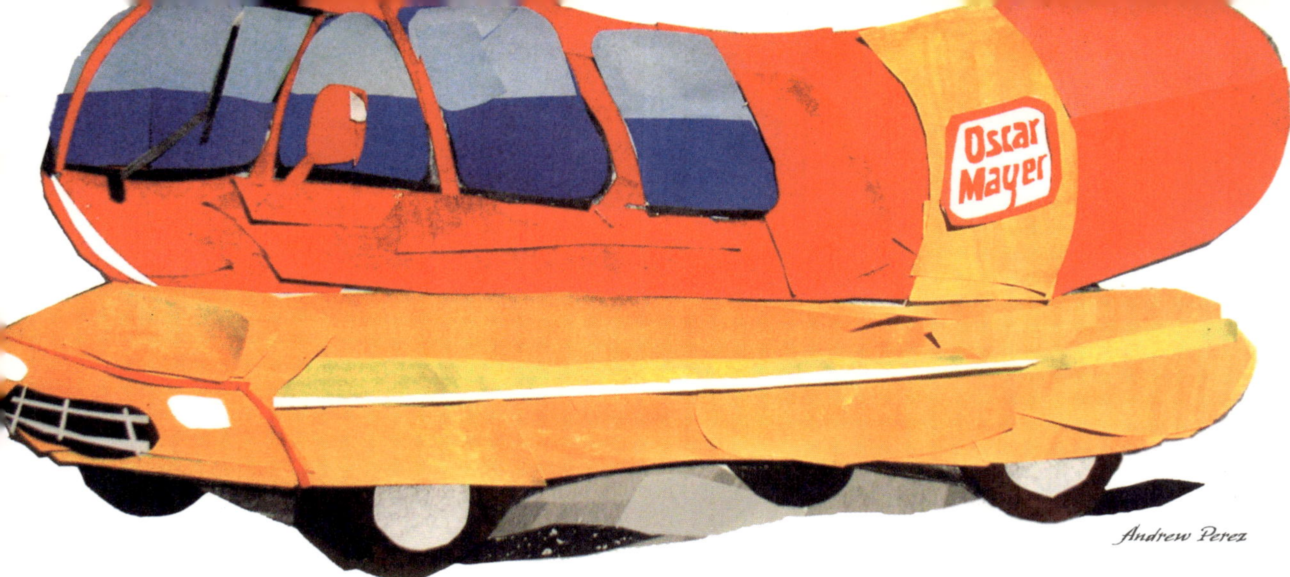

Famed Milwaukee designer Brooks Stevens is best known for creating sleek boats, cars, and trains. One of his most recognizable and whimsical works is this "internal combustion hot dog" that is now known worldwide.

Andrew Perez

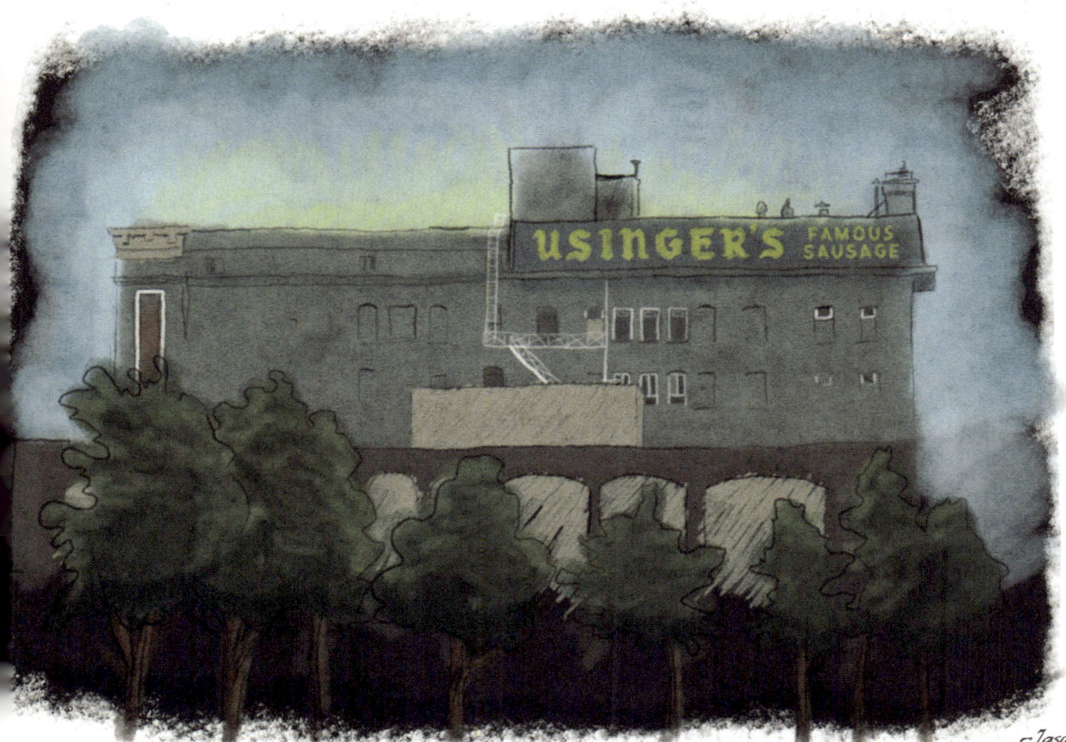

Jason McDowell

The Germans loved sausage and no one made it better than Fred Usinger who arrived in the late 1870s, just as Milwaukee saloons were offering a free lunch to promote their beers. With Prohibition came the saying "no more free lunch." But Usinger's sausages survived, thanks to their popularity.

Rebecca Staszak

Usinger's store still features murals he commissioned in 1906 to depict his old world methods of sausage making, plus the sausage making elves on his sign.

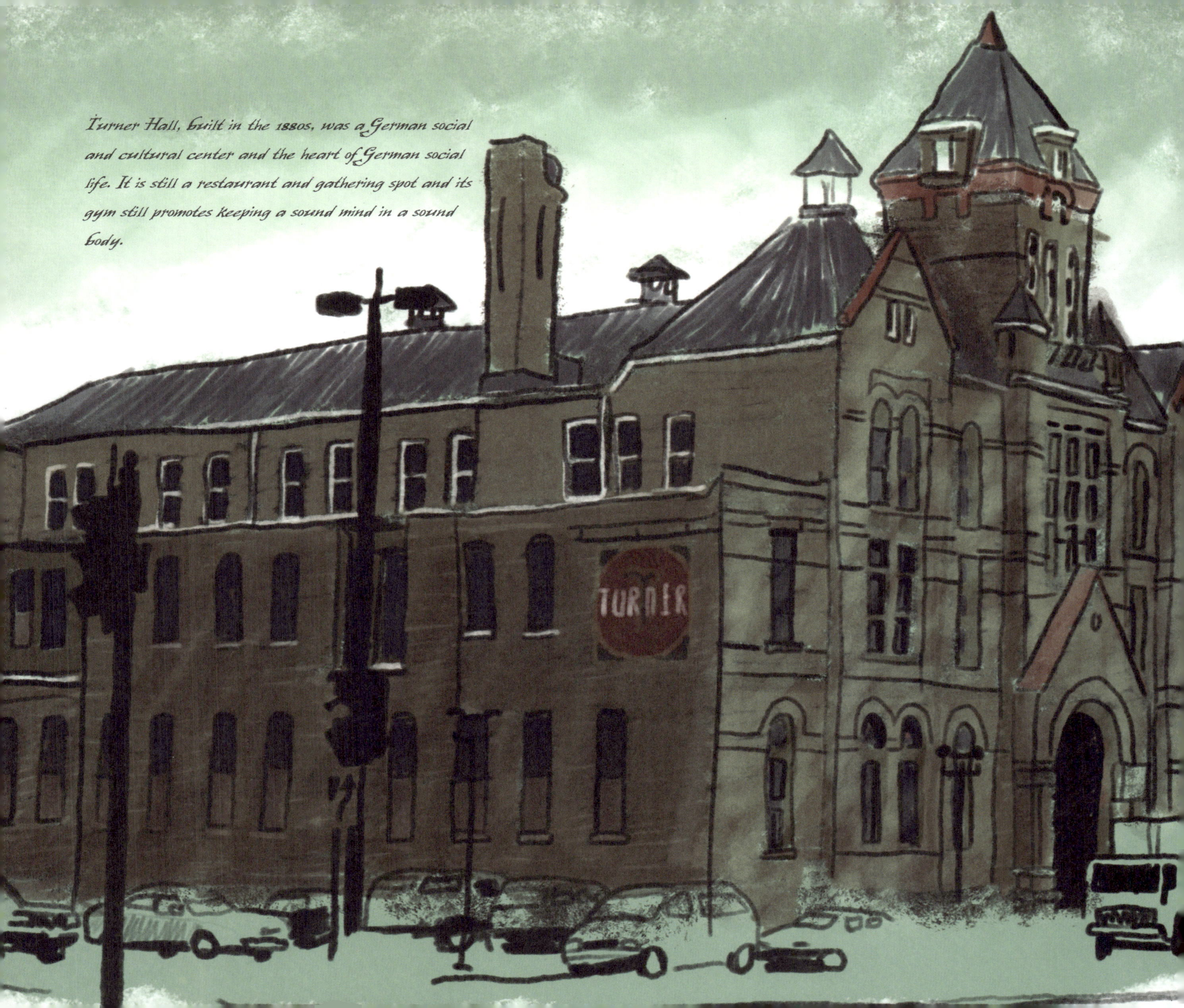

Turner Hall, built in the 1880s, was a German social and cultural center and the heart of German social life. It is still a restaurant and gathering spot and its gym still promotes keeping a sound mind in a sound body.

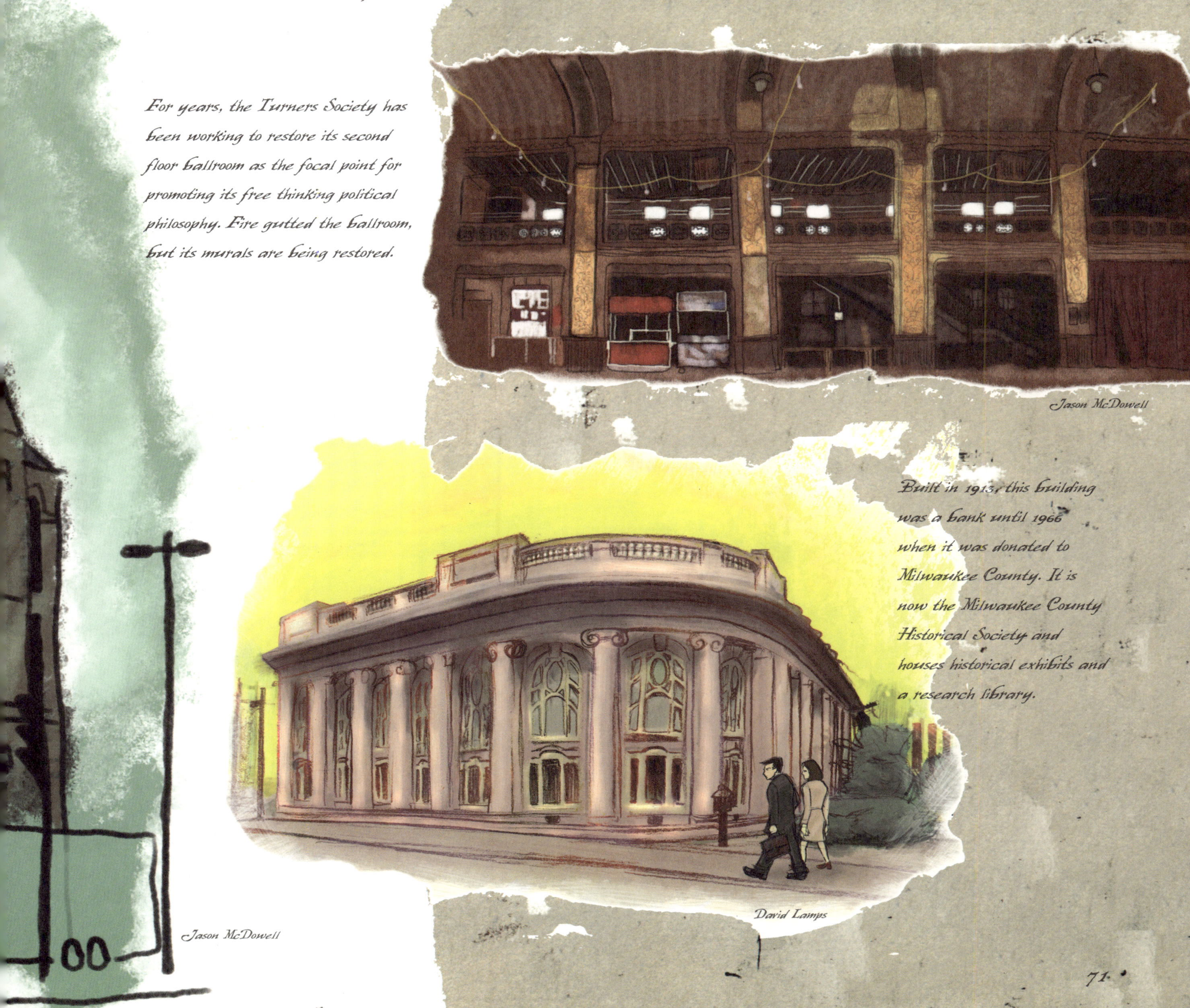

For years, the Turners Society has been working to restore its second floor ballroom as the focal point for promoting its free thinking political philosophy. Fire gutted the ballroom, but its murals are being restored.

Jason McDowell

Built in 1913, this building was a bank until 1966 when it was donated to Milwaukee County. It is now the Milwaukee County Historical Society and houses historical exhibits and a research library.

David Lamps

Jason McDowell

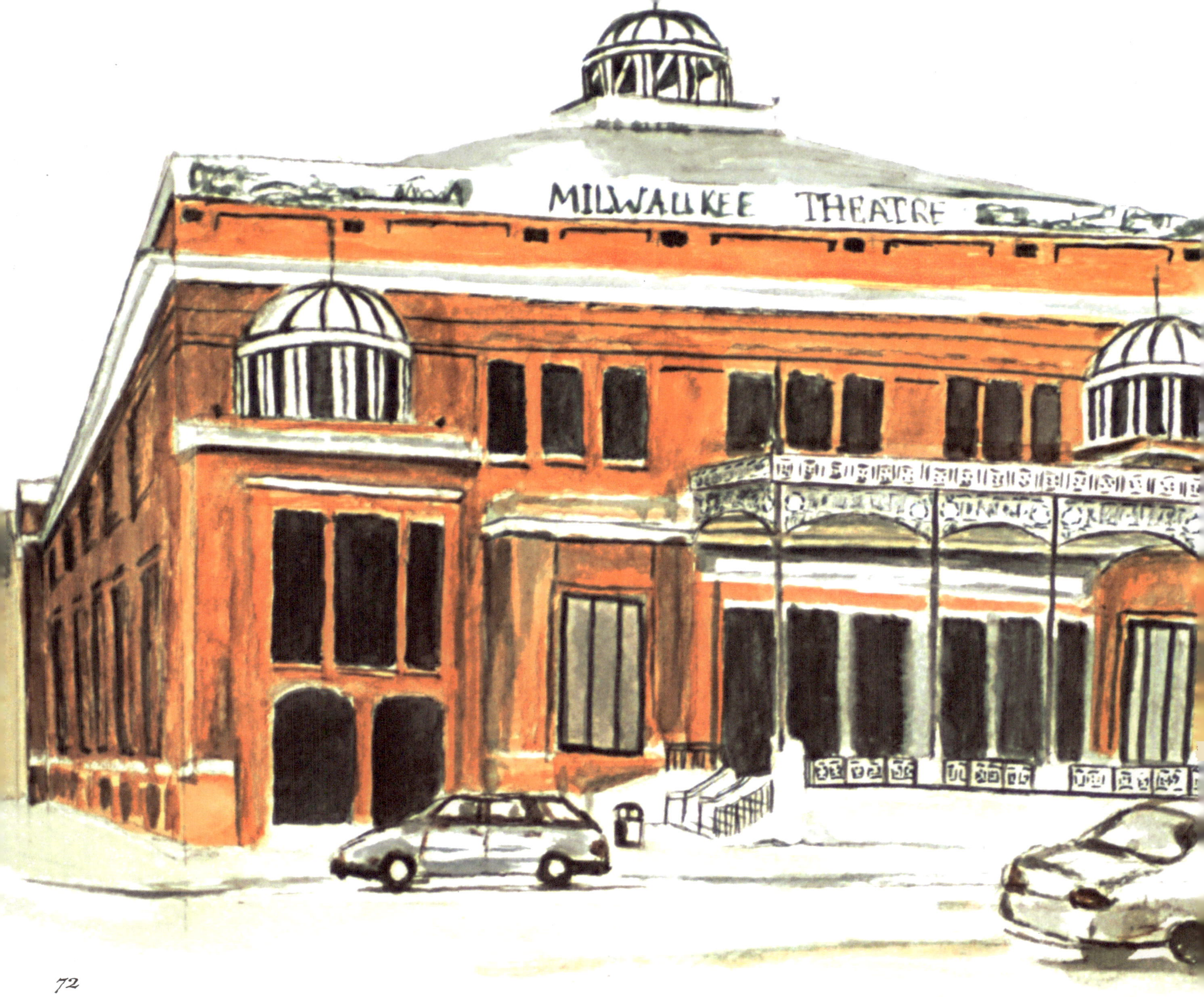
MILWAUKEE THEATRE

The Milwaukee Theater was recently completely renovated. It stands on the site where early leaders built Milwaukee's first industrial exposition hall to promote their businesses. In 1909, the auditorium replaced it as a place for speeches, business shows, and entertainment, a role it still plays today.

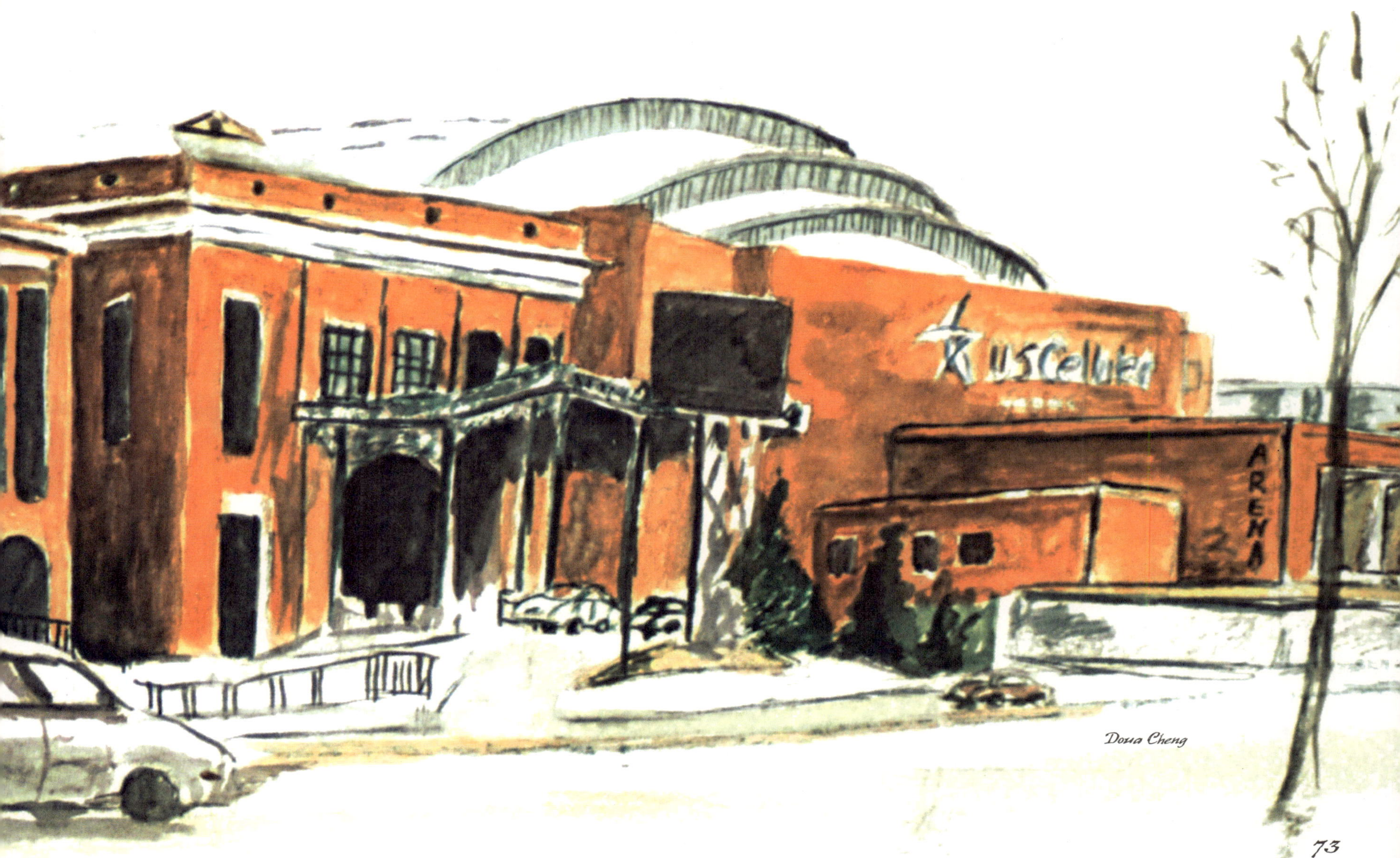

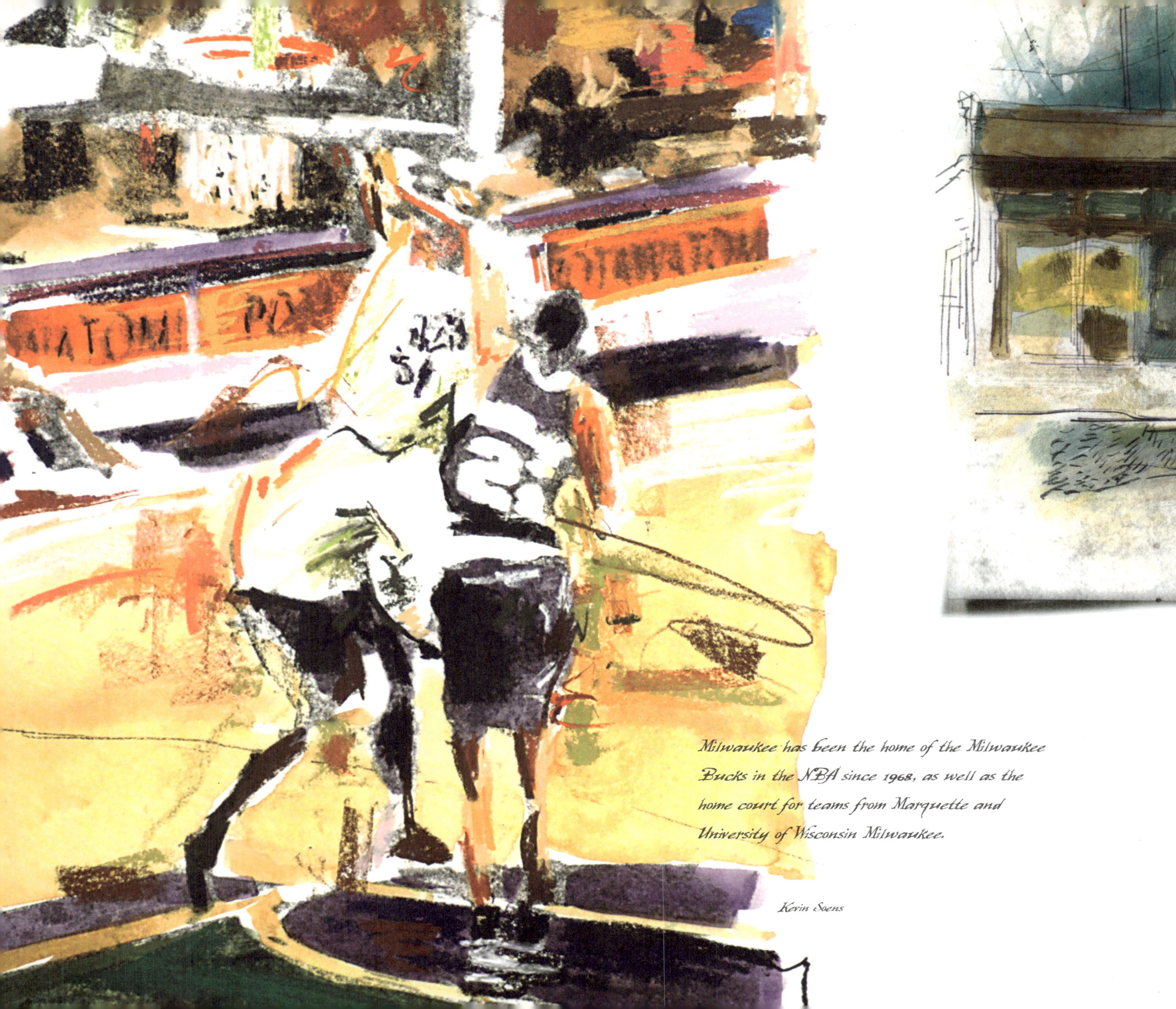

Milwaukee has been the home of the Milwaukee Bucks in the NBA since 1968, as well as the home court for teams from Marquette and University of Wisconsin Milwaukee.

Kevin Soens

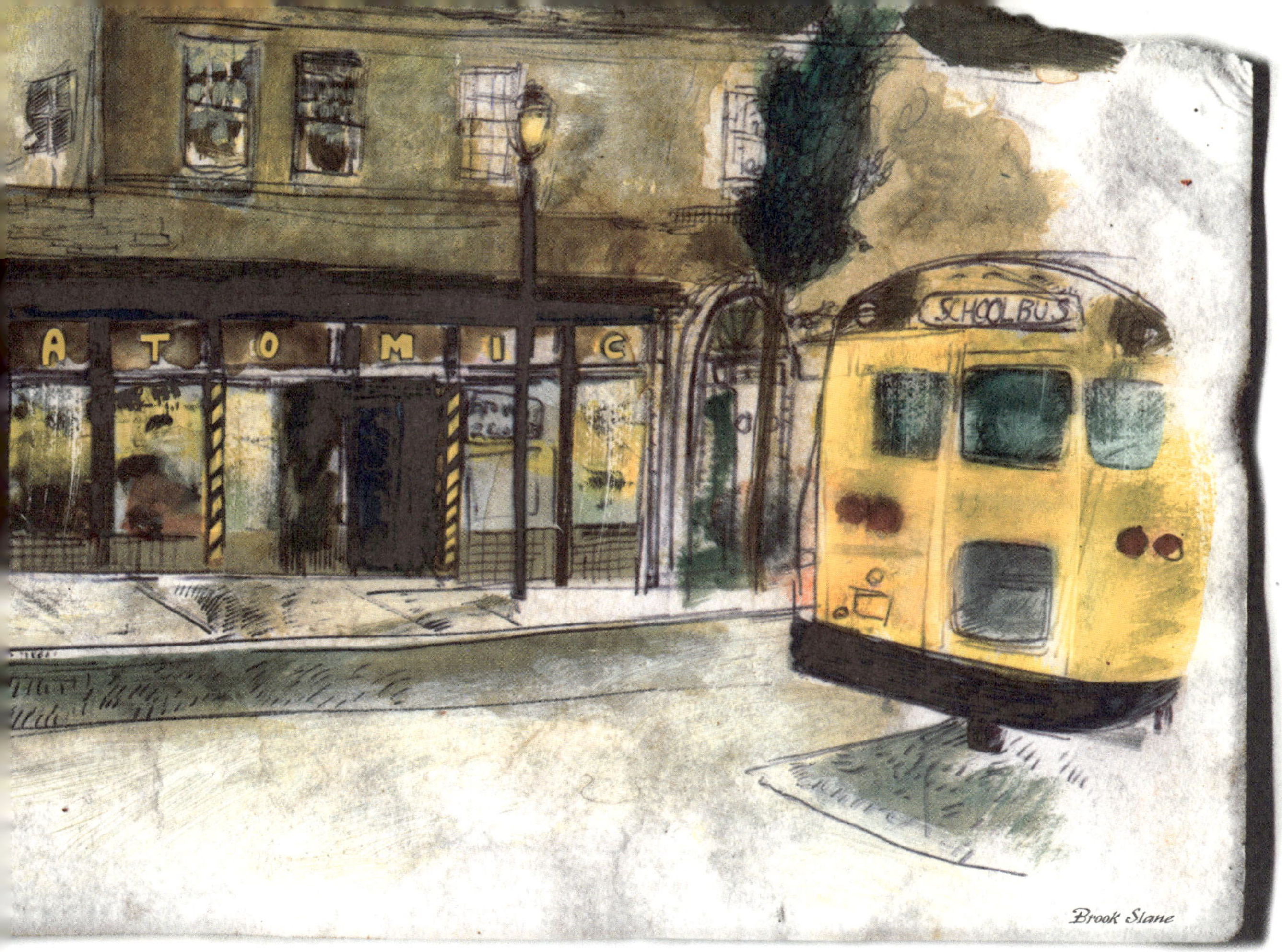

Brook Slane

Stores like Atomic Records have made the intersection of Oakland and Locust a popular business district for students at nearby University of Wisconsin Milwaukee and young people throughout the city.

At the turn of the last century, city leaders envisioned creating the tree lined boulevard which now extends from City Hall on the east to the top of the hill on 9th Street where a new courthouse was completed in 1931.

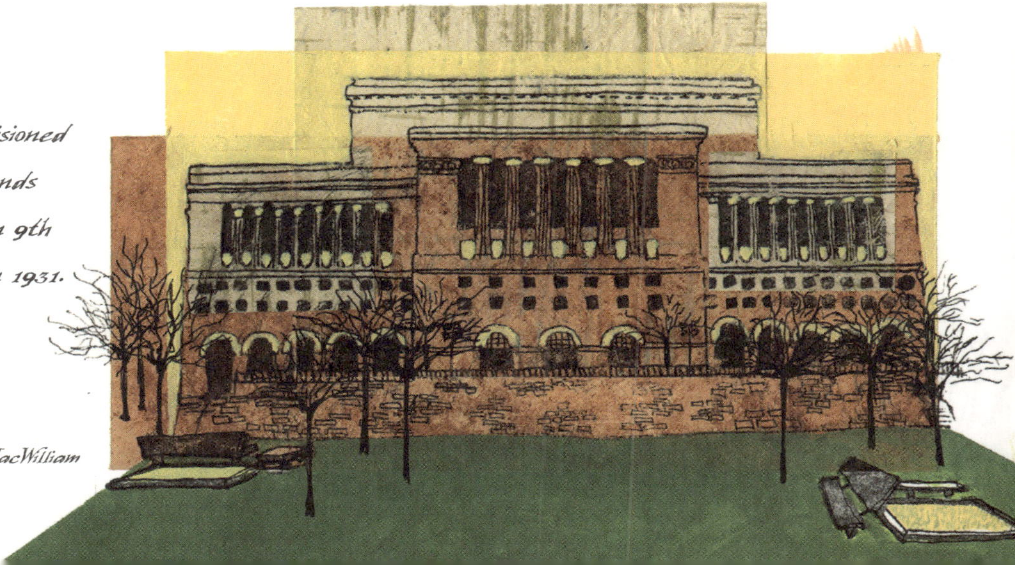

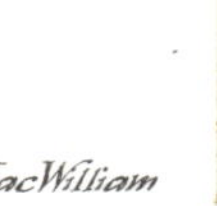

Briana MacWilliam

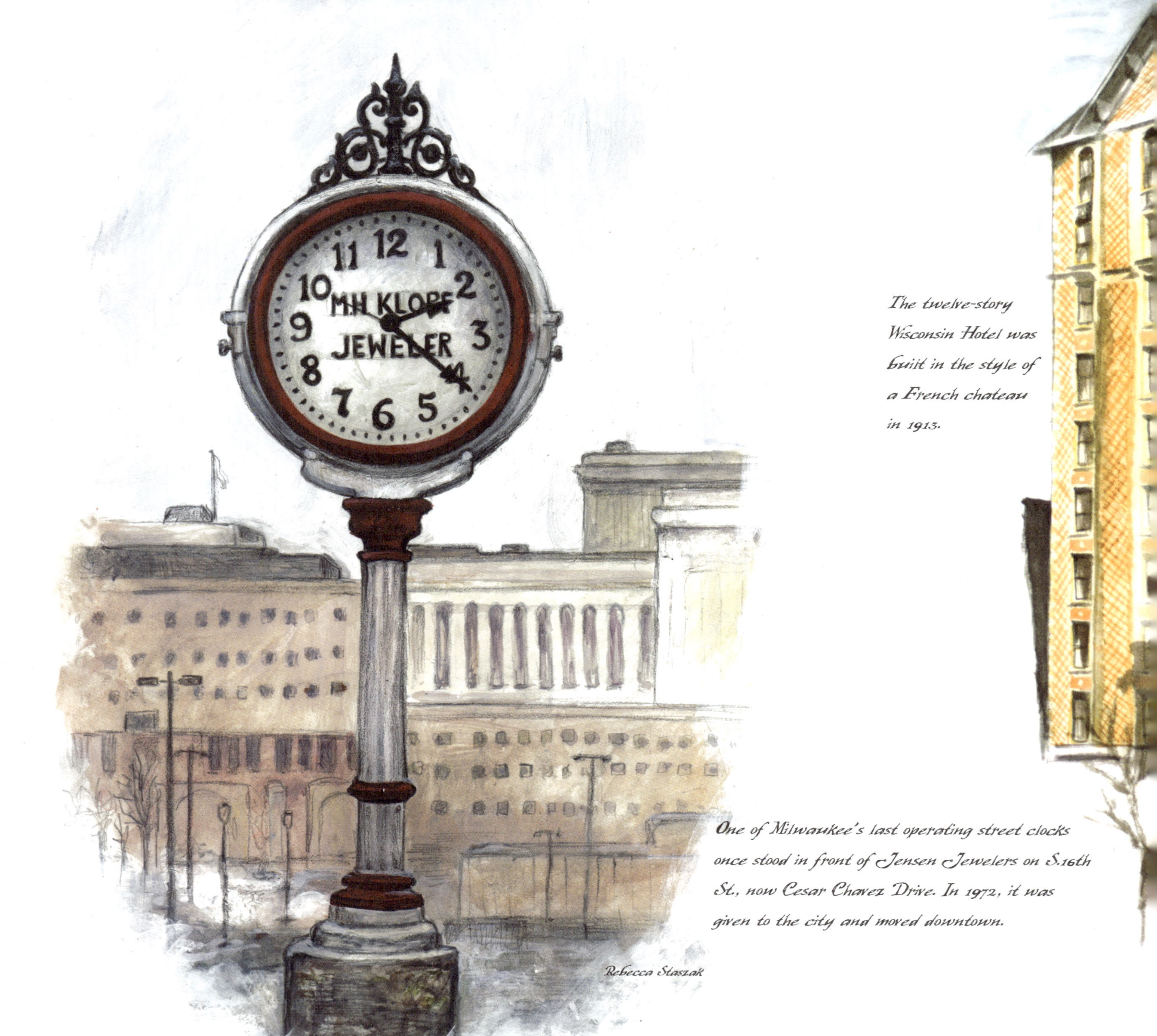

The twelve-story Wisconsin Hotel was built in the style of a French chateau in 1913.

One of Milwaukee's last operating street clocks once stood in front of Jensen Jewelers on S.16th St., now Cesar Chavez Drive. In 1972, it was given to the city and moved downtown.

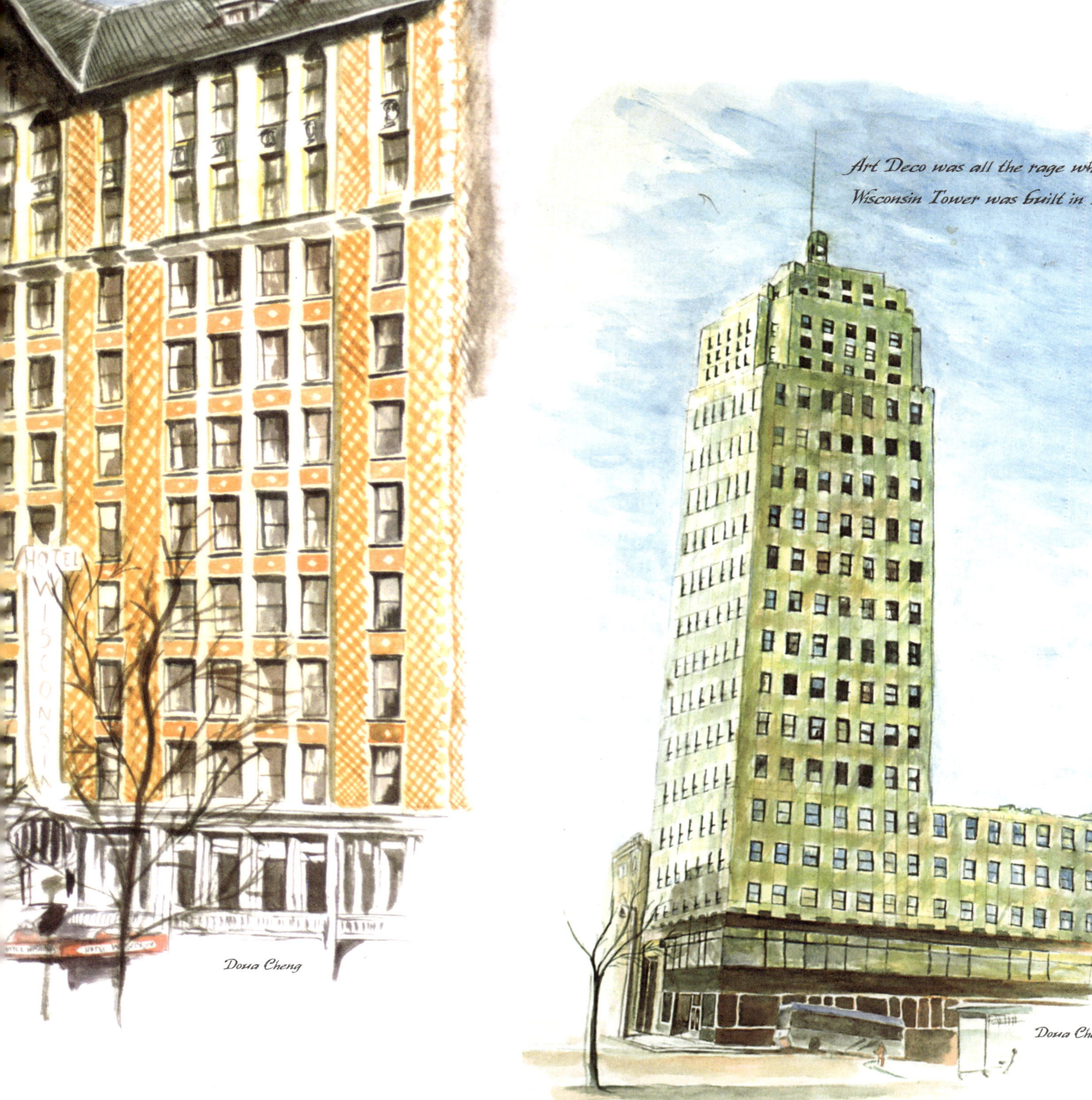

Art Deco was all the rage when The Wisconsin Tower was built in 1930.

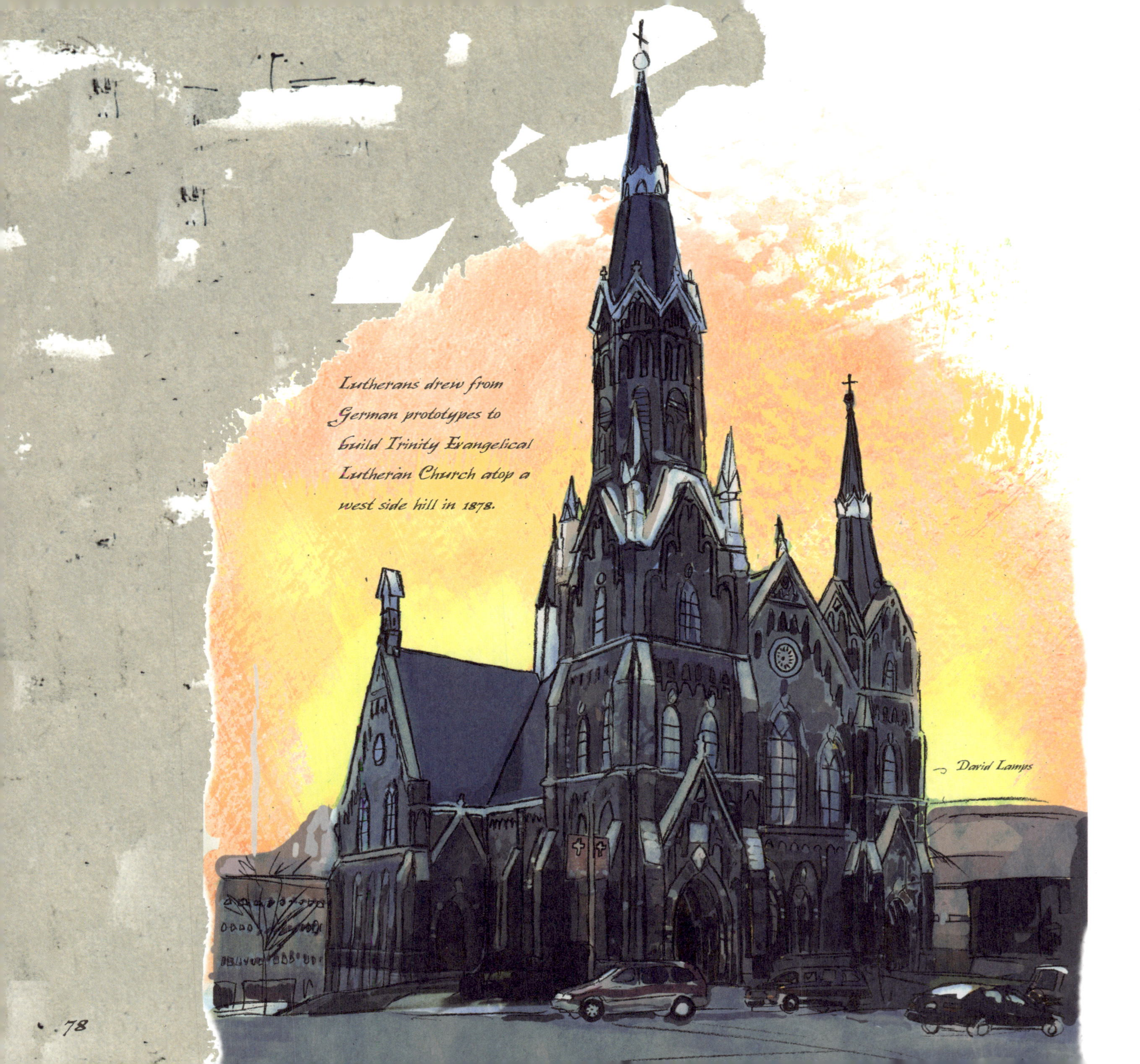

Lutherans drew from German prototypes to build Trinity Evangelical Lutheran Church atop a west side hill in 1878.

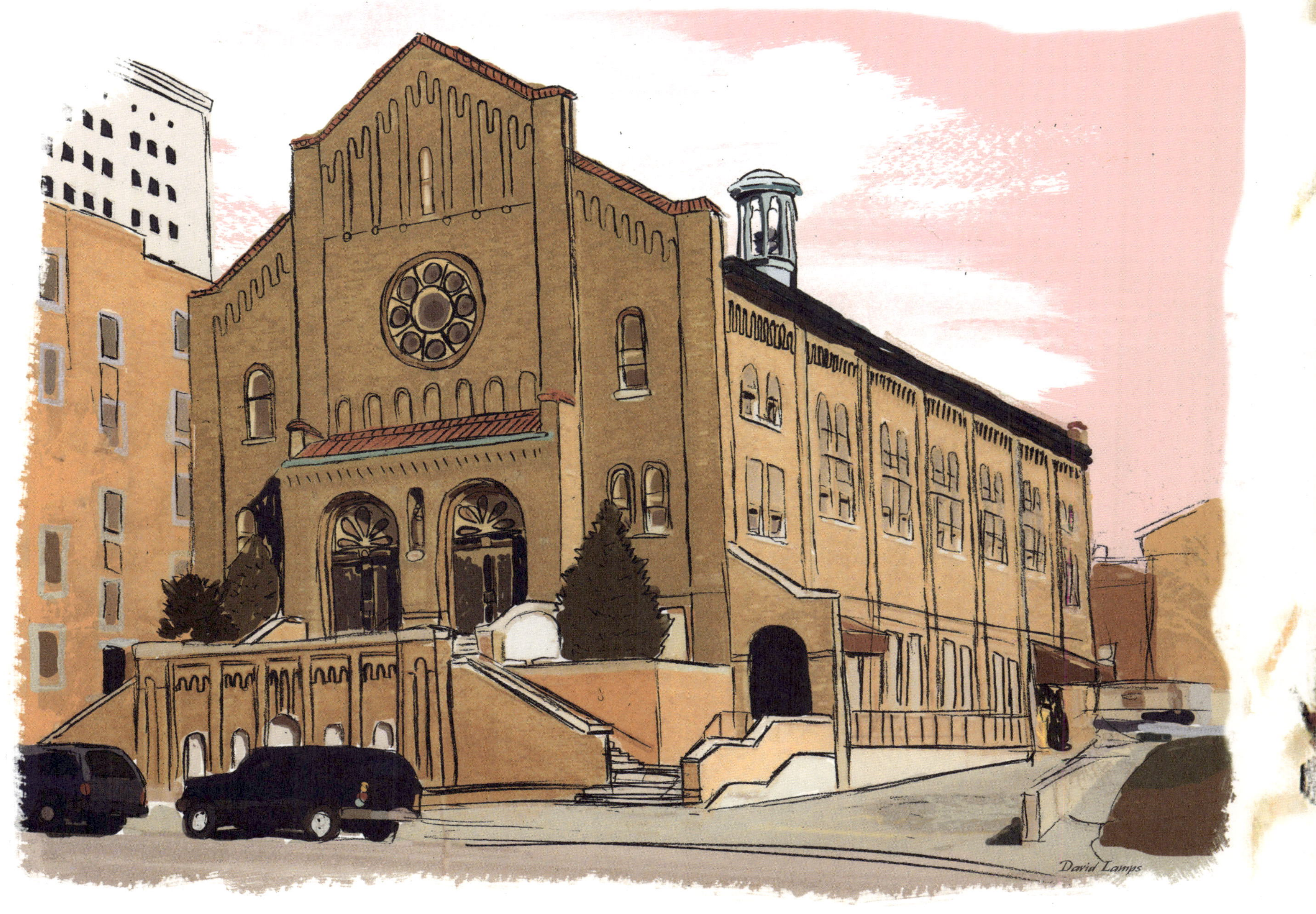

St. Benedict the Moor Church is best known for its mission of feeding the hundreds of homeless who line up at its doors for a free meal every day.

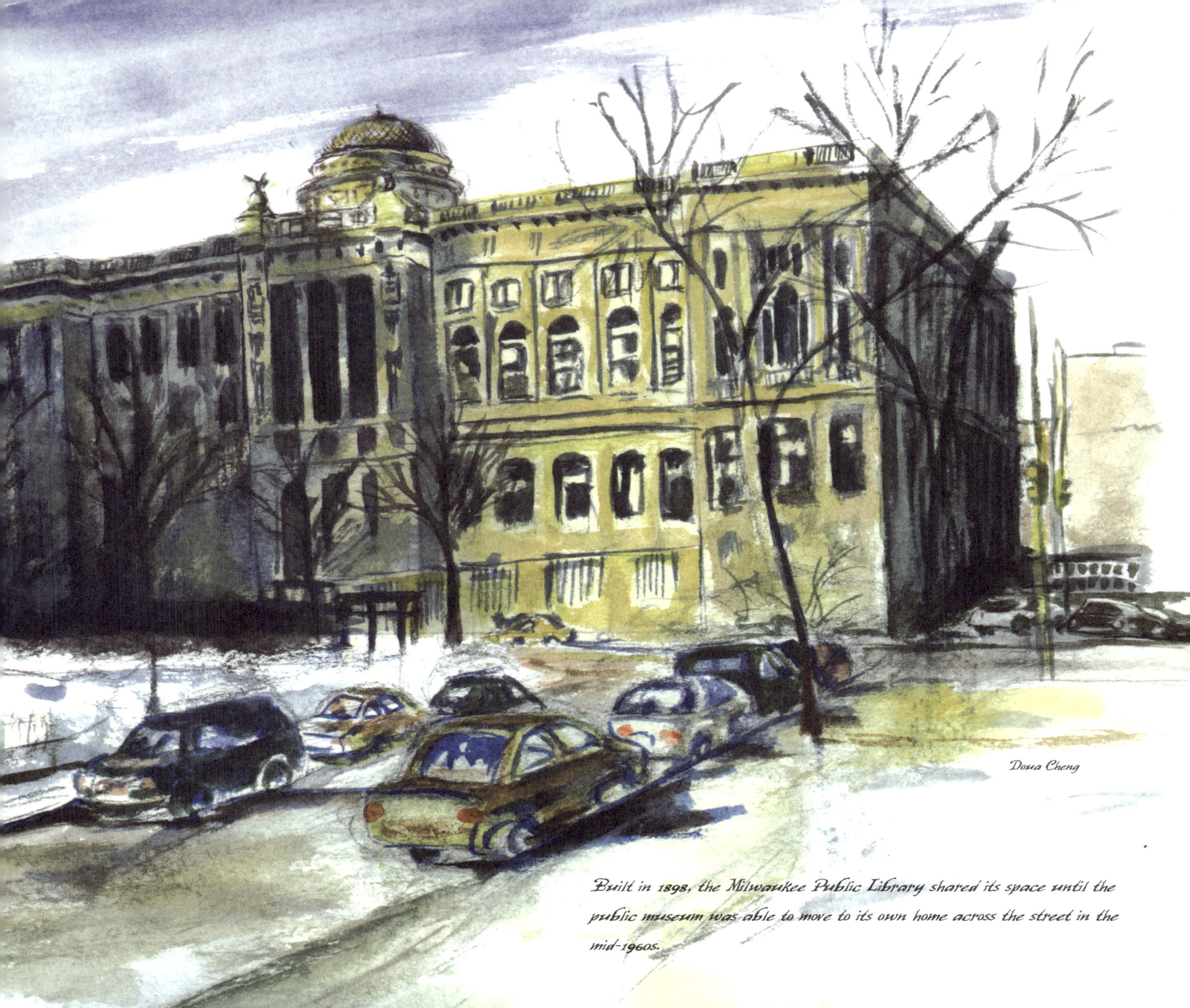

Built in 1898, the Milwaukee Public Library shared its space until the public museum was able to move to its own home across the street in the mid-1960s.

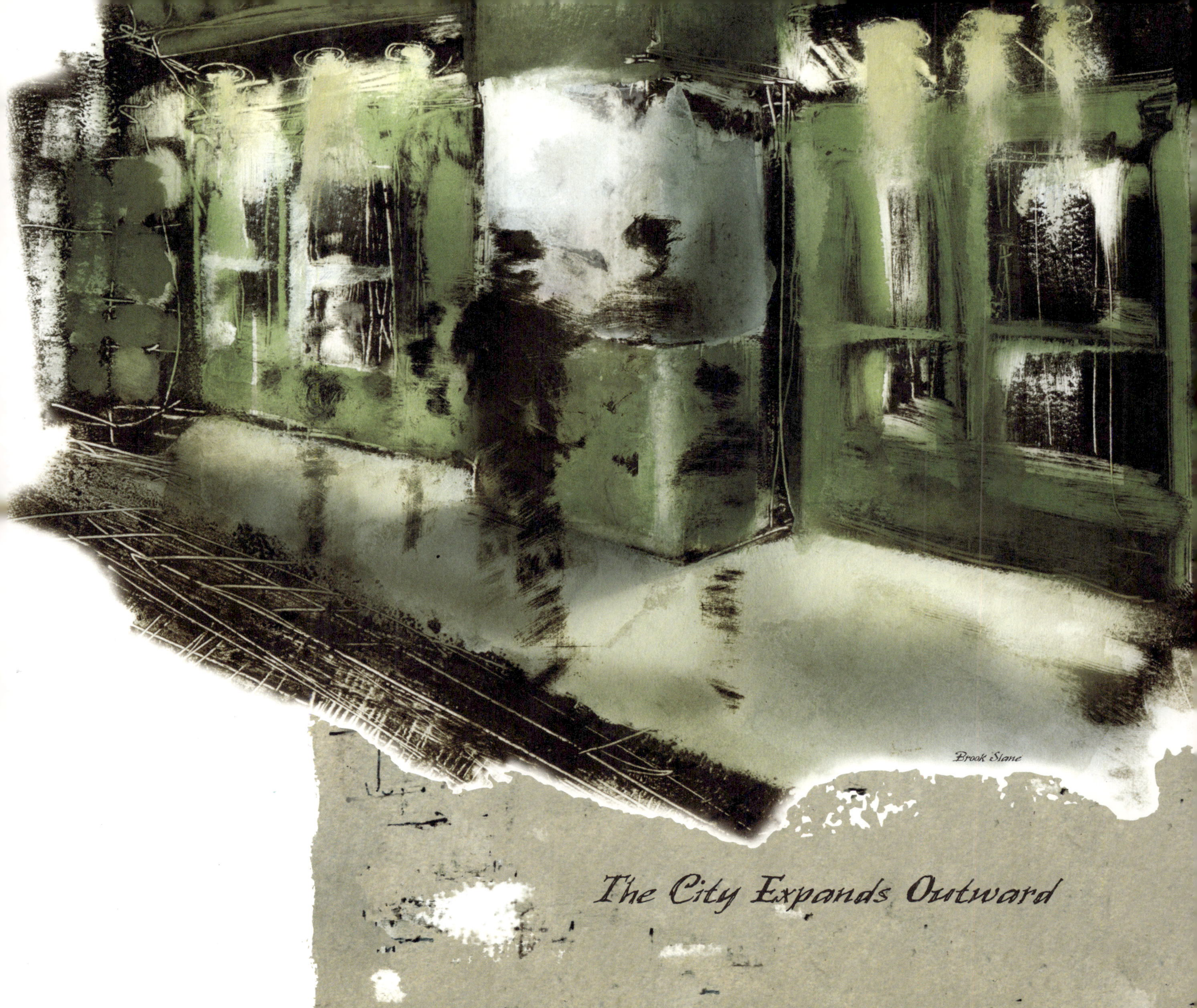
Brook Slane
The City Expands Outward

Still elegant today are the homes the well-to-do built on the east side overlooking the lake.

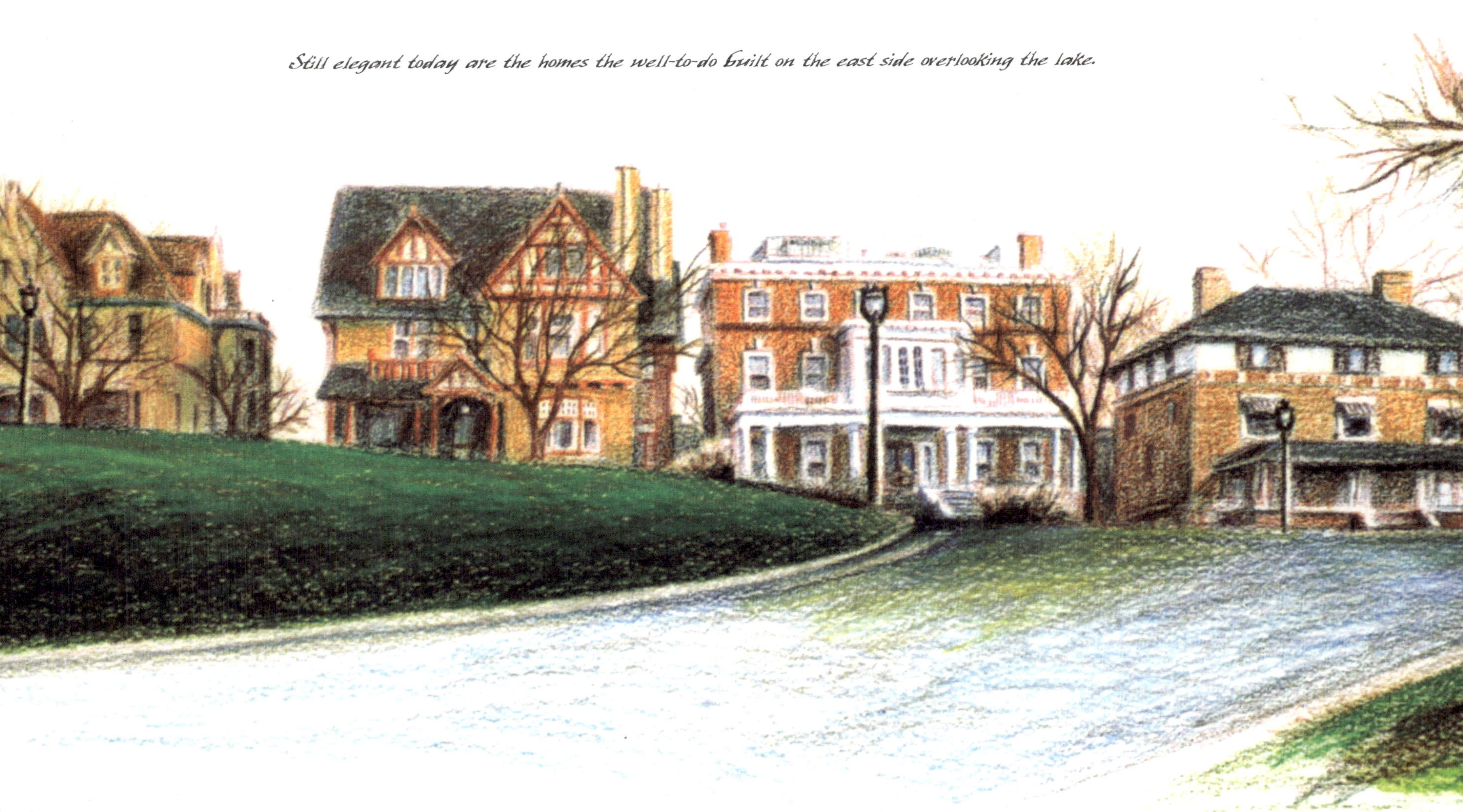

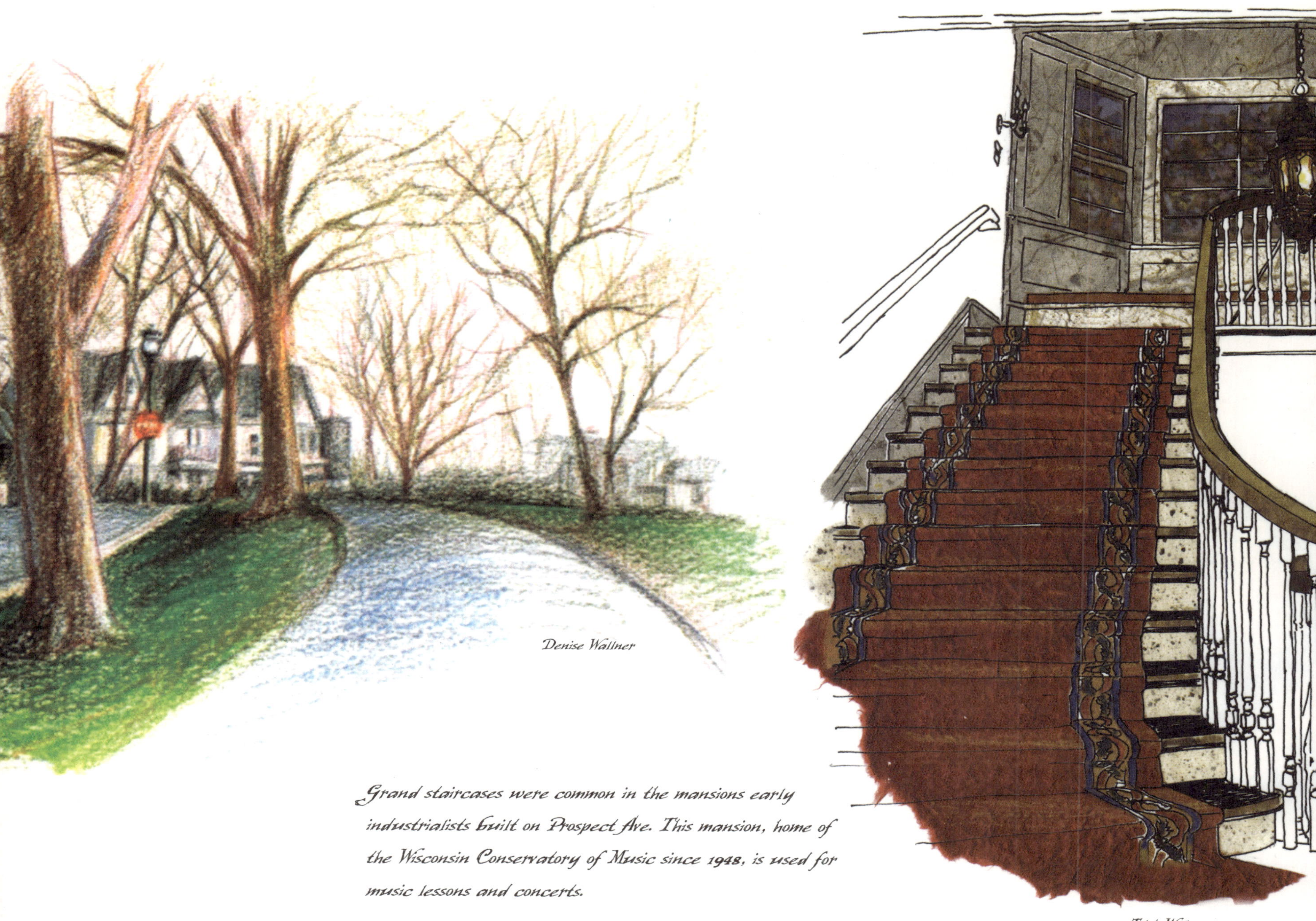

Denise Wallner

Grand staircases were common in the mansions early industrialists built on Prospect Ave. This mansion, home of the Wisconsin Conservatory of Music since 1948, is used for music lessons and concerts.

Trish Williams

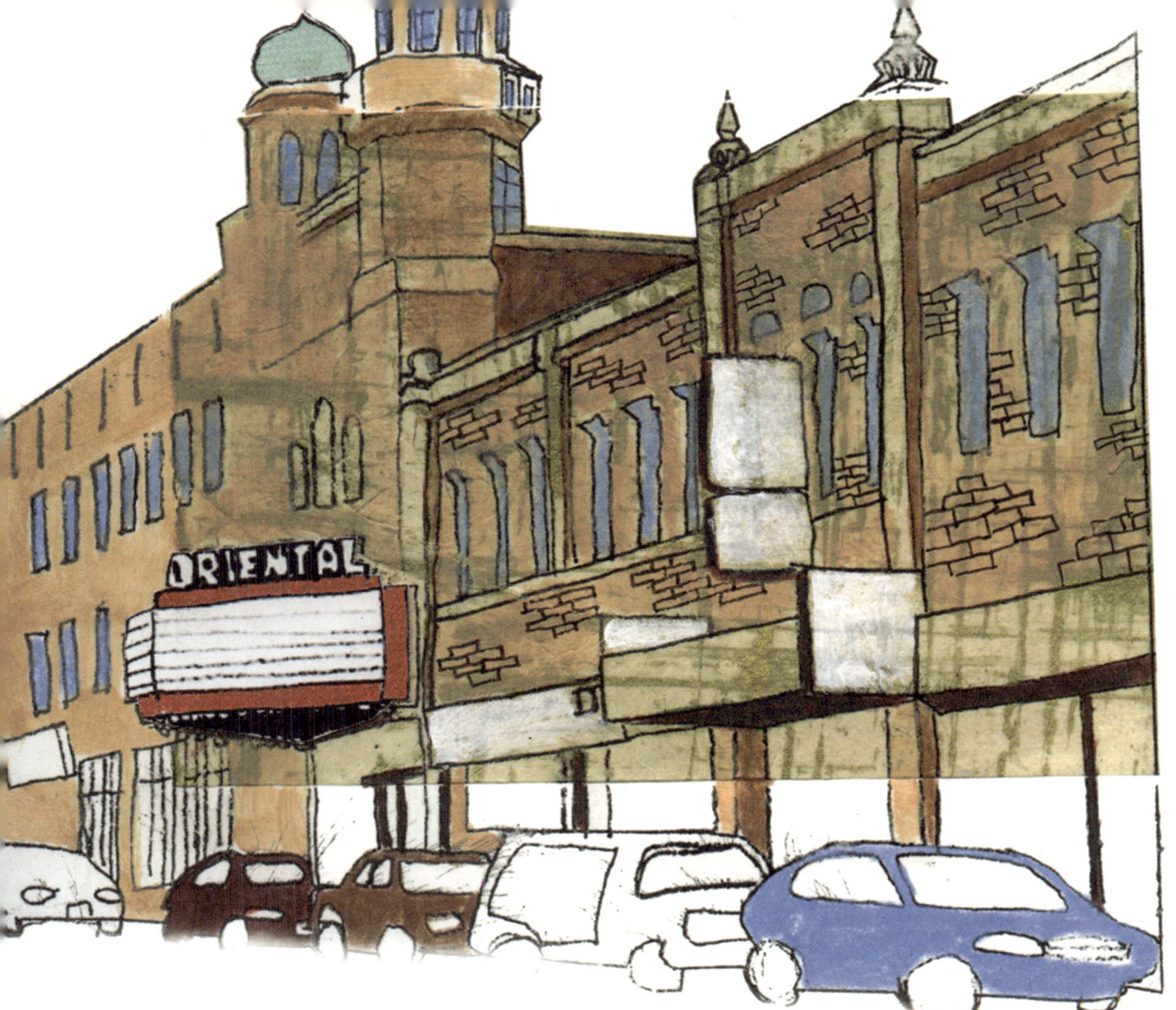

Briana MacWilliam

The Oriental Theater is one of Milwaukee's last great movie palaces. Its two Turkish inspired minarets and exotic architecture are east side landmarks.

The Oriental's lobby has been restored to its original splendor and still surrounds movie-goers with glazed lions, elephants, and ornate tiles.

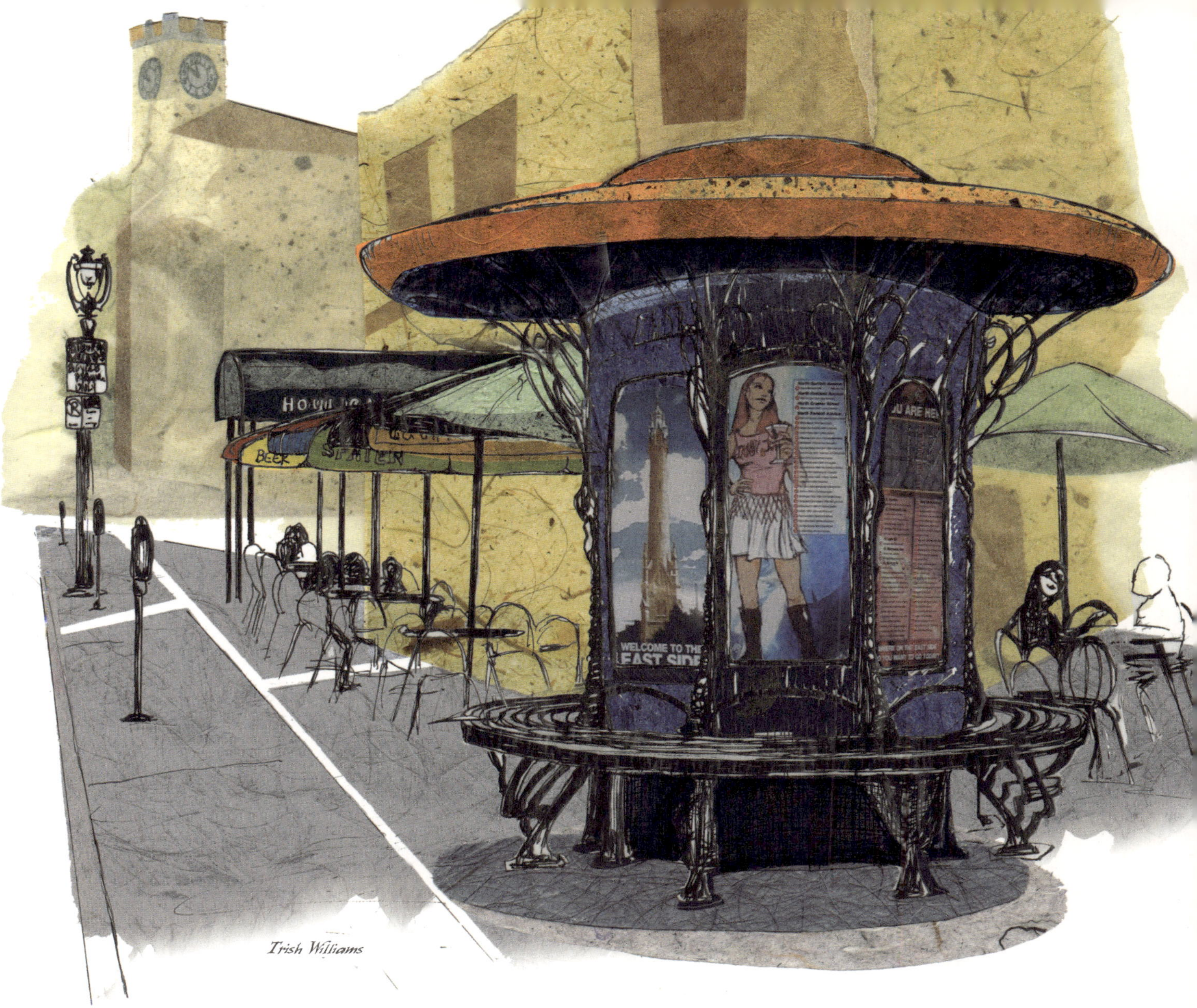

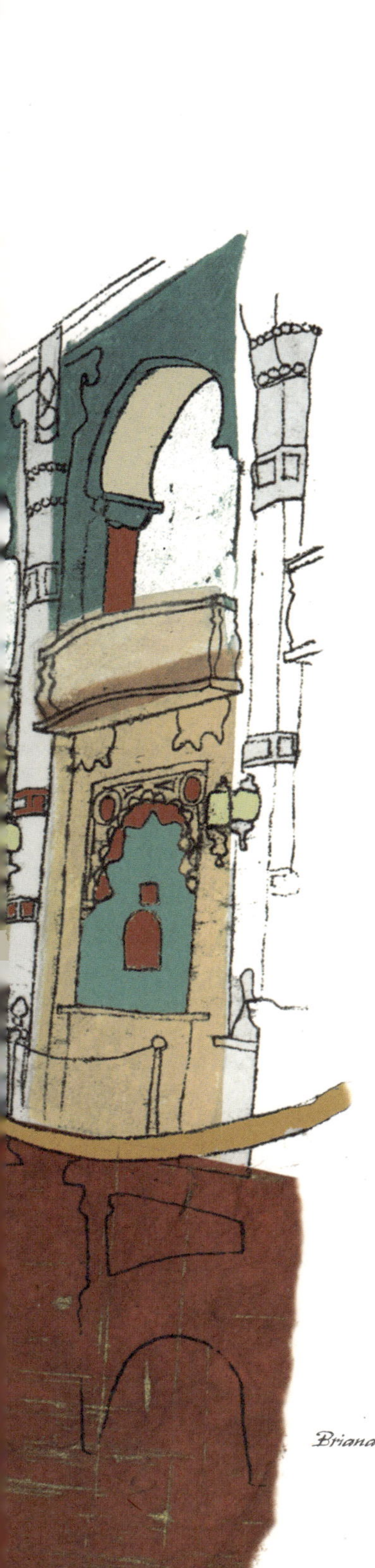

Briana MacWilliam

Trish Williams

Businesses banded together with the city's help to add colorful kiosks and street décor that make this east side corner distinctive.

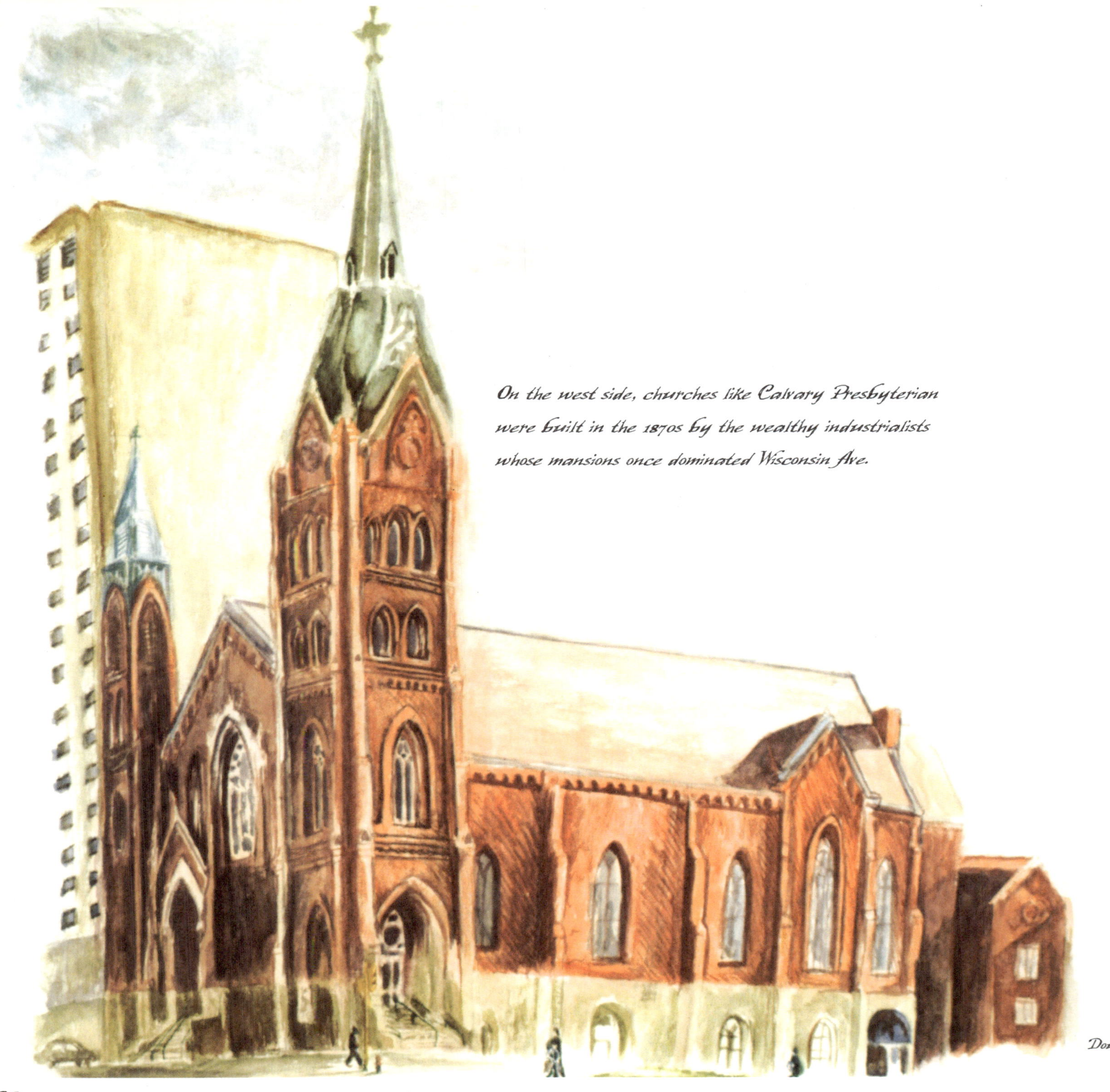

On the west side, churches like Calvary Presbyterian were built in the 1870s by the wealthy industrialists whose mansions once dominated Wisconsin Ave.

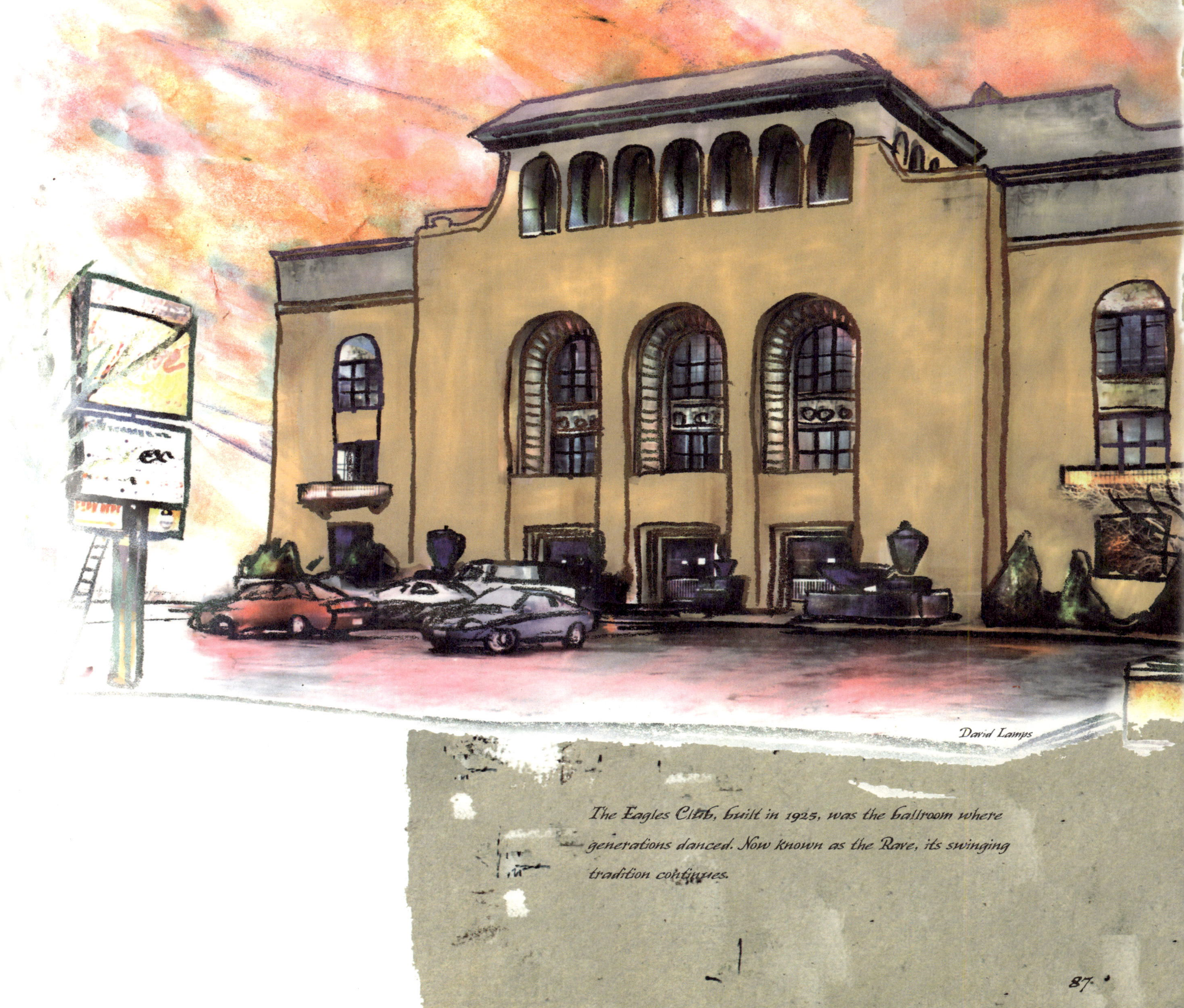

David Lamps

The Eagles Club, built in 1925, was the ballroom where generations danced. Now known as the Rave, its swinging tradition continues.

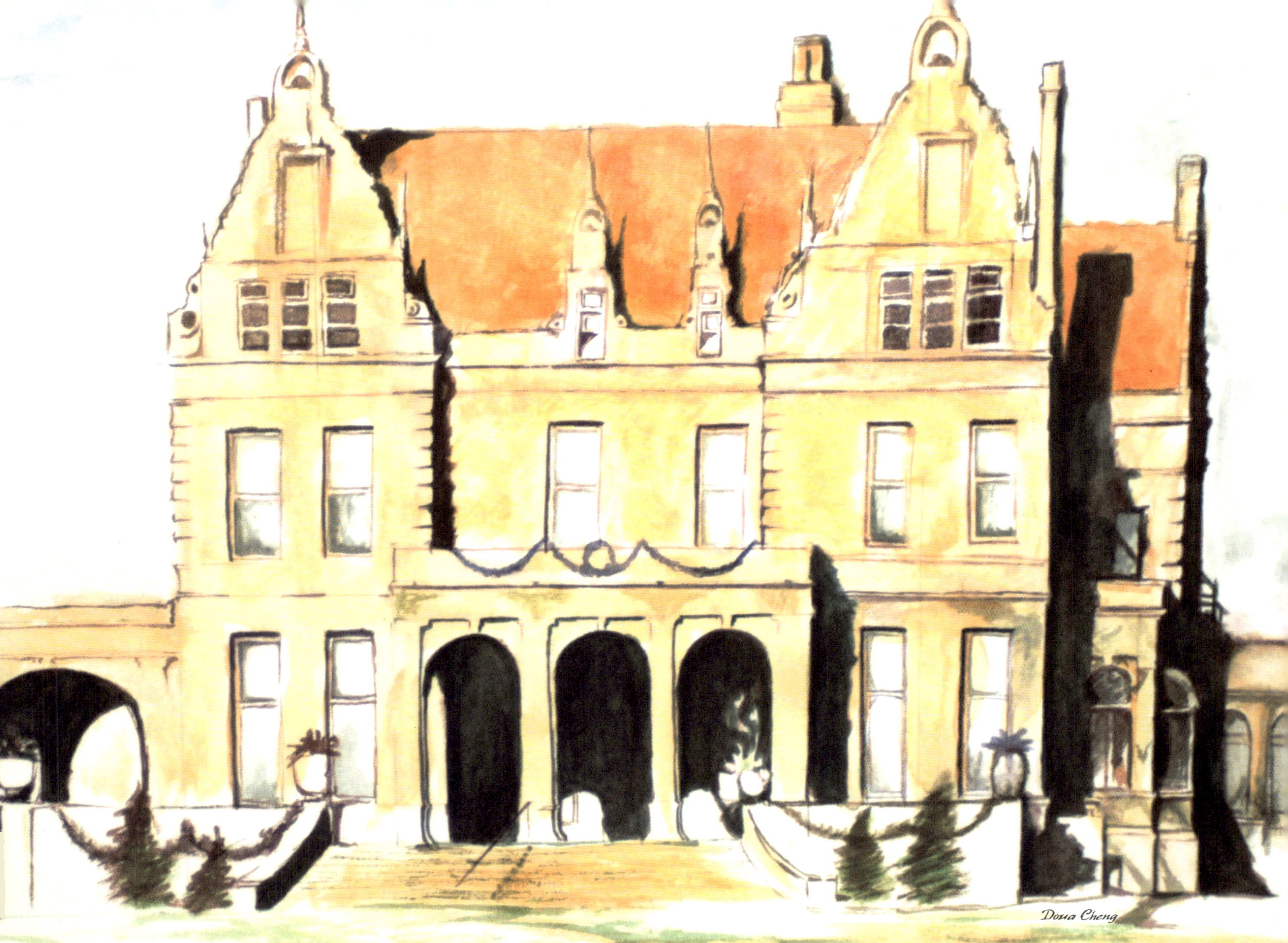

By 1893, the brewery owned by Captain Frederick Pabst was the largest in the nation so he could well afford his elegant new mansion. For 70 years after his death, the Catholic archdiocese owned it. In 1978, a nonprofit group bought, restored, and turned it into a popular museum.

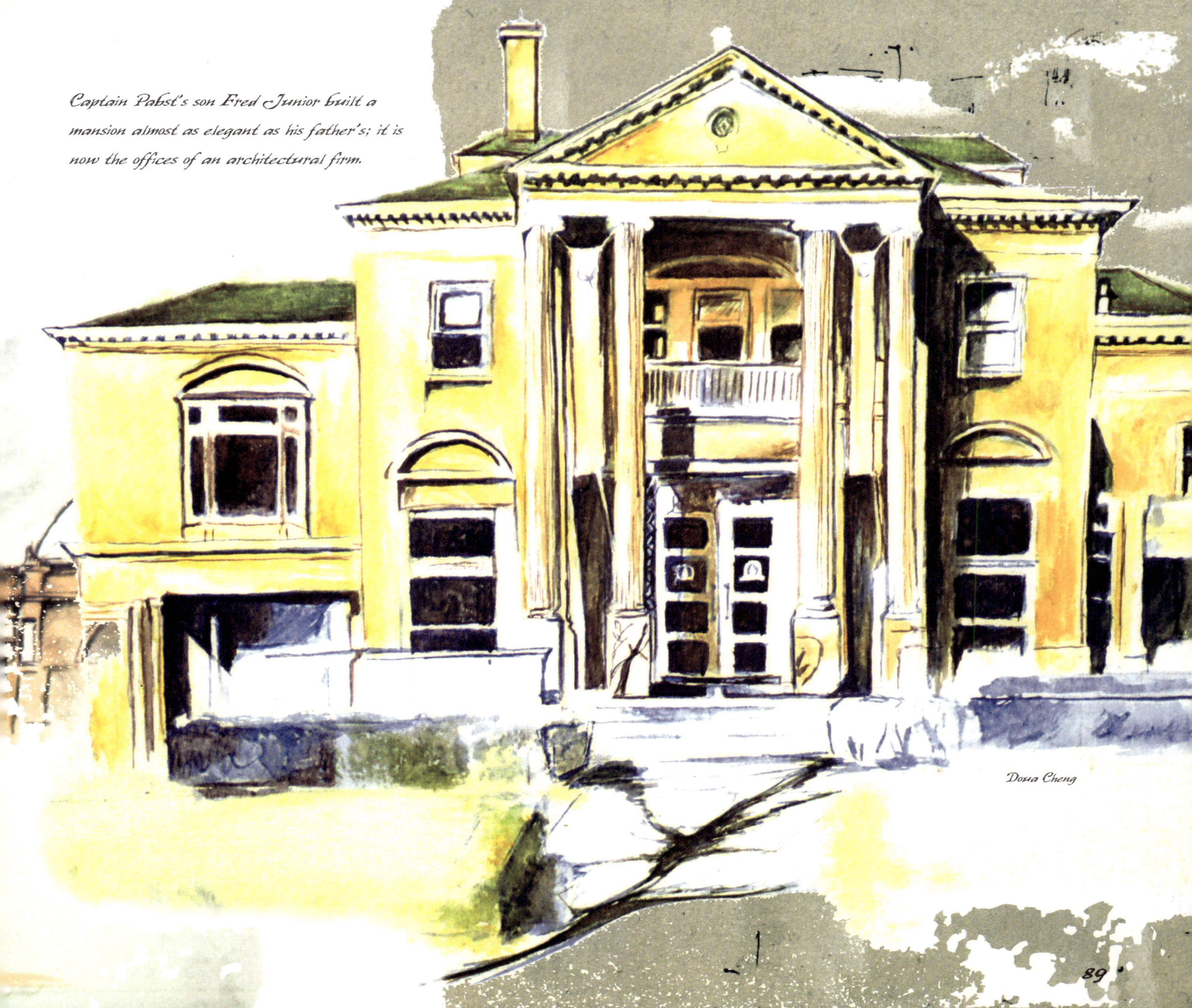

Captain Pabst's son Fred Junior built a mansion almost as elegant as his father's; it is now the offices of an architectural firm.

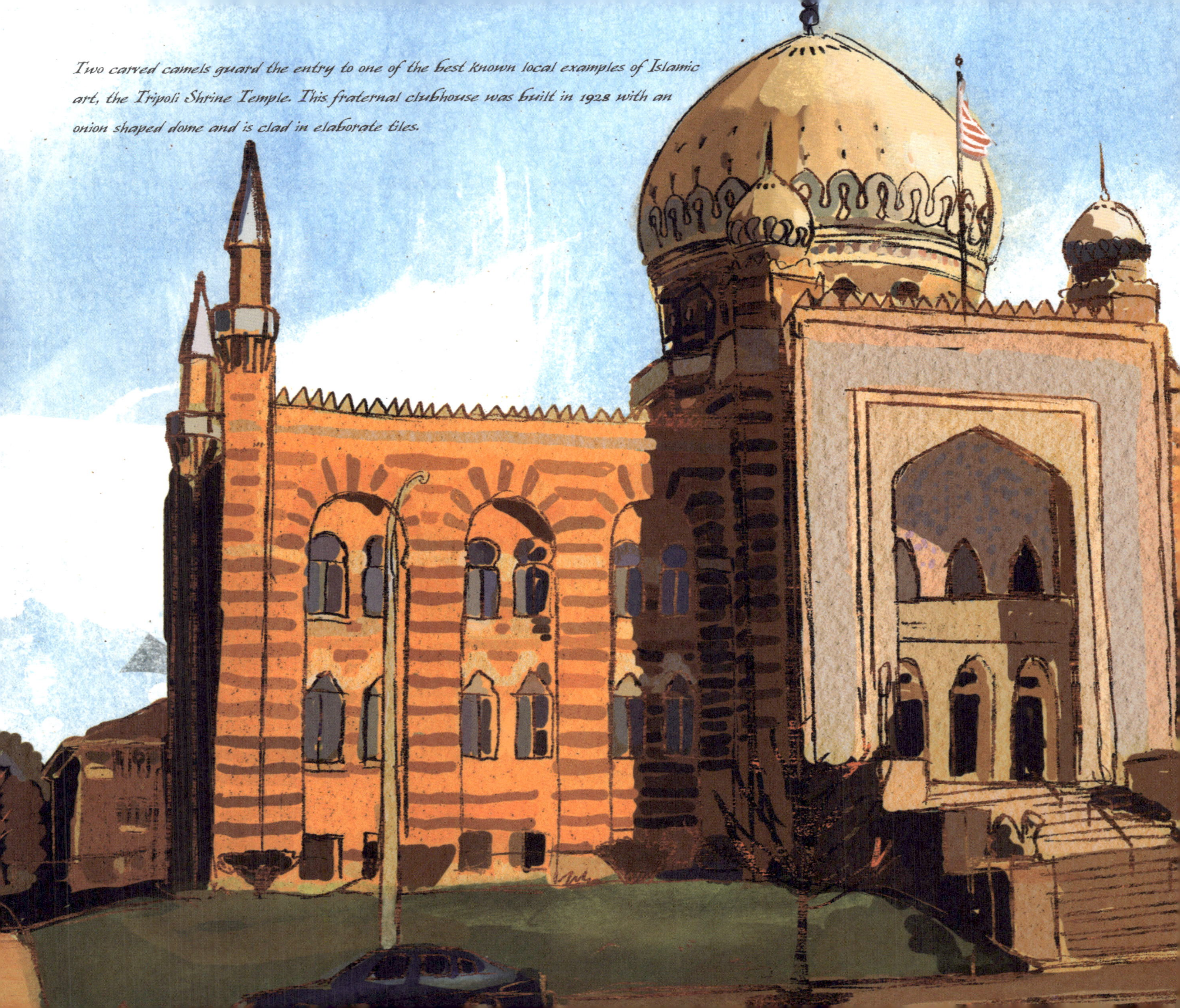

Two carved camels guard the entry to one of the best known local examples of Islamic art, the Tripoli Shrine Temple. This fraternal clubhouse was built in 1928 with an onion shaped dome and is clad in elaborate tiles.

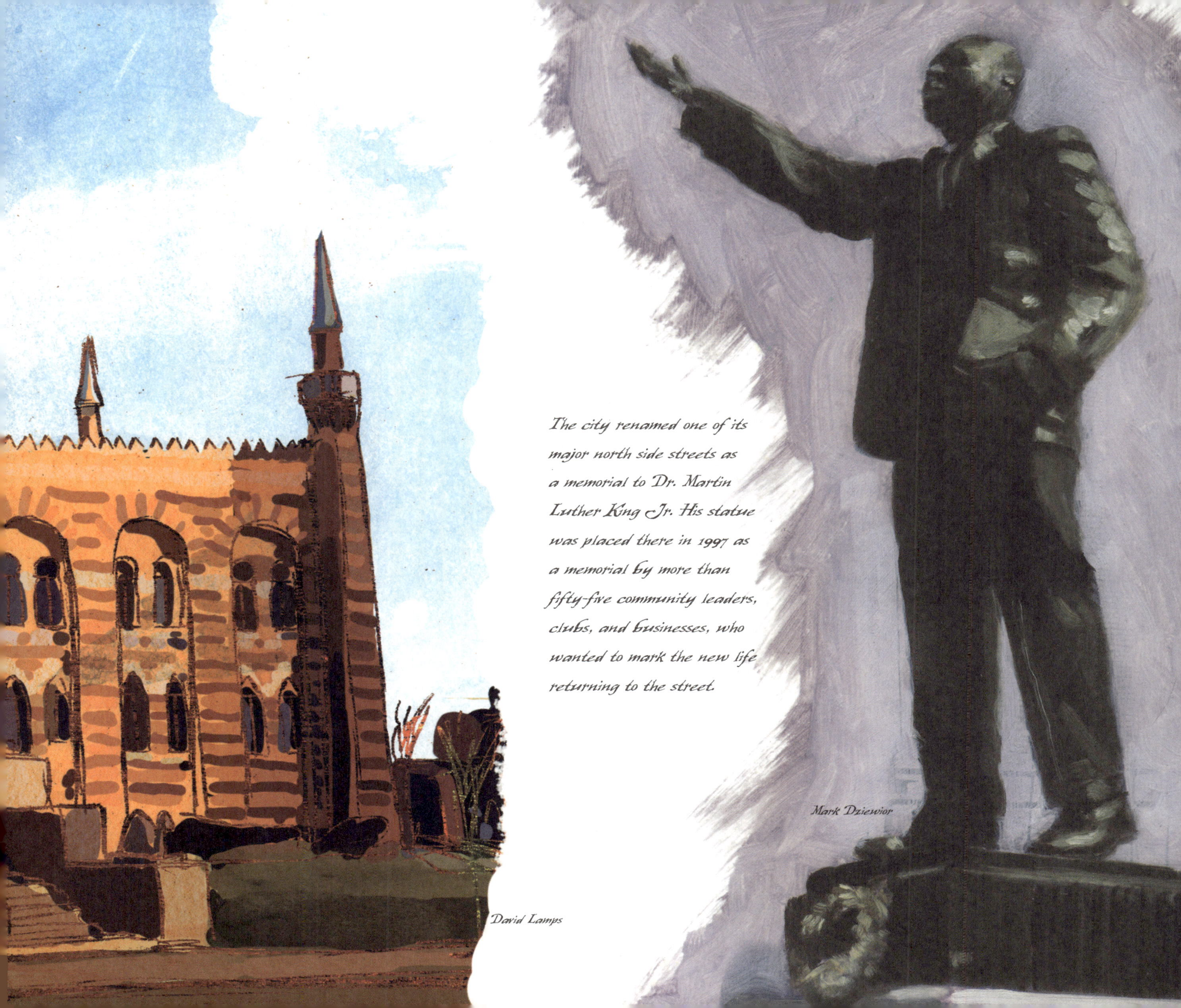

The city renamed one of its major north side streets as a memorial to Dr. Martin Luther King Jr. His statue was placed there in 1997 as a memorial by more than fifty-five community leaders, clubs, and businesses, who wanted to mark the new life returning to the street.

David Lamps

Mark Dziewior

James Cameron was nearly lynched as a young man. His experience led him to create the Black Holocaust Museum to tell in photos and displays the history of African Americans. A library is also available.

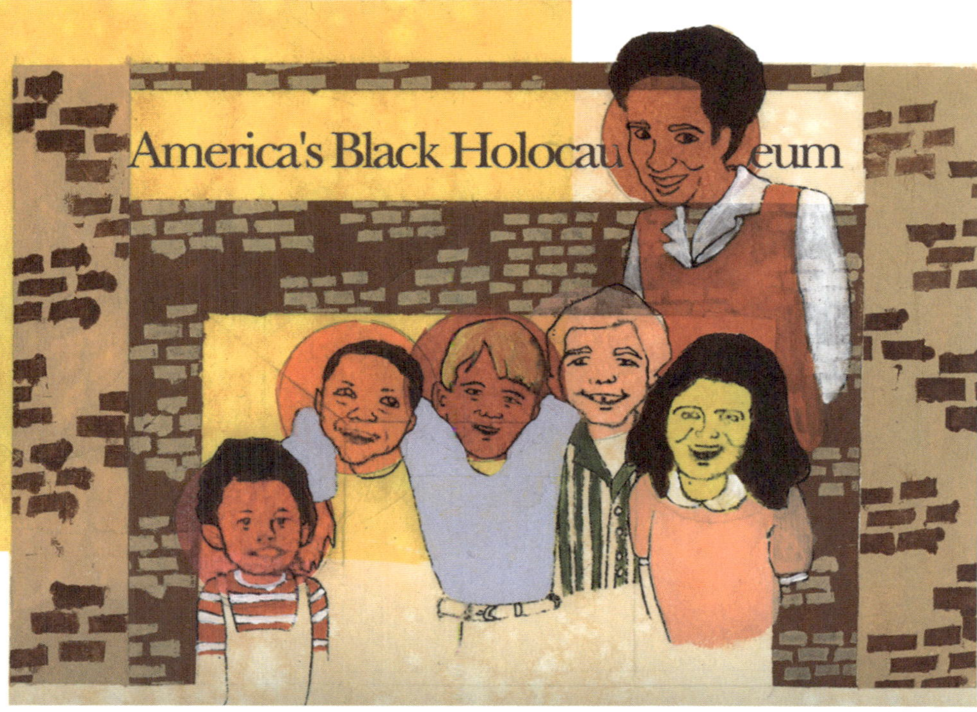

Briana MacWilliam

A statue of animal welfare leader Henry Bergh with an injured dog stands in front of the new headquarters of the Wisconsin Humane Society.

Mark Dziewior

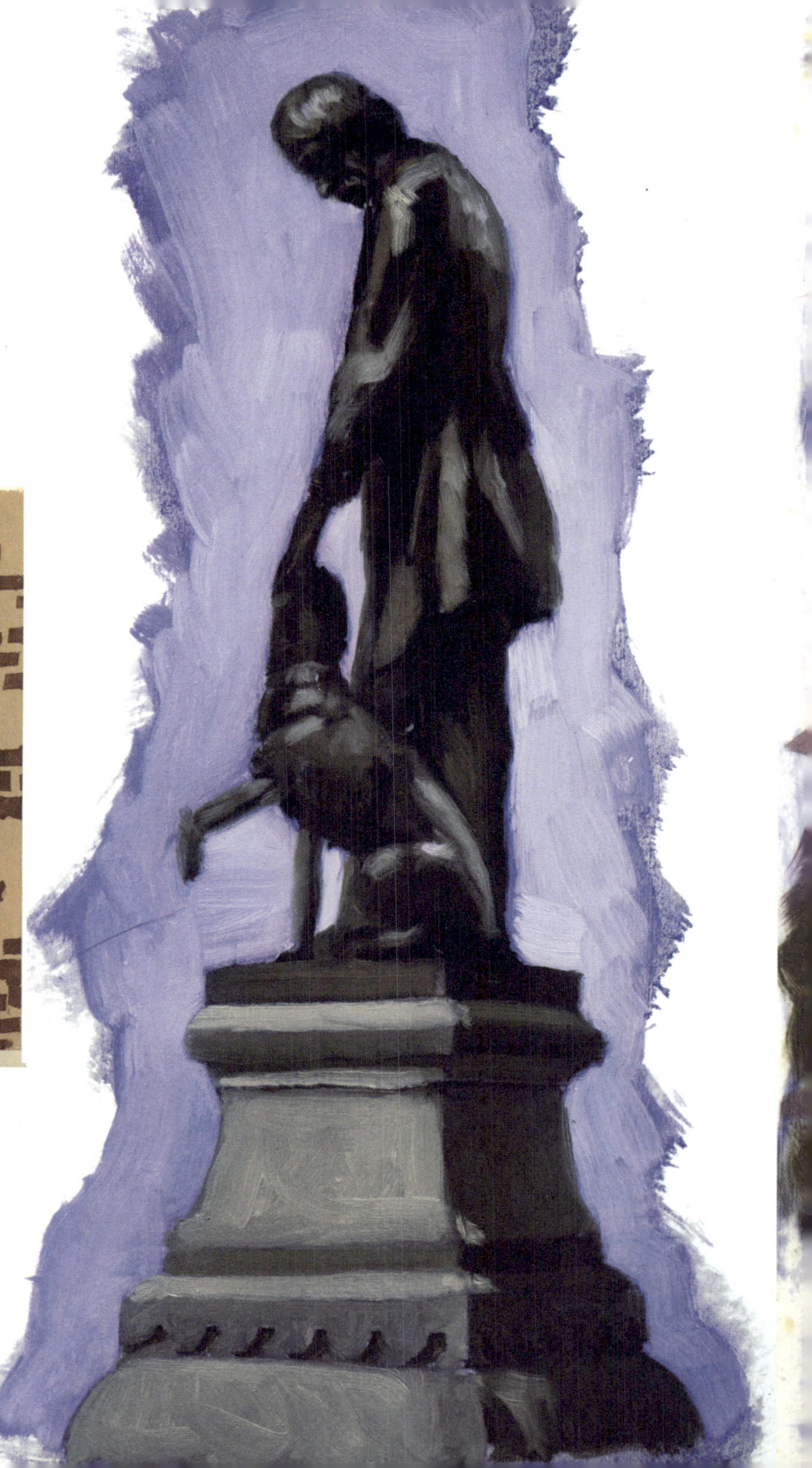

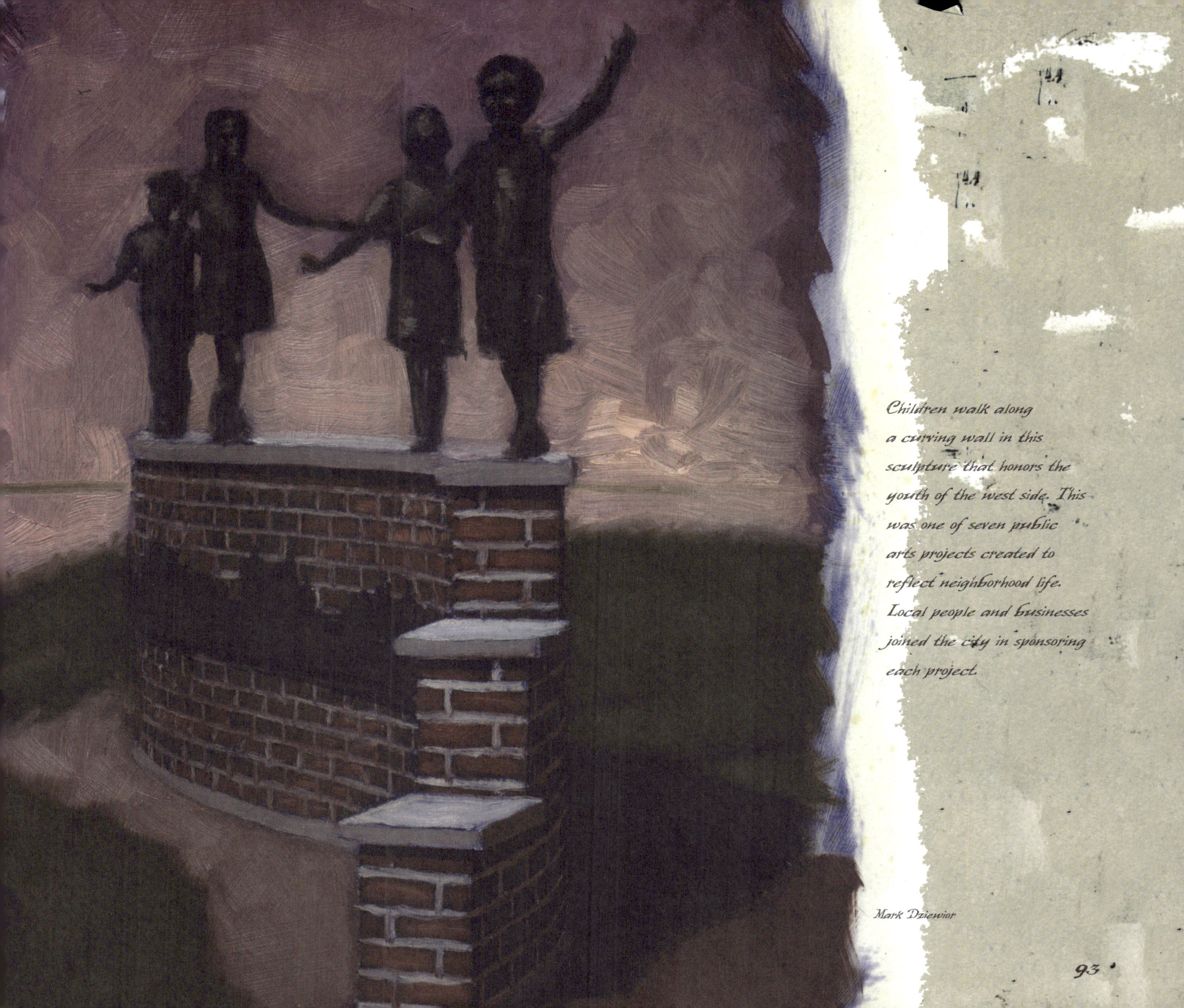

Children walk along a curving wall in this sculpture that honors the youth of the west side. This was one of seven public arts projects created to reflect neighborhood life. Local people and businesses joined the city in sponsoring each project.

Mark Dziewior

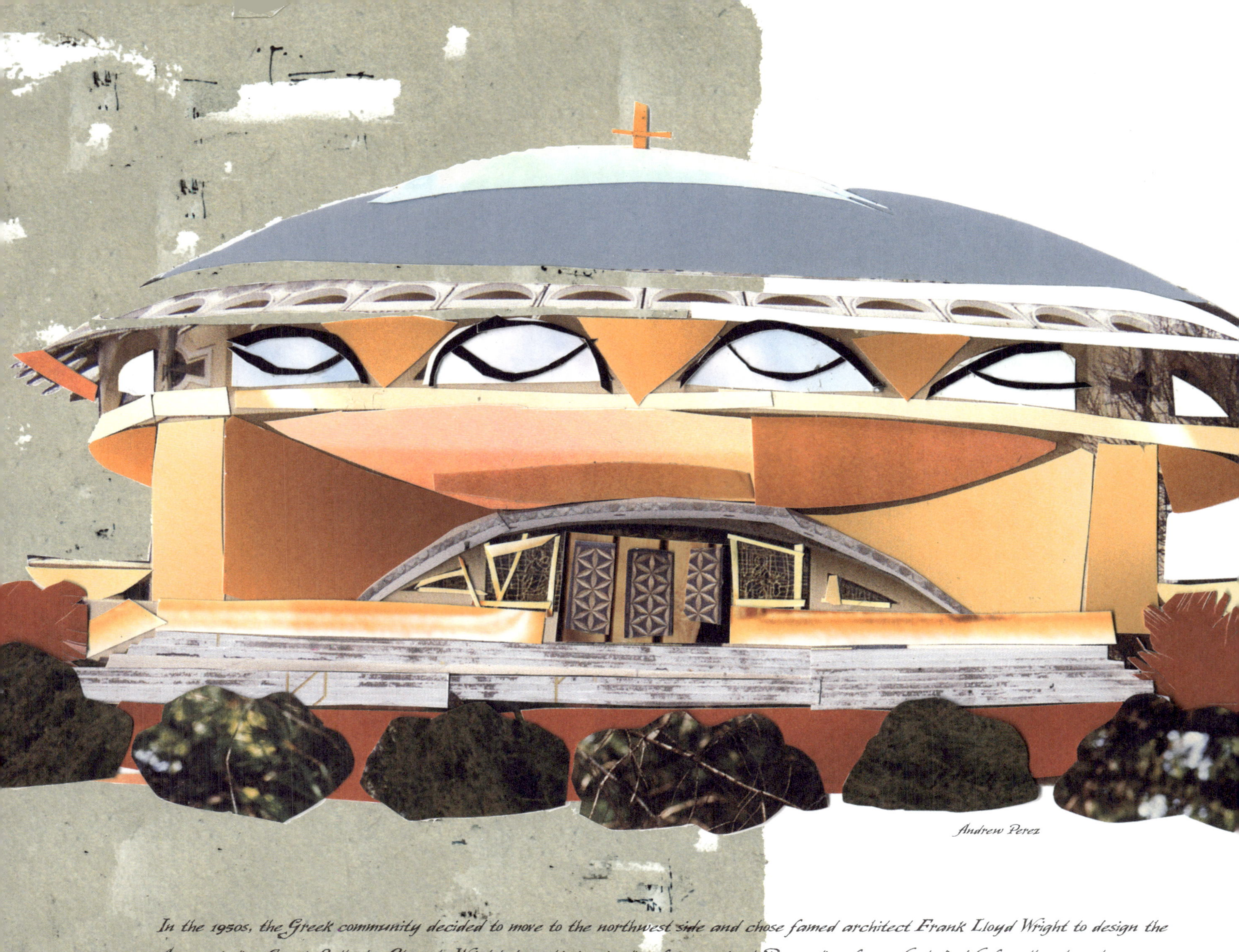

Andrew Perez

In the 1950s, the Greek community decided to move to the northwest side and chose famed architect Frank Lloyd Wright to design the Annunciation Greek Orthodox Church. Wright drew his inspiration from ancient Byzantine forms, but died before the church was completed in 1961.

The Wisconsin State Fair moved to West Allis in 1892, and over the years has added a modern new race track to the barns and exhibit halls that still showcase the state's agriculture. New gates show off the renovations now underway.

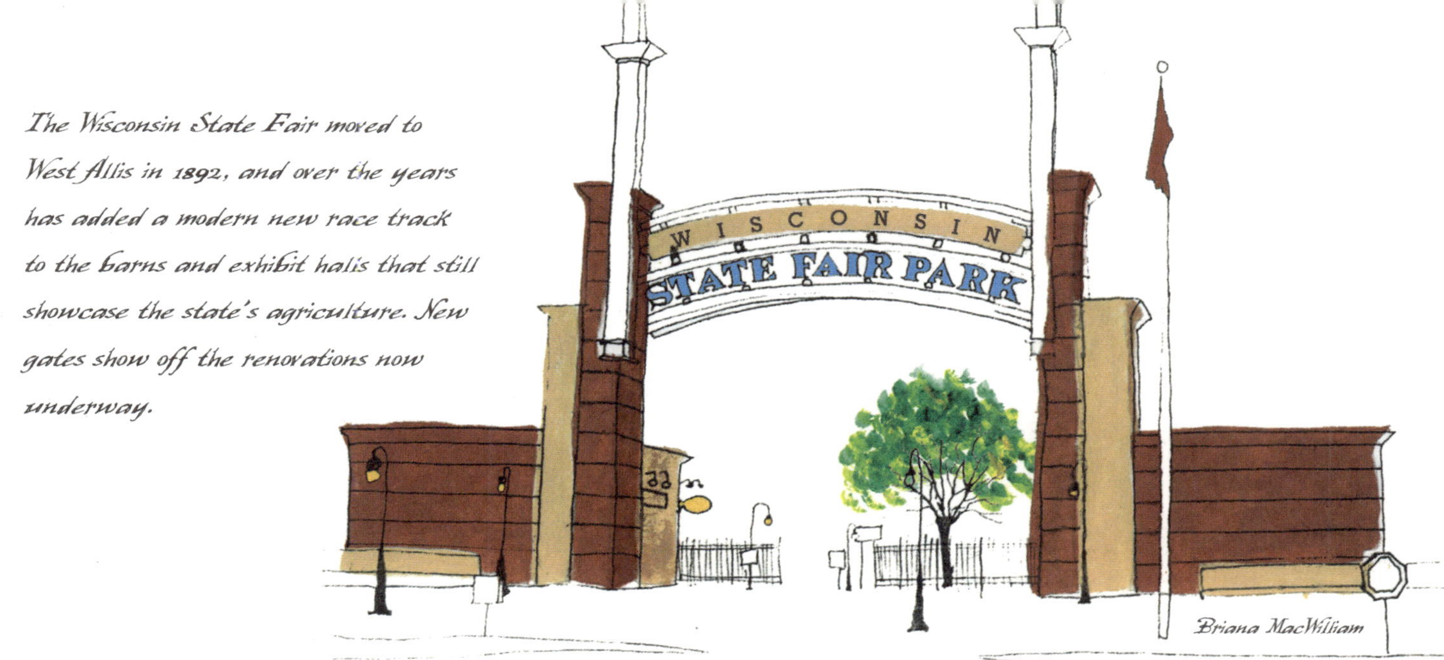

Briana MacWilliam

West Allis has preserved one of the last remaining pagoda shaped gas stations that once were the trademark for Wadhams. Frank Seneca ran the station for years on S. 76th Street.

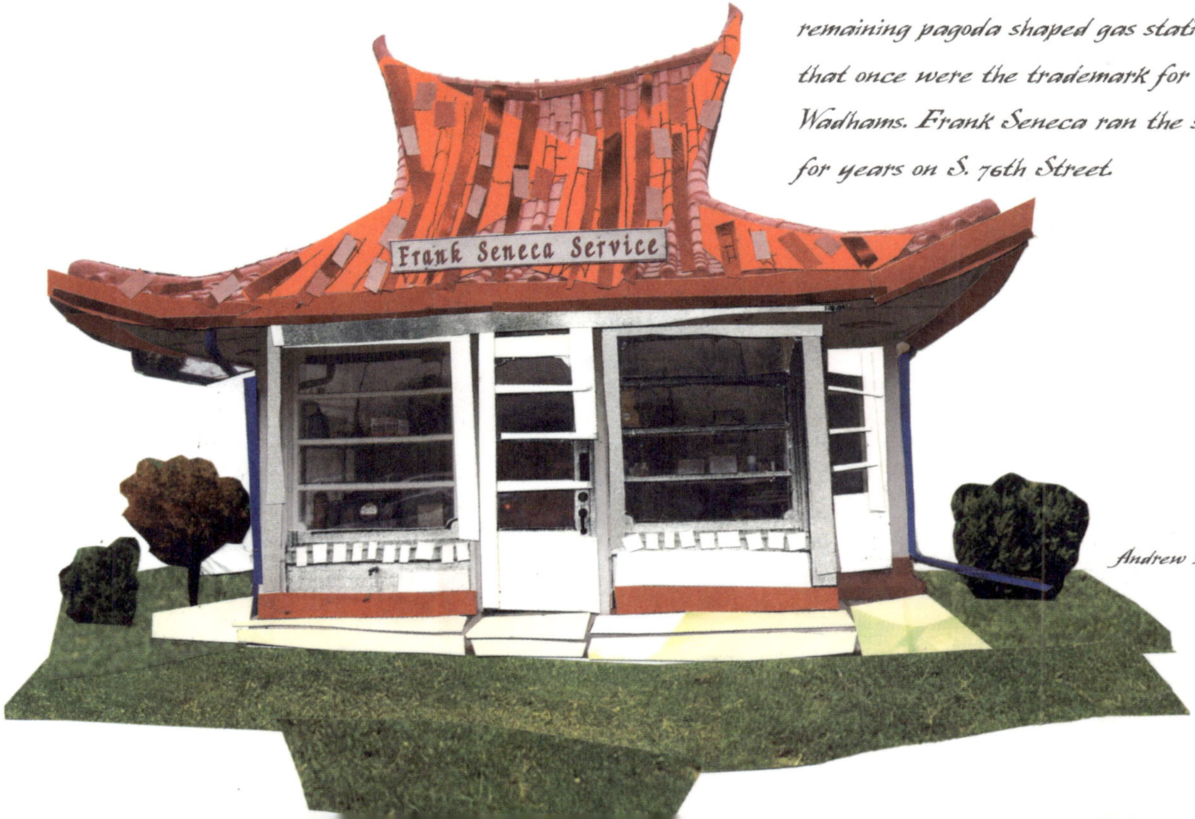

Frank Seneca Service

Andrew Perez

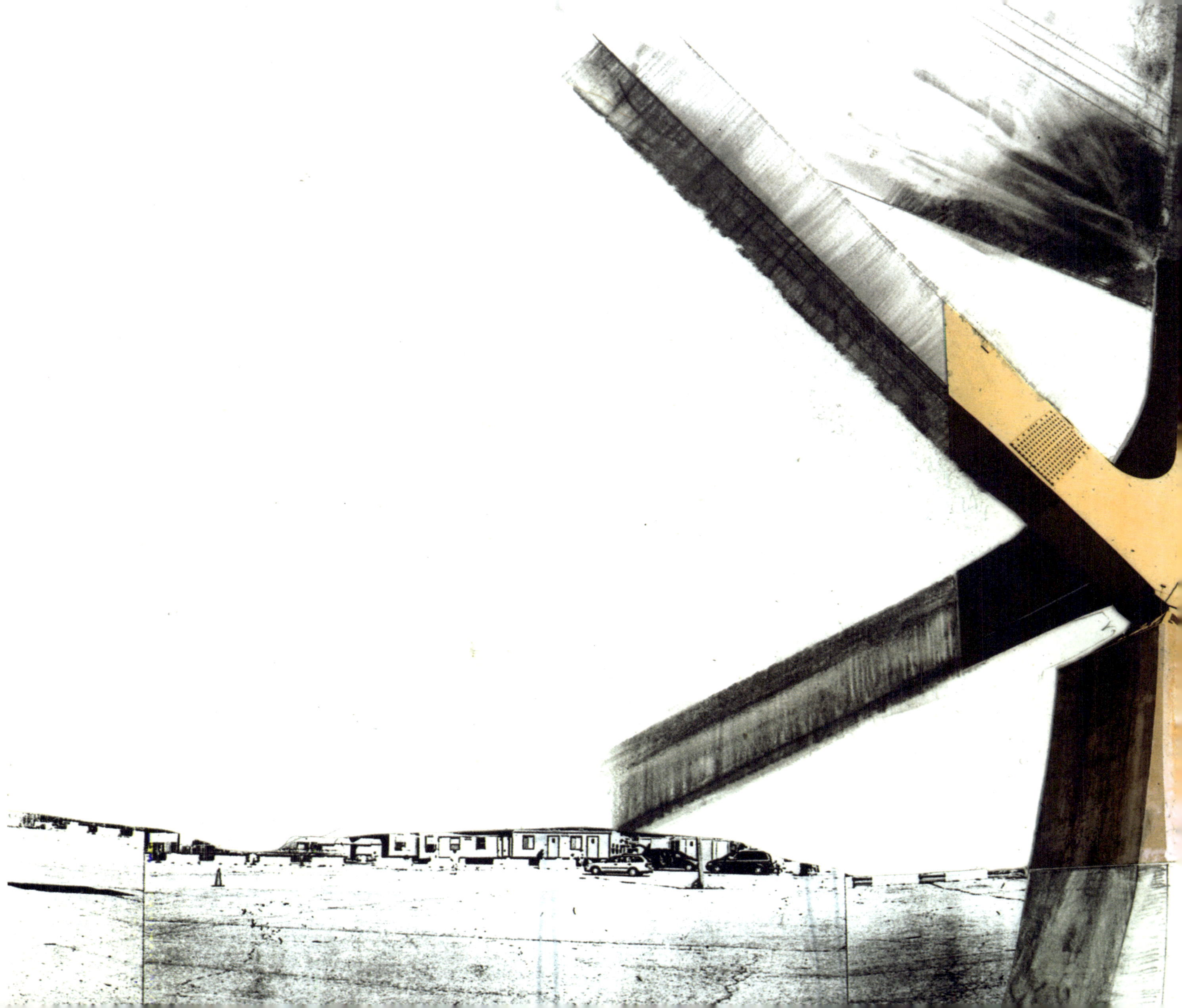

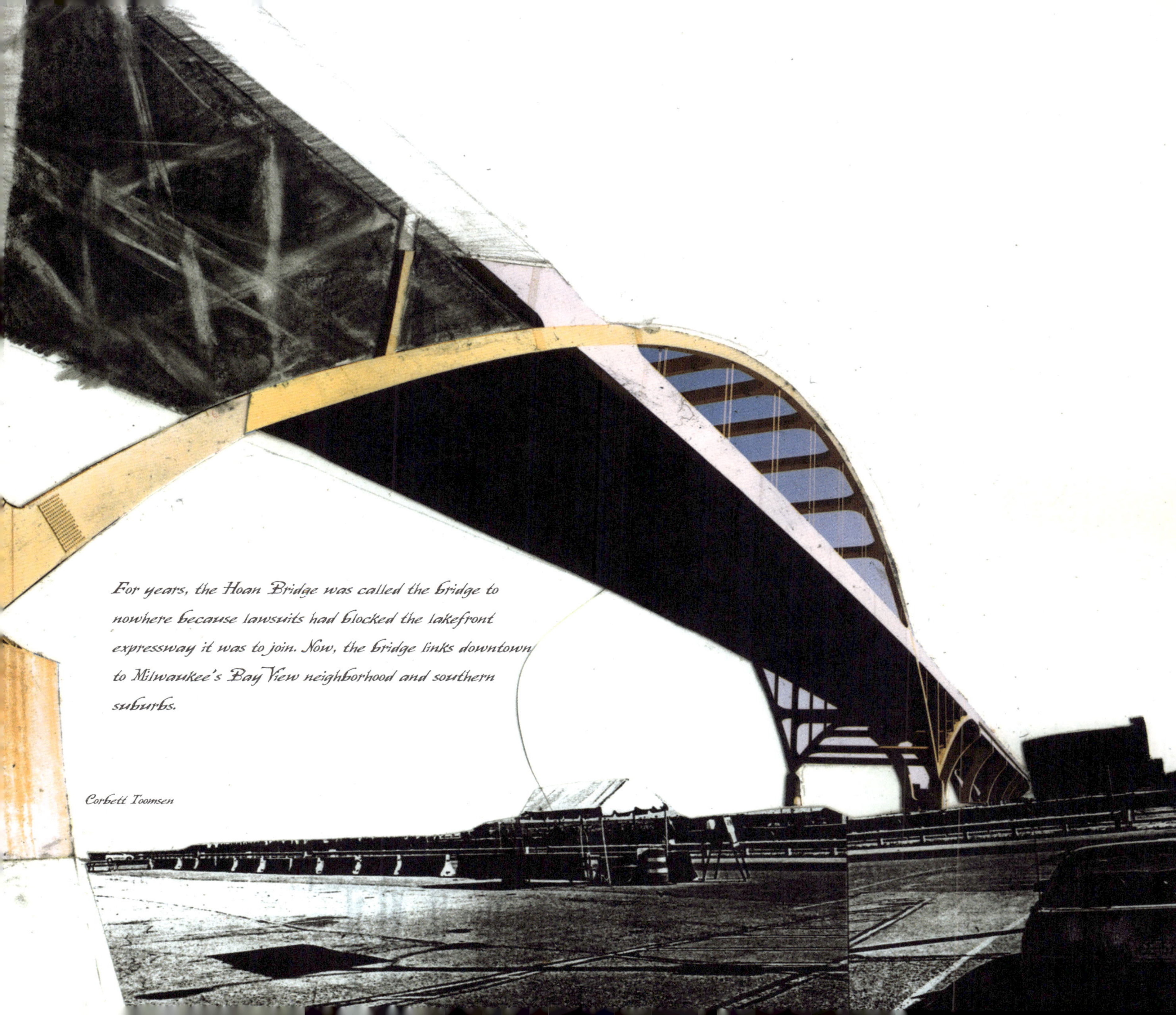

For years, the Hoan Bridge was called the bridge to nowhere because lawsuits had blocked the lakefront expressway it was to join. Now, the bridge links downtown to Milwaukee's Bay View neighborhood and southern suburbs.

Corbett Toomsen

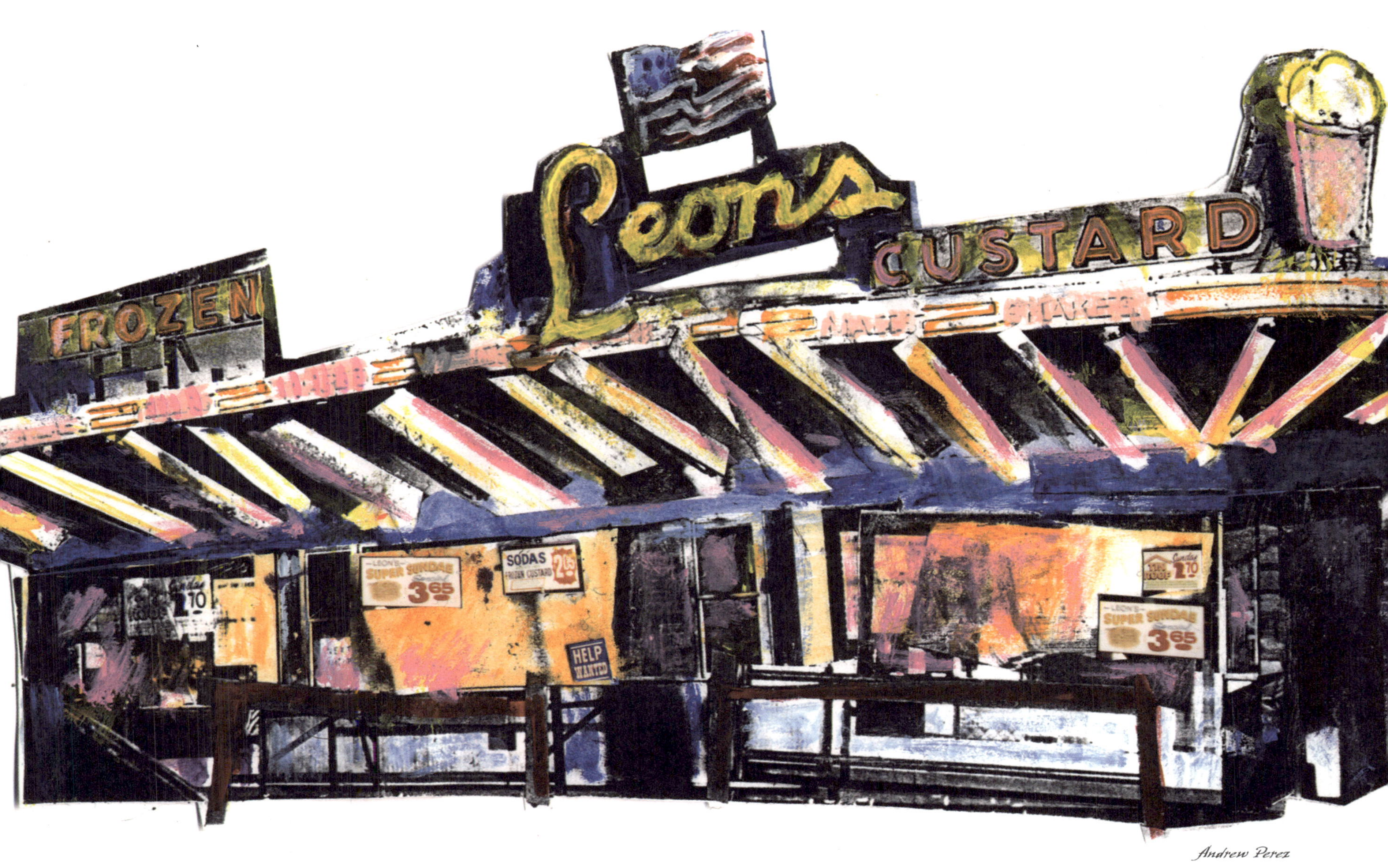

Andrew Perez

Leon's is famous for its frozen custard cones and sundaes and a trip to its drive-in on S. 27th St. is almost a "must" for any visiting dignitary or political hopeful hoping to get a taste of the real Milwaukee.

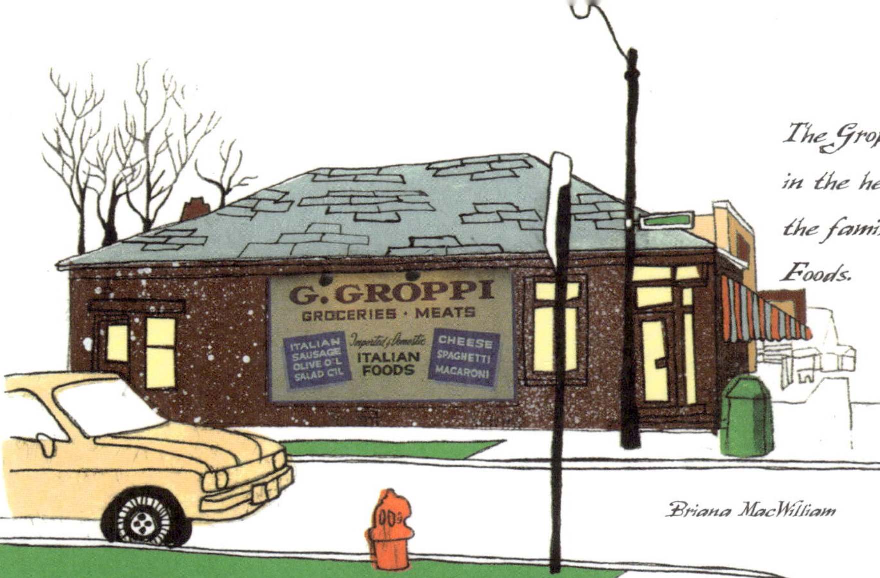

The Groppi family ran this tiny grocery that was for years in the heart of the Italian community in Bay View. When the family retired, the grocery became a new Sendiks Foods.

Briana MacWilliam

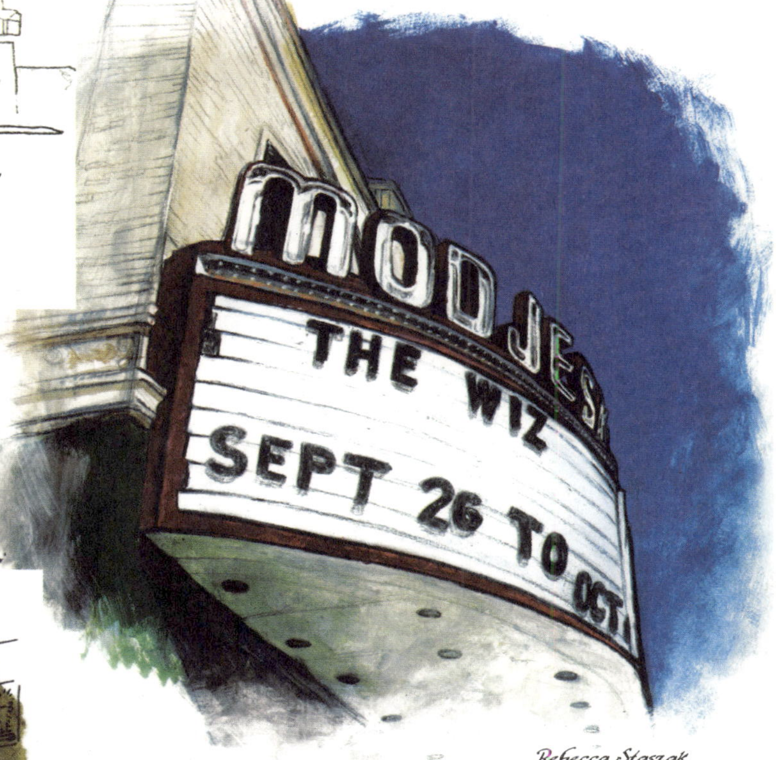

Mitchell St. was for years the shopping hub of the largely Polish south side. The Modjeska, built in 1924 in the heyday of the movie palaces, now sponsors a theater company for area teens, as well as a few stage shows.

Rebecca Staszak

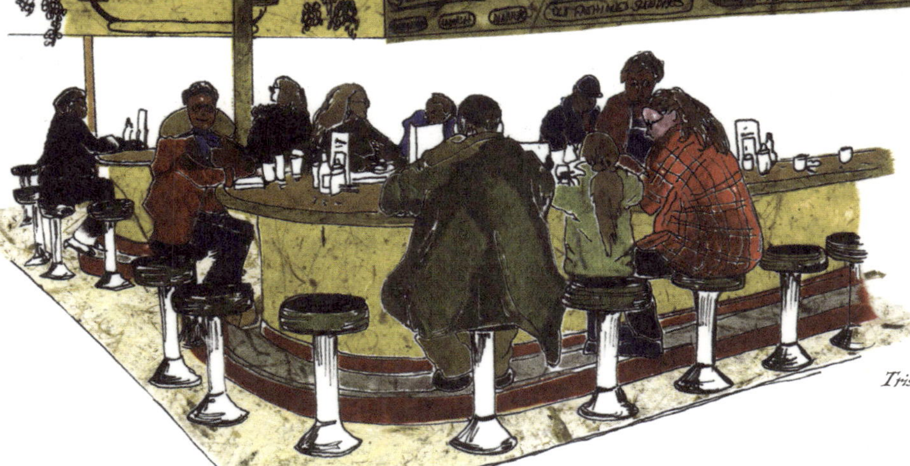

One of the city's last remaining lunch counters at Goldmann's Department store still fills with regulars every day. The store has stubbornly refused to go modern and still stocks items that can't be found anywhere else.

Trish Williams

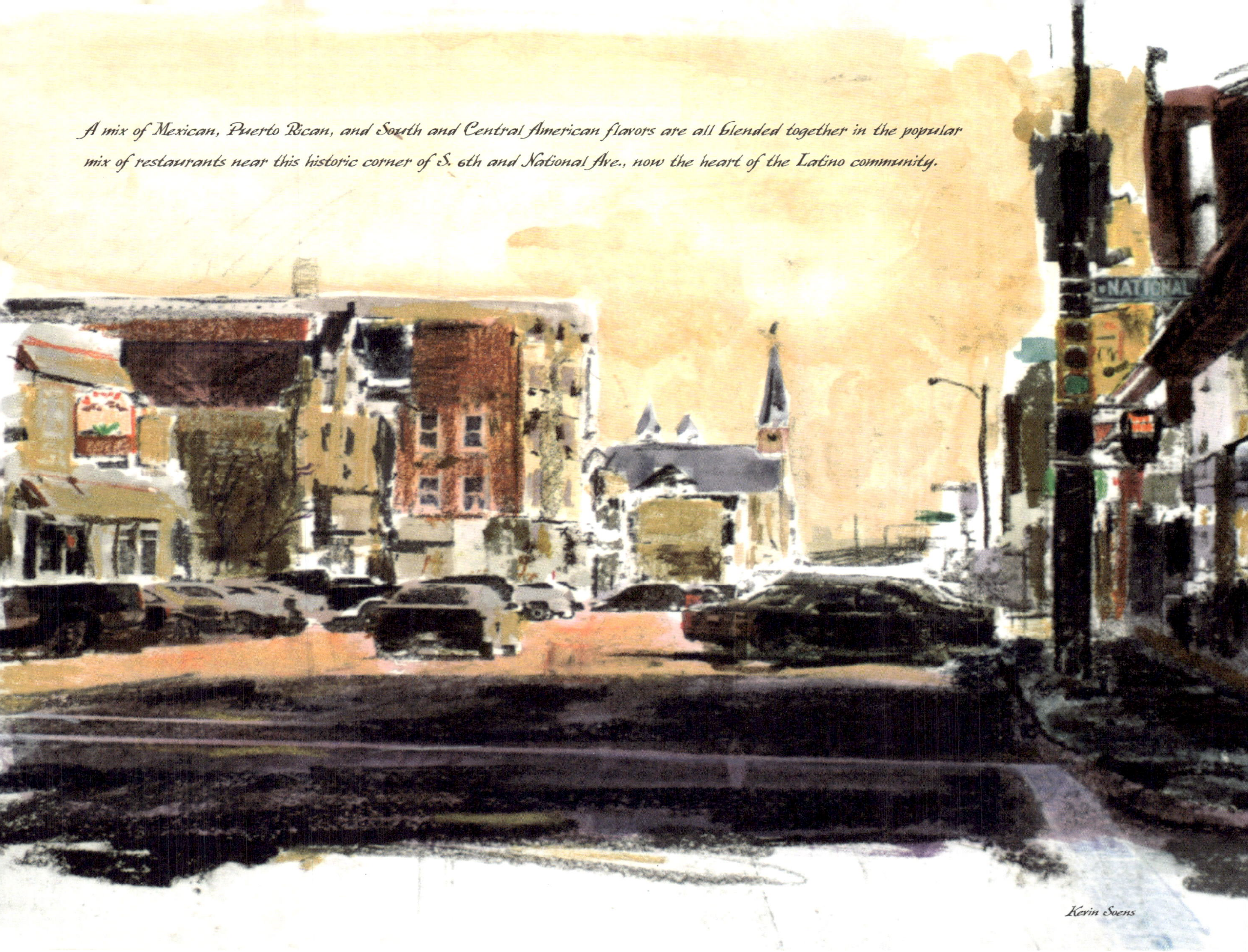

A mix of Mexican, Puerto Rican, and South and Central American flavors are all blended together in the popular mix of restaurants near this historic corner of S. 6th and National Ave., now the heart of the Latino community.

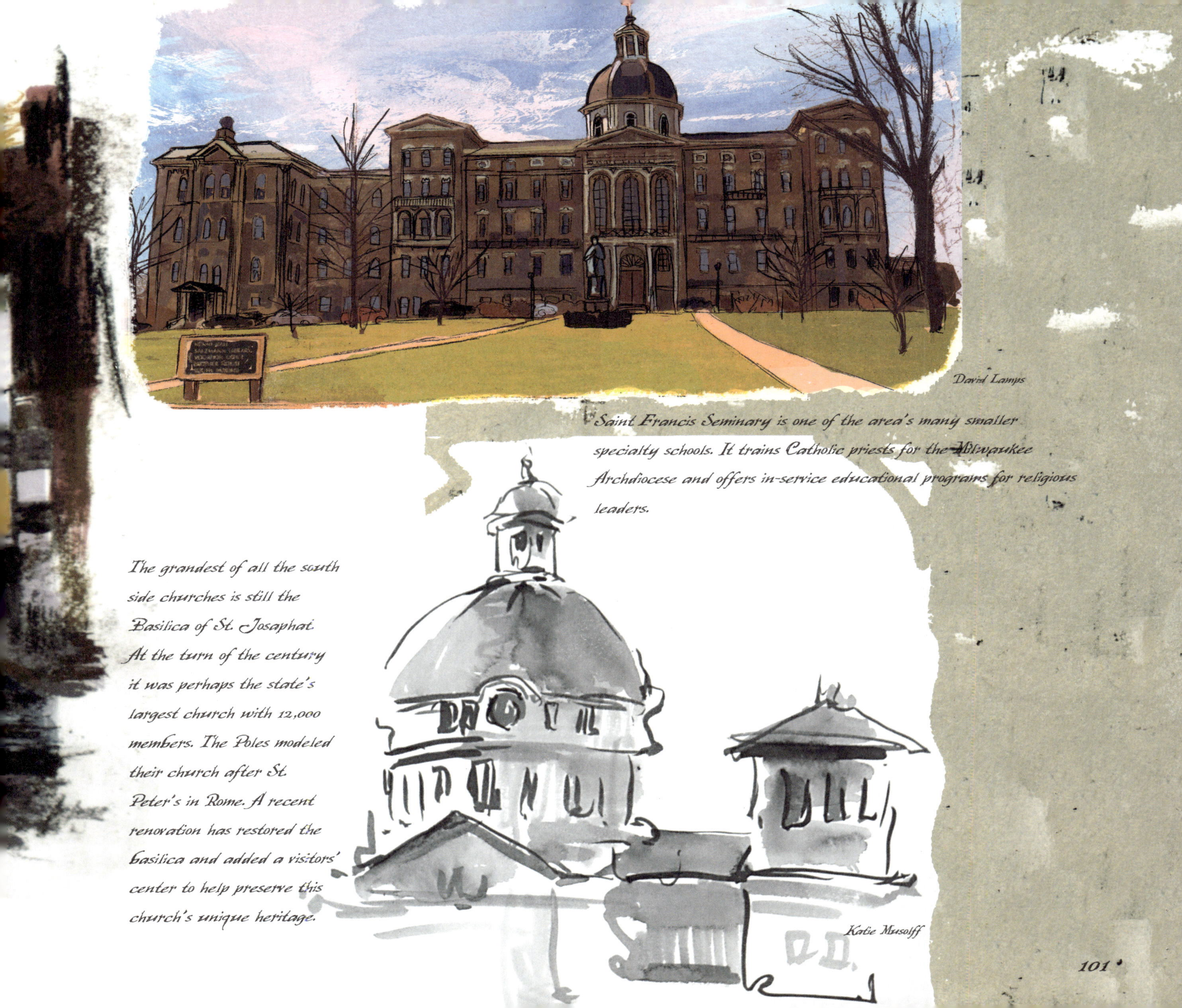

David Lamps

Saint Francis Seminary is one of the area's many smaller specialty schools. It trains Catholic priests for the Milwaukee Archdiocese and offers in-service educational programs for religious leaders.

The grandest of all the south side churches is still the Basilica of St. Josaphat. At the turn of the century it was perhaps the state's largest church with 12,000 members. The Poles modeled their church after St. Peter's in Rome. A recent renovation has restored the basilica and added a visitors' center to help preserve this church's unique heritage.

Katie Musolff

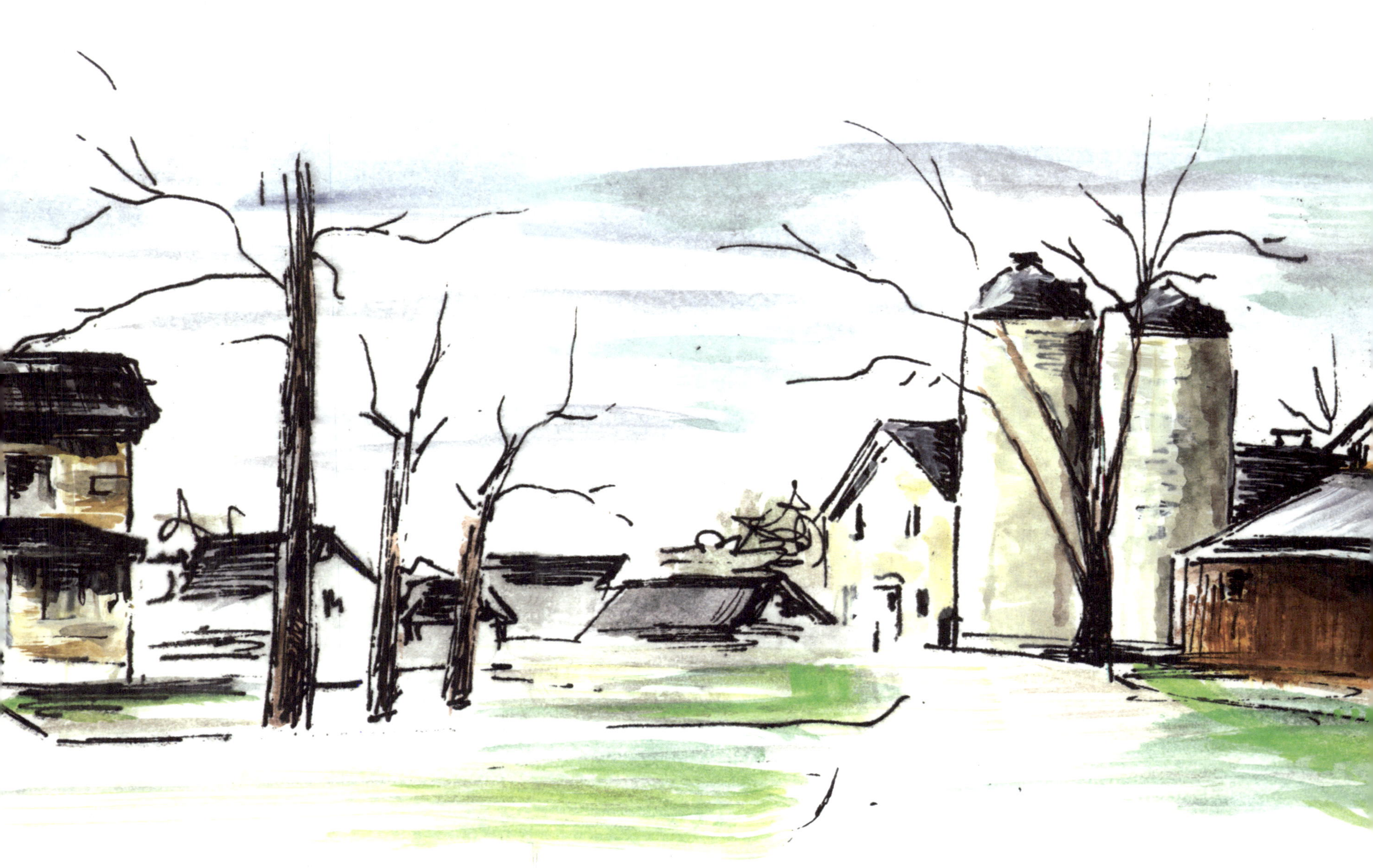

Milwaukee became known for its fine brick houses thanks in part to the lime produced at Trimborn Farms in Greenfield. Werner Trimborn in 1851 began digging limestone from a nearby quarry that he baked in kilns to produce the essential ingredient in mortar. The farm has been preserved in hopes of becoming a county park.

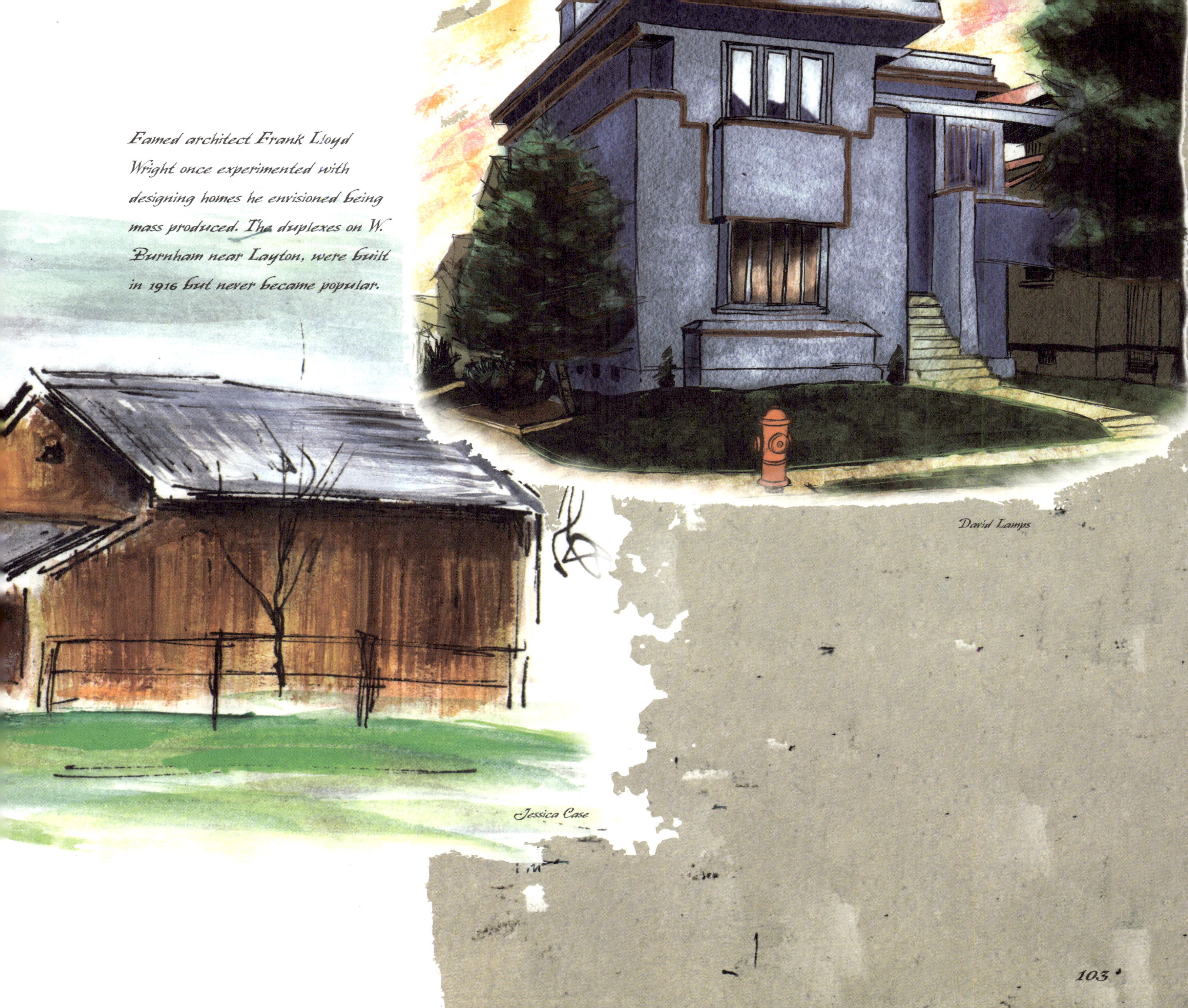

Famed architect Frank Lloyd Wright once experimented with designing homes he envisioned being mass produced. The duplexes on W. Burnham near Layton, were built in 1916 but never became popular.

David Lamps

Jessica Case

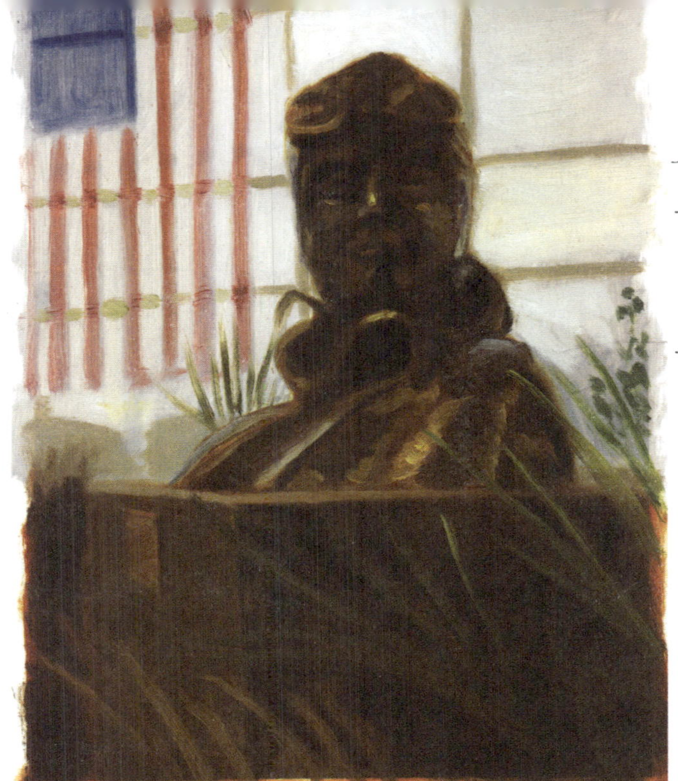

Billy Mitchell, the grandson of early city leader Alexander Mitchell, devoted his life to aviation and tried for years to convince the military of its importance. Though punished for being so outspoken, his vision became reality by World War II. The Milwaukee airport is named for him.

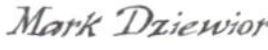

Mark Dziewior

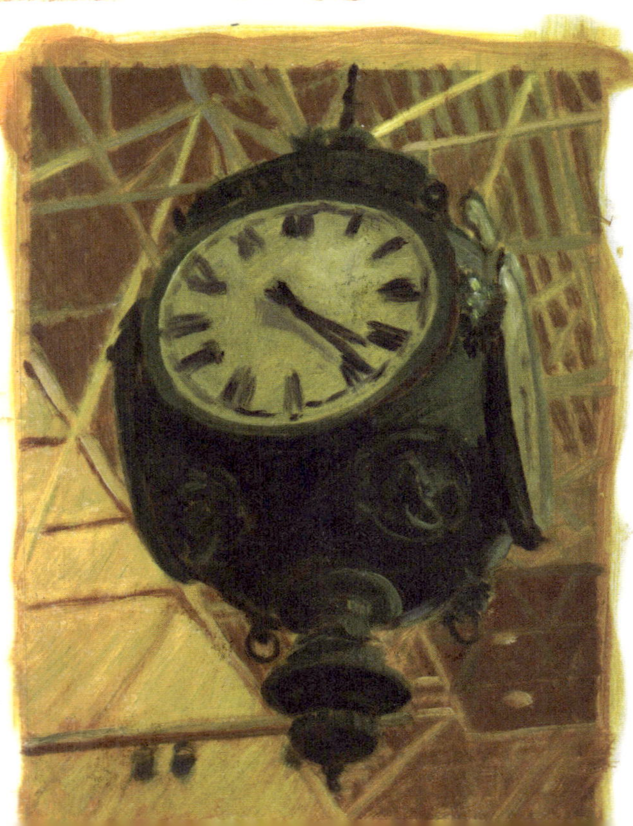

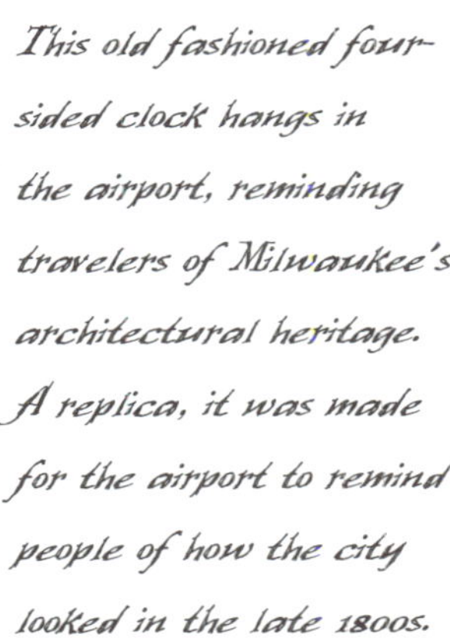

This old fashioned four-sided clock hangs in the airport, reminding travelers of Milwaukee's architectural heritage. A replica, it was made for the airport to remind people of how the city looked in the late 1800s.

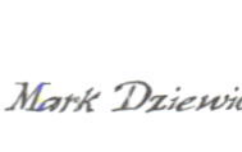

Mark Dziewior

Mark Dziewior

Henry Aaron has been a hometown hero every since he played for the Milwaukee Braves, and went on to beat Babe Ruth's title for hitting the most homeruns. He's now immortalized in a statue at Miller Park.

Milwaukee and MIAD

Milwaukee's sites and scenes have captured hearts for generations. No wonder, then, that they have captured so completely the imaginations of the talented students at the Milwaukee Institute of Art & Design.

MIAD, as it's often called, is Wisconsin's only college devoted exclusively to the education of professional artists and designers. Students come from throughout Wisconsin and across the nation to pursue its degree offerings in communication design, drawing, illustration, industrial design, interior architecture and design, painting, photography, printmaking, or sculpture. Founded in 1974, it has become one of the region's leading providers of artists and designers.

For its students, Milwaukee is more than the place their college is named after. It's home to a wonderful array of internship opportunities. It offers a rich repository of subject matter to study and enjoy.

And as the art they've produced in this book shows, it's also a delightful place to explore, a visual feast of landmarks stately and quirky. Led by illustration professor Christiane Grauert and painting professor Michael Howard, a group of fifteen MIAD students devoted most of 2003-04 to creating art about Milwaukee. The results presented here are a visual record as original as Milwaukee itself.

As the "visual authors" of this book, and on behalf of MIAD's board, faculty, staff, students and alums, we hope you enjoy this affectionate collection of some of the many places that make Milwaukee so memorable.

Milwaukee Institute of Art & Design

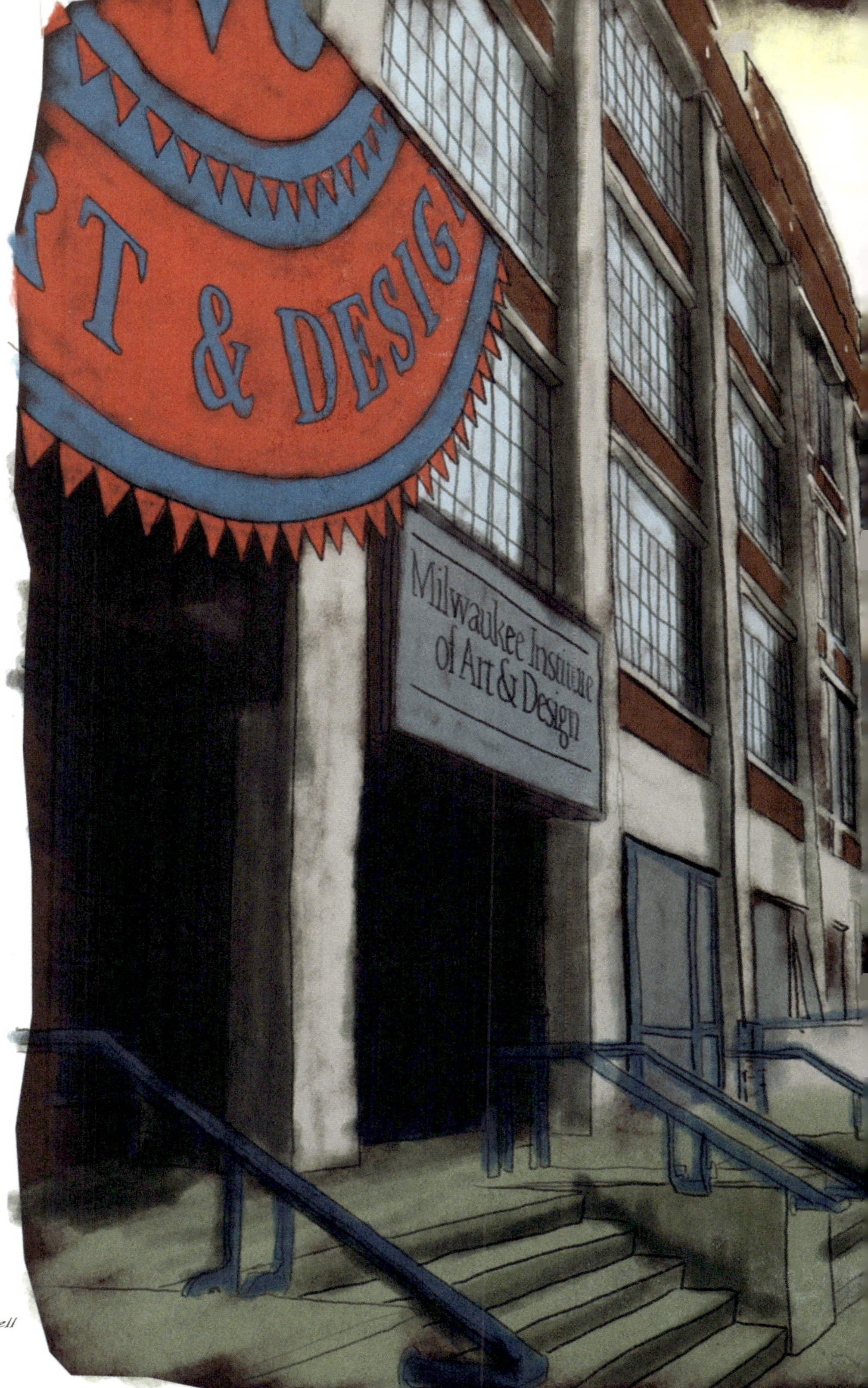

Jason McDowell

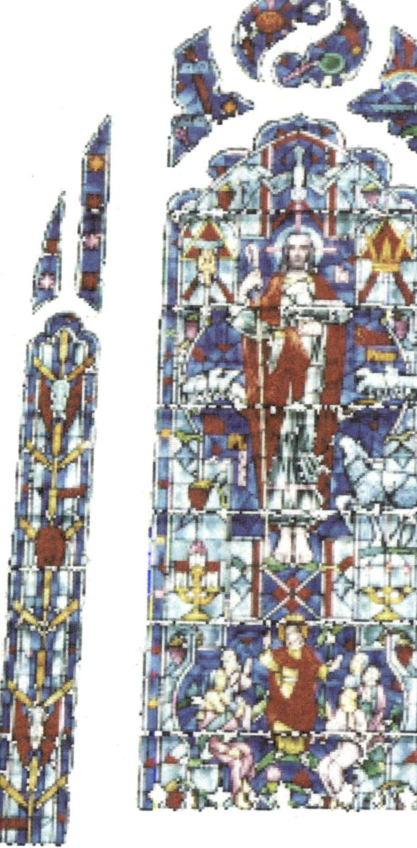

Albright United Methodist Church

Through its rich history, the community, now known as Albright, has dedicated itself to spiritual growth and community outreach. As our neighborhood and world change, the community outreach is changing to meet the spiritual needs of its members, community, and world. It is the church's hope that as people of faith we will walk in common discipleship, reach out in mission, and through the United Methodist connection support ministry throughout the world.

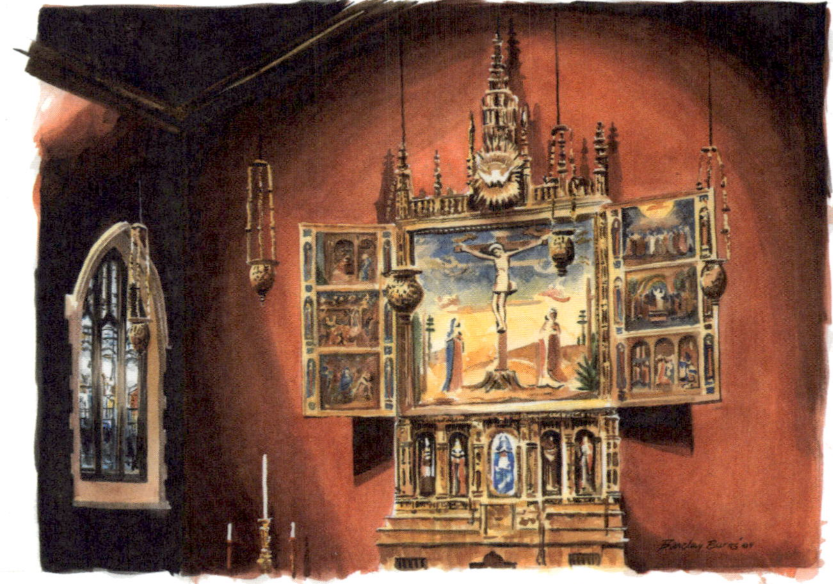

All Saints' Cathedral

We are committed to a life of service to the world in Christ's name. We are best known for our well-established Hunger Book Sale, contributing over $250,000 to local, regional, and international food-related agencies for well over twenty years. Opportunities abound throughout the year to enhance knowledge and spiritual growth through daily Eucharists, Offices, Quiet Days, and study and prayer groups. Our Cathedral family is drawn from throughout the greater Milwaukee area. We reflect the full diversity of the Anglican Communion, committed to reaching across all cultural lines. We welcome visitors and enjoy worship and fellowship together throughout the year.
All Saints' Cathedral. Ordinary People doing Extraordinary Things!

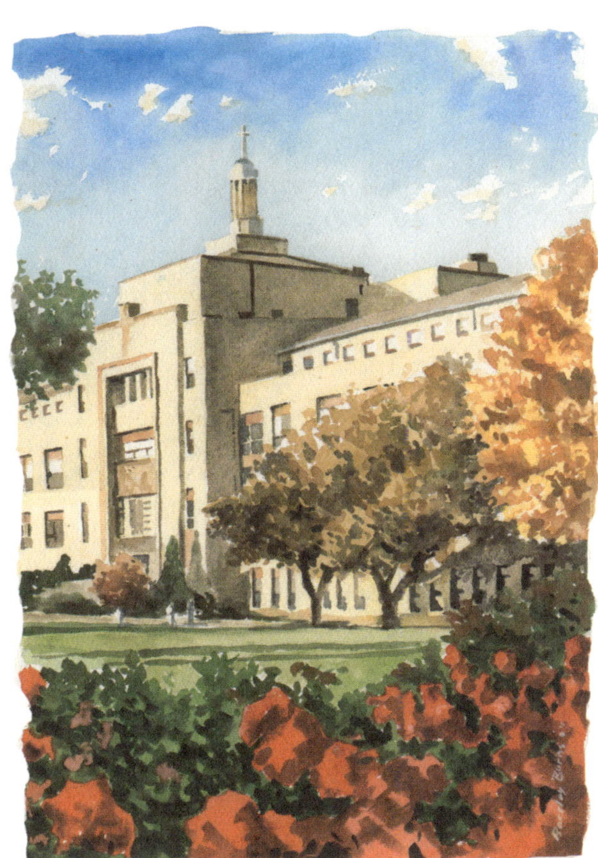

Alverno College

The Alverno approach to education requires students to master eight abilities within the context of their classes and through their education as a whole. These skills are: communication, analysis, problem solving, valuing in decision-making, social interaction, developing a global perspective, effective citizenship, and aesthetic engagement. This unique, assessment-as-learning, outcome-based education promotes a deeper level of understanding, a greater degree of retention, and strengthens a student's ability to use what is learned.

This credo defines the college's long-term aims and daily pursuits. As a result of their education, Alverno graduates enter the workforce committed to making a difference in their career and their community.

Associated Bank

Associated Bank has a long and rich tradition of providing superior financial services to the communities that it serves and takes enormous pride in its exceptional customer service. Excellence in personal service is Associated Bank's guiding Principal. From understanding a wide array of product options to a focus on careful listening and understanding, it's each associate's attention to detail and follow-up that make customers' experience with Associated special.

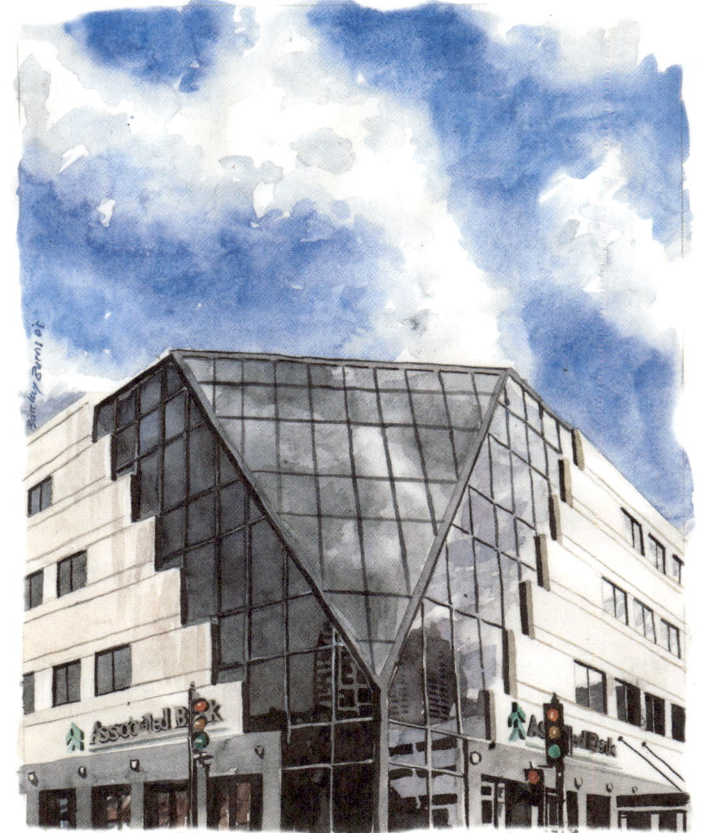

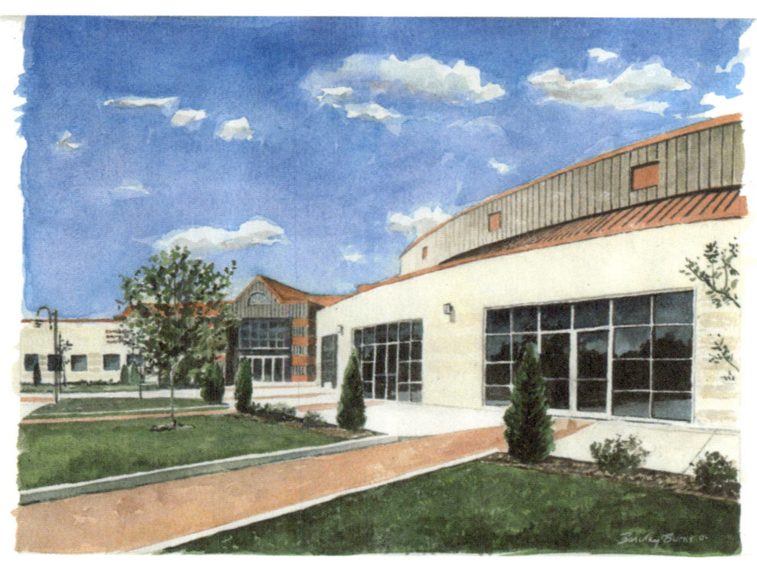

Cardinal Stritch

Cardinal Stritch University is a learning community in which the elements of scholarship and learning – discovery, application, integration and teaching – are embraced by faculty, staff, and students. Its graduates are critical thinkers, ethical decision makers, and lifelong learners, and its vision for its future is best stated as: Cardinal Stritch University is a Franciscan learning community that acts courageously and with integrity to foster the transformation of lives.

Deloitte & Touche

Deloitte Touche Tohmatsu is an organization of member firms devoted to excellence in providing professional services and advice. We are focused on client service through a global strategy executed locally in nearly 150 countries. With access to the deep intellectual capital of 120,000 people worldwide, our member firms, including their affiliates, deliver services in four professional areas: audit, tax, consulting, and financial advisory. Our member firms serve more than one-half of the world's largest companies, as well as large national enterprises, public institutions, locally important clients, and successful, fast-growing global companies.

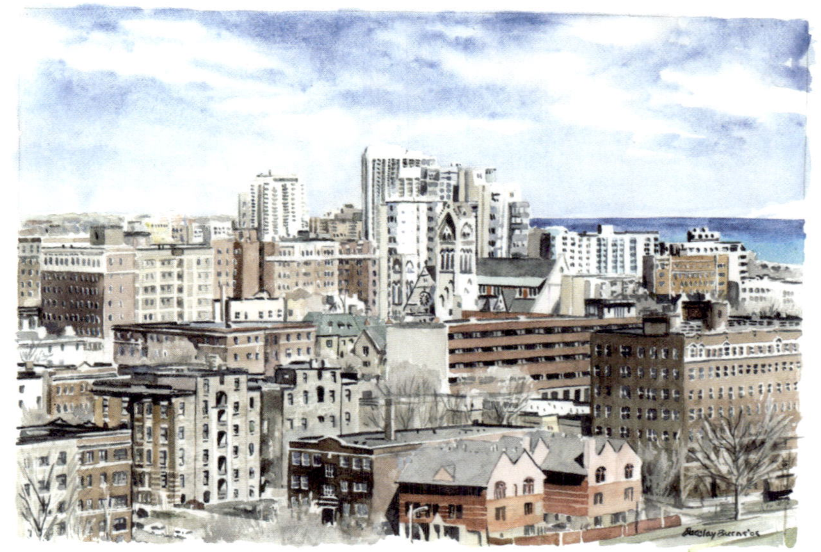

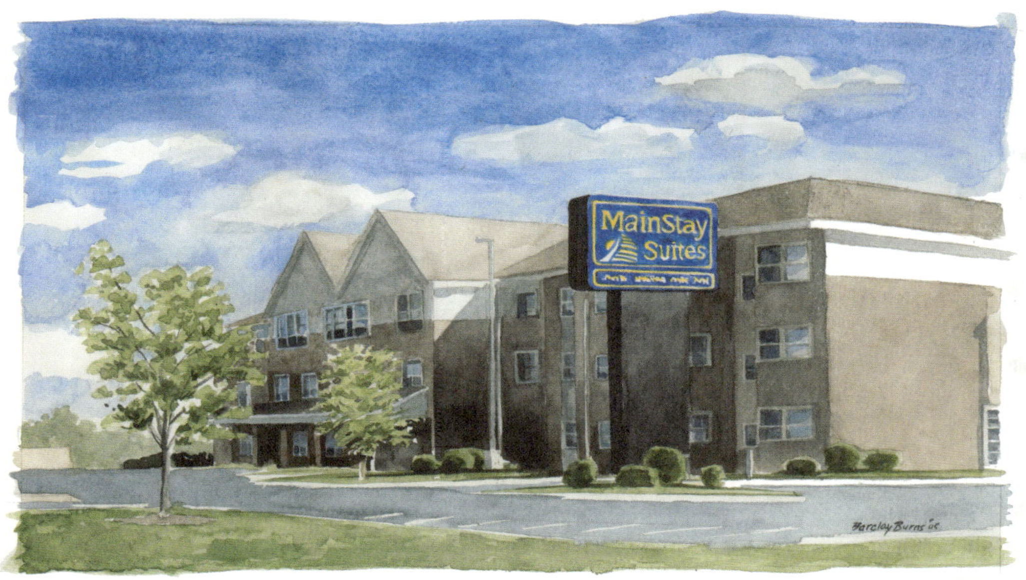

MainStay Suites

At Oak Creek's MainStay Suites, general manager Dale Beckemeier has set an envious standard of excellence in personalized customer service. Dale imbues his staff with a contagious enthusiasm evident in every customer interaction. "When you stay with us, it's like you are staying at home," comments Dale. From serving an enhanced continental breakfast with make-your-own waffles to featuring a patio with a gas grill for those who like to dine al fresco, the subtle details of home have been considered. Dale boasts, "We take pride in the details, like remembering every guest's name."

Michael Best & Friedrich LLP

It is the people at Michael Best who define the firm's quality and service. Attorneys at the firm are recognized as leaders in their fields. They frequently offer perspectives on legal matters including business issues, regulatory issues, and emerging issues in the law. In seminars, in periodicals, and in prominent roles on committees and panels, Michael Best attorneys share their knowledge and analysis.

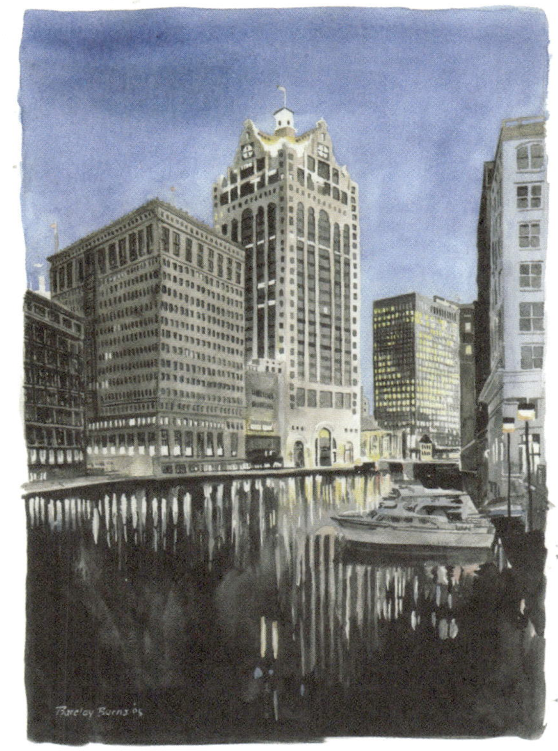

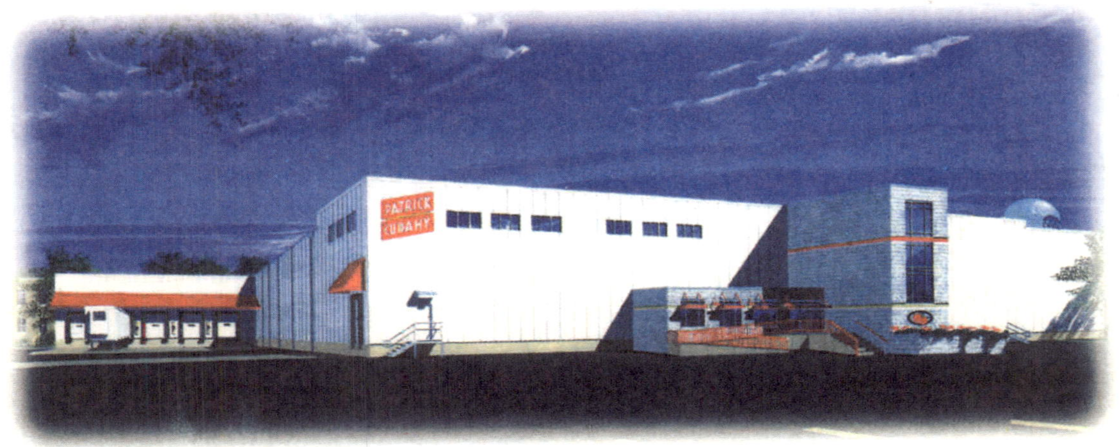

Patrick Cudahy

Management staff and employees alike are committed to earning and keeping consumers' trust and confidence. "We get very high marks from our customers, and we're extremely proud of our products and our plant," says Bill Otis. The company invested approximately $100 million dollars over six years in new plant equipment and construction, but some of the original operations continue, like smoking with real sweet apple wood chips, the moniker the business is known by. "We combine the seasoned operational processes and brand new, state-of-the-art equipment and when you put that all together, that's basically what has allowed Patrick Cudahy the successes it has been able to enjoy for more than a century."

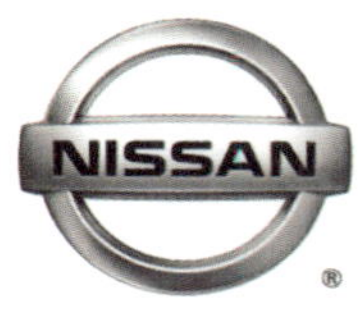

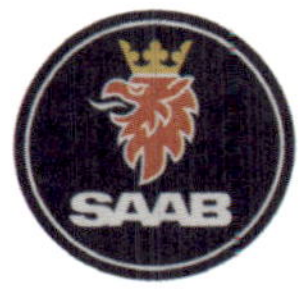

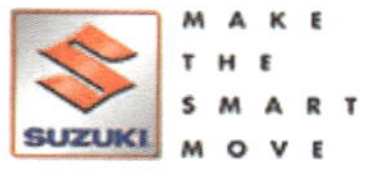

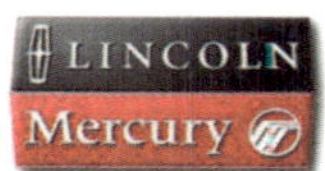

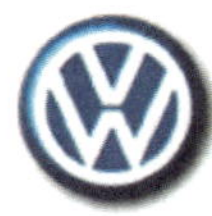
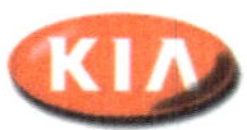

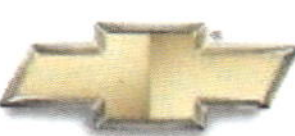
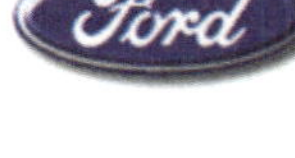

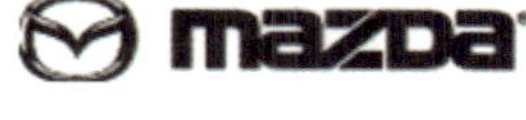

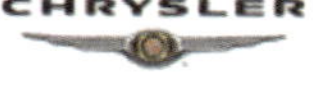

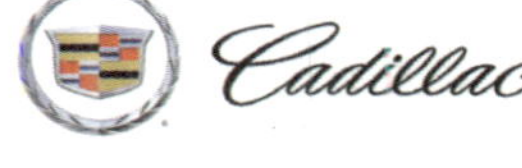

The Boucher Group

Gordon "Gordie" Boucher started the family-owned and -operated business in 1977 when he opened his first dealership in West Allis, Wisconsin. Since then, the Boucher Group has grown to include over 1,000 associates, seventeen dealerships, a full service management company, an in-house advertising agency, a fleet group, and a leasing company. The Boucher Group is ranked in the nation's top 100 dealer groups, and Deloitte & Touche rank Boucher in Wisconsin's top twenty-five largest privately owned companies. Gordon's children, Frank, Gordie Jr., and Julie Boucher Sellars, run the many dealerships in southeastern Wisconsin.

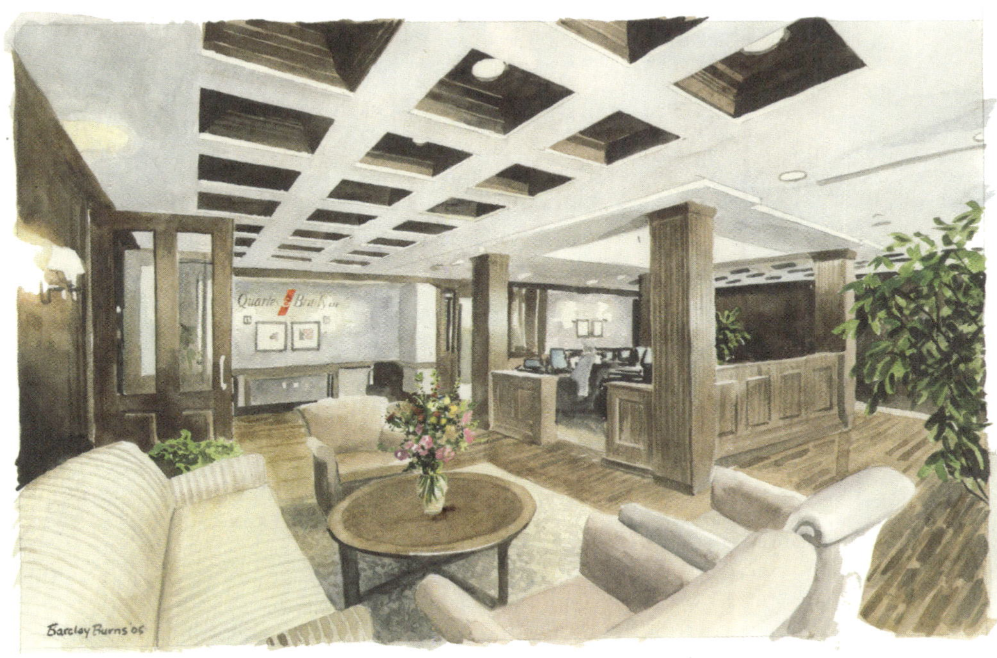

Quarles & Brady LLP

The firm's lawyers and staff are considered the firm's most valuable asset, and Q&B recruits with its clients' high expectations in mind. The firm seeks the most qualified and outstanding candidates from a variety of law schools, with a commitment to diversity and equal opportunity in employment. Attorneys at the firm include graduates of 165 colleges and universities and seventy-three law schools. Notably, the firm has 94 lawyers listed in The Best Lawyers in America, which is the third highest ranking nationally.

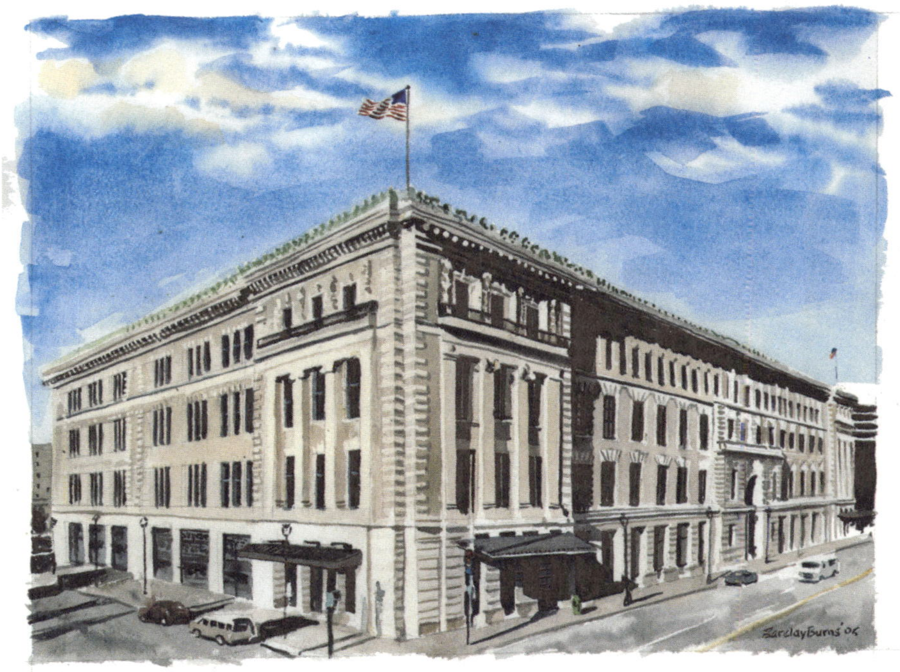

We Energies

One architectural detail, a stained-glass window above the main entrance, symbolizes the activities conducted in the Public Service Building (PSB); it depicts a swarm of bees buzzing around a beehive. The PSB has always been the site of busy enterprise. In fact, the April 1908 Architectural Record gave the PSB national standing when it stated: "Under its roof are carried on a greater variety of occupations than in any other building in the country."

Index